OCCUPATIONAL HEALTH AND SAFETY ACT REFERENCE GUIDE

for

Joint Health and Safety Committees
and
Health and Safety Representatives

536B Fourth Line East
Sault Ste. Marie, ON P6A 5K8
(705) 254-3752

Fax : (705) 254-7365
Toll Free : 1-877-254-3752
E-mail : info@hspinc.ca

Developed by: Louise Caicco Tett, MPH, CRSP, RN
President, Health & Safety Professionals Inc.

Produced by: **B**usiness **O**ffice **S**upport **S**ervices
1496 Wellington St. E., 2nd Floor
Sault Ste. Marie, ON P6A 1R2

ISBN 978-1-928108-18-4   © 2020 Version 1.0

Table of Contents

Foreword

This Reference Guide is in its second revision. This update was done in April 2020, in the midst of the historic COVID-19 pandemic. Just as we thought we were done, we decided to add a section to Chapter 12 Biological Hazards.

The first edition was for members of Joint Health and Safety Committees (JHSC), as per Sec. 9 of the Ontario *Occupational Health and Safety Act (OHSS)*. This second edition includes health and safety representatives (HSR), as per section 8 of the *OHSA*.

Workplaces with more than five but fewer than 20 workers must appoint a worker health and safety representative (Sec. 8(1)). The health and safety representative carries out most of the functions of the worker member of a JHSC, with the following exceptions: there is no requirement for meetings, there is no provision for the certification of a health and safety representative, and they do not have the right to initiate a stop-work procedure.

New in this second edition is Chapter 6 for Health and Safety Representatives.

In keeping with the Ministry of Labour, Training and Skills Development's new Supporting Ontario's Safe Employers Program, Chapter 22 entitled Occupational Health and Safety Management Systems has been added to the book.

1 HEALTH, SAFETY, AND THE LAW

Chapter

Chapter 1

Occupational Health and Safety in Ontario

- The Internal Responsibility System

- The Reference Guide

- Health and Safety Hazards

- Dealing with Health and Safety Hazards

- Certified Member

- Health and Safety Representative

Occupational Health and Safety in Ontario

According to Workplace Safety and Insurance Board (WSIB)'s Report Builder: By the Numbers, Ontario workers suffer nearly 200,000 injuries and illnesses each year that are directly related to their jobs. This includes lost-time and no-lost time injuries for Schedule 1 and Schedule 2 employers. Tragically, more than 300 people are killed at work or die of occupational illnesses every year.

These numbers are only for claims that have been allowed by the WSIB. The true extent of the health and safety problem is really much greater. These statistics are all the more bitter because they are needless. Occupational illnesses and injuries are preventable. Workplace hazards can be systematically identified, assessed and controlled. But it takes a strong commitment by all workplace parties to get results. In spite of the passage of the *Occupational Health and Safety Act* (*OHSA*) more than thirty years ago, too few workplaces have implemented effective health and safety programs.

The consequences of these illnesses and injuries are severe. Workers and their families suffer lost income, damaged careers, and a lower quality of life. Employers lose productivity and pay higher compensation costs and society as a whole is affected by excessive health care costs and reduced economic performance.

Words in the law are not enough. Action in the workplace is needed.

The Internal Responsibility System

An occupational health or safety hazard is anything in the workplace that has the potential to cause harm to the human body. Health and safety hazards vary greatly depending on the type of work involved. We usually associate work hazards with mines, construction sites, and other industrial workplaces. Workplaces like schools, offices, hospitals, and stores have their own particular hazards.

Many aspects of working life can cause health or safety hazards. Equipment, processes, chemical, biological or physical agents, work procedures, and the design of the workplace are all potentially hazardous. We are also acknowledging that workplaces can contribute to mental health disorders.

Workers, employers and government all have an interest in tackling these problems at their source. It is now clear that employers, who design and direct work, and their employees, who actually carry out the work, must be equally involved in finding solutions to eliminate all incidents in the workplace. This understanding has guided the evolution of Ontario's *OHSA*.

The OHSA depends on the participation of both workplace parties to translate its principles into action. The joint participation of workers and employers with equal powers to act on health and safety matters is known as the internal responsibility system.

For this participation to be effective, all workers and employers need special knowledge, training and skills. Along with equal knowledge, training and skills, employers and workers need to share an understanding of the advantages of the internal responsibility system.

The Reference Guide

This reference guide is divided into **three sections**.

Section one is an introduction to occupational health and safety in Ontario. It outlines the fundamental principles of health and safety and of the *OHSA* and offers a clear understanding of the *OHSA* and regulations. It describes the roles of joint health and safety committees and the certified members of those committees. It also describes the role of health and safety representatives, in workplaces with 6-19 workers.

Sections two deals separately, and in greater detail, with health hazards and safety hazards. This section covers physical, chemical, biological, musculoskeletal, psychosocial, and safety hazards. The means of recognition, the assessment methods, and the controls that apply to each type of hazard are explained. This section also introduces a hazard management tool and how it is used to evaluate hazard controls.

Section three describes the tools used by certified members of joint health and safety committees and health and safety representatives to carry out their responsibilities. It covers inspections, investigations and monitoring strategies, basic research and statistical skills, and communication skills. A chapter is dedicated to Occupational Health and Safety Management Systems.

The organization of this reference guide reflects principles that underlie the *OHSA* and its regulations. It will be useful at the outset to understand some of the main concepts involved. This section provides a brief overview.

Incidents and Occupational Illnesses

Statistics on injuries and illnesses are collected by the Workplace Safety and Insurance Board (WSIB). The WSIB collects this information from insured workplaces that are required under the *Workplace Safety and Insurance Act* (WSIA) to report injuries and illnesses to the WSIB. The data that follows does not included injuries and illnesses for workplaces that are not covered by the WSIB.

According to WSIB's By The Numbers online Report Builder there were 65,485 allowed lost-time claims and 129,759 allowed no lost-time claims for a total of 194,614 approved claims in Ontario for 2018. This includes Schedule 1 and Schedule 2 employers.

There is no complete record of occupational injuries and diseases that occur in Ontario workplaces. The principle source of health and safety statistics is reports submitted to the WSIB, but many workplaces are not covered by the WSIB. Even where coverage is in effect, many occupational injuries and health incidents go unreported.

Traumatic and Occupational Disease Fatalities

Traumatic Fatalities (By Year of Death)

Year	Total Traumatic Fatalities in Ontario (WSIB & MOL)
2005	86
2006	102
2007	102
2008	79
2009	77
2010	85
2011	94
2012	78
2013	102
2014	81
2015	72
2016	72
2017	81
2018	85

According to the Workplace Safety and Insurance Board statistics over the past 10 years (2009 to 2018), 92 per cent of all traumatic fatality claims were from men, mostly between the ages of 55 to 59 years old. Construction, transportation, manufacturing and services sectors accounted for 76 per cent of these workplace traumatic incidents.

Most of these traumatic fatalities were due to motor vehicle incidents and falls and struck by/caught in object.

In 2018, 85 traumatic workplace fatalities were reported in Ontario. This number reflects the total traumatic fatalities reported to the Ministry of Labour, Training and Skills Development (MLTSD)and the fatality claims allowed by the Workplace Safety and Insurance Board based on year of death. From 2005 to 2018, the number of traumatic fatalities reported to the MLTSD and the Workplace Safety and Insurance Board ranged between 72 and 102 and did not show a clear trend.

WSIB Allowed Occupational Disease Fatalities
(By Year of Entitlement)

Year	Schedule 1 (Year of Entitlement)	Schedule 2 (Year of Entitlement)	Total Allowed Occupational Disease Fatalities
2004	161	36	197
2005	231	30	261
2006	196	34	230
2007	228	51	279
2008	221	36	257
2009	229	32	261
2010	250	51	301
2011	190	38	228
2012	190	32	222
2013	158	23	181
2014	167	42	209
2015	175	37	212
2016	161	70	231
2017	175	40	215
2018	212	48	260

**WSIB Allowed Occupational Disease
Fatalities (By Entitlement Year)**

Year	Total Allowed Occupational Disease Fatalities
2009	261
2010	301
2011	228
2012	222
2013	181
2014	209
2015	212
2016	231
2017	215
2018	260

Occupational disease fatalities are stated in two formats. The Workplace Safety and Insurance Board's Schedule 1 and 2 fatalities are stated by the year of entitlement (the year a decision was made on the claim). Occupational disease fatalities are also stated by the year of death (the year the workplace fatality occurred). Numbers based on year of entitlement can be affected by many factors including the speed of claims processing and the definition of allowable occupational diseases in a specific year.

Schedule 1 and Schedule 2 employers are defined in the *Workplace Safety and Insurance Act (WSIA)*. Schedule 1 employers pay premiums based on the WSIB's classification system. Since the Board pays benefits to injured workers out of money pooled in the insurance fund, Schedule 1 employers are relieved of individual responsibility for actual incident costs. Schedule 2 employers pay the full injury claim plus an administration fee.

In 2018, the Workplace Safety and Insurance Board in Ontario allowed 260 occupational disease fatality claims based on year of entitlement. Between 2009 and 2018, the number of occupational diseases fatalities ranged between 181 and 301. There are no clear trends in the data.

According to the Workplace Safety and Insurance Board, between 2009 and 2018, the highest percentage of allowed occupational disease fatality claims among Schedule 1 employers occurred among males (97%), individuals 65 years of age and over, and those who worked in the construction and manufacturing sections. Allowed occupational disease fatality claims were primarily due to cancers, including mesothelioma and lung cancer. Occupational disease fatalities generally have a long latency period, which means that the cause may have occurred many years or even decades before the onset of illness.

All of these statistics, and more, can be found on the WSIB website at www.wsibstatistics.ca

Health Hazards

A health hazard is something that has the potential to cause an adverse health effect. *The OHSA* defines an occupational illness as "a condition that results from exposure in a workplace to a physical, chemical or biological agent, to the extent that the normal physiological mechanisms are affected, and the health of the worker is impaired." An adverse health effect might be a minor skin rash, or it might be a life-threatening disease like lung cancer.

The OHSA recognizes three major categories of agents which can be hazardous to health. They are physical agents, biological agents, and chemical agents.

Physical agents are forms of energy or force. They include noise, vibration, electricity, heat and cold, pressure and radiation. Some, like electricity, are usually a deliberate part of a production process. Others, like noise and vibration, are most often unwanted byproducts of a process.

Chemical agents take many forms. They can appear in the workplace as gases, liquids or solids. Chemicals may be the product being manufactured. They may be an input to a process, or they may be a by-product of a process.

Biological agents are living things or products of living things. Most biological agents found in the workplace are microscopic organisms. They include bacteria, viruses and fungi, all of which feed on plant or animal tissue.

This reference guide contains separate chapters on physical, chemical, and biological hazards (see Chapters 10 to 15 inclusive). Some health hazards do not fit into these classifications. For this reason, the reference guide also includes chapters on musculoskeletal and psychosocial hazards (Chapters 13 and 14 respectively).

Safety Hazards

A safety hazard (Chapter 15) is something that has the potential to cause an injury. An injury is physical harm or damage to a person resulting from contact between the body and an outside agent or from exposure to environmental factors. It can range in severity from a minor scratch or burn to the loss of a limb or even death. Injuries are usually the result of incidents. An incident is an occurrence arising in the course of work that resulted in or could have resulted in an injury, illness, adverse effect to health, or fatality (see Chapter 18).

In order to carry out their responsibilities under the *OHSA*, certified members of joint health and safety committees and health and safety representatives must learn how health and safety hazards are recognized, assessed, controlled, and evaluated (also known as RACE).

Hazard Recognition

Recognizing a workplace hazard is the first step in overcoming it. Health and safety hazards are not always obvious. Hazard recognition means:

- identifying potential hazards in the workplace;
- identifying the adverse effects that may be associated with these hazards; and
- determining whether there is a possibility of people being exposed or affected.

If a potential hazard is recognized using these three steps, the hazard must then be assessed.

Hazard Assessment

Hazard assessment is a process of evaluating an identified workplace hazard. The assessment covers equipment, processes and work procedures. An assessment considers which workers, if any, are exposed — or likely to be exposed — to an identified workplace hazard and for how long.

Hazard Control

Recognition and assessment prepare the way for control or elimination of a hazard. Where an assessment finds that a hazard is likely to adversely affect one or more workers, some form of control is needed.

The principles of hazard control are often described by the location of the control: at the source of the hazard; along the path between the hazard and the worker; or at the worker.

- *Control at the Source.* The best control is the elimination of the hazard from the workplace. If this is not feasible, the best alternative is substitution of a non-hazardous or less hazardous material or process. Where no acceptable substitute is available, enclosing or isolating the hazard can protect against exposure. Removing a hazardous gas or dust with a local ventilation system is another example of controlling a hazard at the source.

- *Control Along the Path.* Some processes, by their nature, cannot be enclosed or isolated. A general ventilation system can reduce exposure to heat by cooling the air. Other examples of control along the path are screens to prevent welding flash from reaching the eyes of nearby workers, and energy lockout procedures.

- *Control at the Worker*. Where neither control at the source nor control along the path is effective, control at the worker may be necessary. Control at the worker often consists of special protective equipment or clothing that must be worn during certain work functions. Gloves for hand protection are the most common example. Ear muffs or plugs for noise protection and respirators for breathing protection are other examples of control at the worker.

Evaluating Hazard Controls

Once controls are in place, they must be evaluated. New hazards may have been introduced. Control measures need to be assessed to ensure that they provide the degree of protection expected. The job to which the hazard controls have been applied, must be reevaluated to assess the risk to the workers, with the control measures in place. If any risk remains, the company must decide if further controls are required, or if they are comfortable with the control measures that will protect the workers. In order to formalize this process, it is recommended that the employer, along with the joint health and safety committee or health and safety representatives use a Hazard Management Tool. One type of tool will be discussed in Chapter 15.

Certified Member

The 1990 amendments to the *OHSA*, introduced certified members who receive special training and have special powers and functions under *the OHSA*. At least one management member and one worker member of each JHSC must be certified. They have an important role to play in workplace health and safety. This reference guide has been designed to help certified members carry out their rights, duties, and responsibilities. The role of certified members of joint health and safety committees is discussed in detail in Chapter 5.

Health and Safety Representative

In workplaces that regularly employ 6-19 workers, a worker who does not exercise managerial function, must be chosen to represent the health and safety needs of his/her co-workers. A health and safety representative is also required on construction projects that are completed in under three months, regardless of the number of workers. There are special provisions for farming operations.

Chapter 2
Health and Safety Law

- Rights and Responsibilities of Workers

- The Workplace Safety & Insurance Board

- The *Occupational Health and Safety Act*

- Occupational Health and Safety Regulations

- Other Health and Safety Legislation

- Review

Health and Safety Law

In the late 1970s, the Government of Ontario began a process of updating the province's health and safety laws. Separate laws covering different industrial sectors were replaced with a comprehensive law covering almost all Ontario workplaces. This law, the *Occupational Health and Safety Act* (*OHSA*), was passed in 1978. The philosophy behind the law is known as the *internal responsibility system*. Although this term is not mentioned in any legislation, the Ministry of Labour, Training and Skills Development's guide to *the OHSA* makes it clear that the government expects employers and workers to cooperate to control health and safety hazards.

A turning point came in 1974. Uranium miners in Elliot Lake became alarmed about the high incidence of lung cancer and silicosis, and they went on strike over health and safety conditions. The government appointed a Royal Commission to investigate health and safety in mines. Chaired by Dr. James Ham, it became known as the Ham Commission.

The Ham Commission Report included more than 100 recommendations concerning mine health and safety. Dr. Ham was also concerned about the administration of health and safety. He developed the idea of an internal responsibility system, which would require government, employers and workers to cooperate to improve health and safety. To implement this system, he advocated the creation of joint labour-management health and safety committees, with worker members.

Subsequent amendments to *the OHSA* established new procedures as well as new rights and duties for workers, employers, supervisors and others in the workplace. Most importantly, they established joint health and safety committees in the workplace and gave them the right to participate in health and safety recommendations.

Another turning point in Ontario's history came on Christmas Eve 2009, in Toronto, where six workers fell while working from a suspended work platform. The swing stage from which they were working, collapsed and fell 14 floors, killing four workers and seriously injuring a fifth. The only survivor was wearing his fall arrest harness. This high-profile tragedy led to a comprehensive review of the *OHSA*.

Evolution of the Internal Responsibility System	
1975	Ham Commission Report recommends joint committees.
1976	Bill 139 establishes the Employee's *Health and Safety Act*. The Minister can order joint committees.
1978	Bill 70 establishes the *Occupational Health and Safety Act*. It mandates joint committees in many workplaces.
1987	Bill 79 adds Workplace Hazardous Materials Information System to the *Occupational Health and Safety Act*.
1990	Bill 208 amends the *Occupational Health and Safety Act*, broadening the requirement for joint committees. It establishes certified members and the right to stop work.
2010	"Expert Advisory Panel on Occupational Health & Safety Report" released.
2011	Bill 160 transfers prevention responsibilities from the WSIB to the MOL. Ontario's first prevention officer appointed.

In December of 2010, a panel of nine experts, chaired by Tony Dean, released a report entitled, "Expert Advisory Panel on Occupational Health and Safety". It was the result of a year-long review of Ontario's Occupational Health and Safety Prevention and Enforcement system.

The report was prepared for the Ministry of Labour, Training and Skills Development (MLTSD) and included 45 recommendations. Some of those recommendations led to changes which affect certified members of joint health and safety committees.

Prevention for occupational health and safety, long the responsibility of the Workplace Safety and Insurance Board, became the responsibility of the Ministry of Labour Training and Skills Development. For the first time ever, the MOL had a prevention officer. His duties included developing a provincial occupational health and safety strategy and an annual report on occupational health and safety. It also led to a reorganization of the Health and Safety Associations from fourteen to six.

Joint Health and Safety Committees (Section 9 of OHSA)
Bill 70 made joint health and safety committees (JHSCs) mandatory in most industrial workplaces with 20 or more workers. Bill 208 expanded the JHSC requirement to cover all workplaces with 20 or more workers, regardless of the industry or occupation involved. One exception is construction projects expected to last less than three months. Other exceptions may also be created by regulation. A committee is required in workplaces of any size where a designated substances regulation applies, or where a Ministry order covering toxic substances is in effect. In workplaces with more than 5 but fewer than 20 employees, a health and safety representative must be selected by the workers.

Joint health and safety committees are discussed in detail in Chapter 4.

Health and Safety Representatives (Section 8 of OHSA)
The rights, duties and responsibilities of health and safety representatives as prescribed by the *OHSA* are very similar to those of JHSCs. The main difference is that there is no provision in the *OHSA* for certification of health and safety representatives. Section 8(5.1) of the *OHSA* states that a health and safety representative is to receive training in order to effectively carry out his/her duties. This training is voluntary. Since they have no management counterparts and thus no committee meetings to attend, they are not entitled to pay for "preparation time", as are JHSC members. However, health and safety representatives are entitled to pay while carrying out their duties. Health and safety representatives are discussed in detail in Chapter 6.

The *Occupational Health and Safety Act* includes three fundamental rights of workers:

- **the right to know** about workplace health and safety;

- **the right to participate** in health and safety recommendations, through their representation on the joint health and safety committee, or their health and safety representative;

- **the right to refuse** work if it endangers health or safety.

The Right to Know

The OHSA places a duty on employers to provide a wide range of information about hazards in the workplace to workers, health and safety representatives, joint health and safety committees. JHSCs and HSRs have a duty to communicate with workers. The right to know was first included in the *OHSA* and further expanded by subsequent amendments.

The Right to Participate

The right to participate is given force by a duty on employers. They must consult with JHSCs or HSRs about testing methods and strategies and about health and safety training programs. Designated worker members of JHSCs or HSRs have the right to be present at the beginning of testing, to participate in Ministry inspections and investigations, and to investigate serious incidents. Certified worker members have the right to investigate complaints dealing with dangerous circumstances. JHSCs and HSRs have the right to make recommendations to employers about health and safety improvements, and the *OHSA* requires employers to reply in writing. The right to participate was established by the *OHSA*.

The Right to Refuse

Bill 139 proposed that workers be given a limited right to refuse work on the grounds that it endangered the health or safety of themselves or another worker. The 1978 *OHSA* expanded on this right by setting out specific work refusal procedures. The *OHSA* contains a two-stage refusal process. The work may be initially refused on the basis of a worker's subjective belief that it is dangerous. Once a supervisor has investigated, the worker must have reasonable grounds for

---

What the Law Says

Rights and Responsibilities of Workers

Rights
- **To know** about workplace health and safety hazards
- **To participate** in making recommendations on health and safety issues
- **To refuse** work if they believe it endangers health or safety

Responsibilities
- To work in compliance with the *Occupational Health and Safety Act*
- To wear protective equipment, devices and clothing required by the employer
- To report to a supervisor any defective equipment, hazard or violation of the *OHSA*
- To work in a manner that does not endanger the worker or others
- Not to engage in horseplay or boisterous conduct.

believing that the work is still dangerous in order to continue refusing. Bill 208 extended the right to refuse to workers who were formerly excluded altogether. For example, police officers, firefighters and correctional workers can refuse dangerous work if the refusal does not endanger others and is not a normal or inherent part of their work.

The Workplace Safety and Insurance Board

The WSIB administers the province's no-fault workplace insurance for employers and their workers. It is funded entirely by employer premiums and receives no funding from the Ontario provincial government. The WSIB also provides major funding to Ontario Health and Safety Associations.

In 1998, the WSIB undertook a new prevention mandate. Part of this mandate included developing standards for the certification of persons to be certified for the purposes of the *OHSA* and to approve training programs for certification and to certify persons who meet the standards. The WSIB oversaw Ontario's workplace safety education and training system.

Ontario Health and Safety Associations

- Infrastructure Health and Safety Association (IHSA) www.ihsa.ca
- Public Services Health and Safety Association (PSHSA) www.pshsa.ca
- Workplace Safety North (WSN) www.workplacesafetynorth.ca
- Workplace Safety & Prevention Services (WSPS) www.wsps.ca
- Occupational Health Clinics for Ontario Workers Inc. (OHCOW) http://www.ohcow.on.ca
- Workers Health and Safety Centre (WHSC) www.whsc.on.ca

2010 resulted in the formation of the Expert Advisory Panel headed by Tony Dean. The Dean Panel made recommendations to the Government of Ontario on occupational health and safety and training requirements in the province. These recommendations called for the prevention mandate at the WSIB to move to the Ministry of Labour, now the Ministry of Labour, Training and Skills Development. The government of Ontario accepted the recommendations of the Dean Panel in the form of Bill 160. The date of effect for this legislation was April 1, 2012 or as prescribed.

The *Occupational Health and Safety Act*

The *Occupational Health and Safety Act* is designed to protect the health and safety of workers by setting minimum standards for safe practices. The *OHSA* is the law, as are the regulations made under the *OHSA*. Both the *OHSA* and regulations incorporate by reference many other regulations, guidelines, codes and standards. Since these separate elements of the law are determined by different processes, it is useful to think of the law as having three parts:

- the *OHSA*;

- the regulations; and

- guidelines, codes and standards incorporated into the *OHSA* or regulations.

For convenience, the Ministry of Labour, Training and Skills Development publishes three booklets. Each contains the *OHSA* and the regulations for one of the three sectors: industrial establishments, mining or construction. These booklets are commonly referred to as the green books. Other companies publish all the regulations into one book. Alternately, the legislation can be found electronically under e-laws.

The OHSA
The *OHSA* sets out the principles of the law and assigns general rights and duties to individuals and organizations.

The Regulations
The *OHSA* authorizes the Minister of Labour, Training and Skills Development or the Cabinet to enact specific regulations that determine how the law operates. Regulations provide many specific requirements. They are not debated and adopted in public. They are usually drafted by Ministry experts and then approved by the Cabinet, but they cannot contradict the *OHSA*. When a provision is made by regulation, it is referred to as being prescribed.

The government may appoint committees, made up of those affected by the law, to provide assistance or advice on specific regulations. For example, labour and management make up the Joint Steering Committee on Hazardous Substances in the Workplace.

Guidelines, Codes and Standards
Guidelines, codes and standards provide additional details that make regulations more precise or apply them to specific situations. They do not require Cabinet approval, and may not even be seen by the Minister. They are not enforceable unless they are specifically named, or cited, in *the OHSA* or in a regulation. Even if they do not have the force of law, they provide an indication of the rules likely to be used by Ministry inspectors and others who oversee the *OHSA*.

Guidelines are usually developed by government experts, outside experts or a combination of both, and do not require formal approval. Guidelines are set in government policy and are used extensively by Ministry inspectors. For examples, see the Guidelines on heat stress or confined spaces on the Ministry of Labour, Training and Skills Development website.

Codes help to refine regulations and make them more specific. They are written by experts, usually outside the government. Codes are often referred to in the regulations of the *OHSA*. An example is the Building Code within Regulation 851, Section 120 for Industrial Establishments.

Standards are usually developed outside government by committees of professionals in a particular industry or field of specialty. For example, there are several Canadian Standards Association (CSA) standards for the components of a fall protection system, in the Construction Projects Regulation 213/91, Section 26.1(3).

The Organization of the OHSA

The provisions of the *OHSA* are discussed in detail elsewhere in this reference guide wherever they are relevant. This section aims to provide an understanding of the law's overall framework. The principle effects of each section of the *OHSA* are briefly described, but the descriptions are not exhaustive. Readers who need to know the precise content of the law should read the relevant sections of the *OHSA*.

The *OHSA* is divided into thirteen parts. Each part contains one or more sections, and there are 71 sections in all. Section 1, Definitions, is not included in any of the parts. It comes before Part I and contains definitions of terms used in the *OHSA*. These definitions are important to understanding the *OHSA*. They help to establish how, when and to whom the *OHSA* applies. For example, Section 1 defines a certified member as a committee member who is certified under section 7.6.

Application

Part I sets out the application of the *OHSA*. This means where, when and to whom it applies. In general, the *OHSA* applies to all workers in Ontario. There are a few exceptions, including workers at federal undertakings, work done by an owner or a servant in or around a private residence. In addition, it is the Ministry's policy that an inmate of a correctional institute is not a worker under the *OHSA* and therefore that the *OHSA* does not apply to inmates.

The Occupational Health and Safety Act	
Definitions	
Part I:	Application
Part II:	Administration
Part II.1	Prevention Council, Chief Prevention Officer and Designated Entities
Part III:	Duties of Employers and Other Persons
Part III.0.1	Violence and Harassment
Part II.1	Codes of Practice
Part IV:	Toxic Substances
Part V:	Right to Refuse or to Stop Work where Health or Safety in Danger
Part VI:	Reprisals by Employer Prohibited
Part VII:	Notices
Part VIII:	Enforcement
Part IX:	Offences and Penalties
Part X:	Regulations Index

The Occupational Health and Safety Act	
Part I: Application	
Section	
2	To whom the act applies
3	Where and to whom the act does not apply
4	Application of the act to the self- employed

Administration

Part II of the *OHSA* deals with administration. It also establishes processes that support joint consultation in the workplace. Some sections give the Minister the authority to delegate powers to government employees. These include inspectors and ministerial advisors. The Chief Prevention Officer may establish and maintain training standards for health and safety programs in Ontario workplaces.

Other administrative items include the collection of levies and the provision of information by the Workplace Safety and Insurance Board. A large portion of Part II sets up the processes that promote joint management-labour participation:

- joint health and safety committees; and
- health and safety representatives.

Joint health and safety committees and health and safety representatives are described in Chapters 4 and 6.

Prevention Council

In Part II.1 of the *OHSA*, one will find information about the Prevention Council, the Chief Prevention Officer (CPO), and Designated Entities such as safe workplace associations, a medical clinic, or a training centre specializing in occupational health and safety. The Prevention Council's role is to advise the Minister of Labour, Training and Skills Development and the Chief Prevention Officer on issues that lead to the prevention of workplace injuries and illnesses, the development of a provincial OHS strategy, and large funding and delivery of services changes. The Prevention Council is made up of representatives from unions, employers, and others with occupational health and safety expertise.

The Chief Prevention Officer (CPO) is appointed by the Minister. The duties include developing a provincial occupational health and safety strategy, preparing an annual report, setting standards and holding Basic Certification and Working at Heights training providers accountable. The CPO certifies members of joint health and safety committees.

The Occupational Health and Safety Act	
Part II: Administration	
Section	
4.1	Powers of Minister
5	Delegation of Powers
6	Appointment of Inspectors and Directors
7	Certificate of Appointment
7.1-7.7	Training Standards
8	Health & Safety Representatives
9	Joint Health and Safety Committees
10	Worker Trades Committees
11	Consultation on Industrial Hygiene Testing
12	Provision of Information by the WSIB
13-19	Repealed
20	Testimony
21	Advisors to the Minister
22	Contribution to Defray Cost
22.1	Powers under Federal Legislation

The Occupational Health and Safety Act	
Part II.1: Prevention Council, Chief Prevention Officer and Designated Entities	
Section	
22.2	Prevention Council
22.3	Chief Prevention Officer Functions
22.4	Changes to Funding and Delivery of Services
22.5-.7	Designated Entities
22.8-.9	Appointment of Administrator/ Board of Directors

Duties of Employers and Others

Part III sets out the duties of employers, workers, supervisors and other persons. Unlike rights that the parties may exercise, duties are things they must do.

More than 30 different parties are mentioned in *the OHSA* and all of them have duties. The duties of nine of them are set out in Part III. The most important duties are summarized below. They are discussed in more detail wherever they are relevant.

Employers – Sections 25 and 26

Employers have many duties under *the OHSA*. They can be grouped into five categories:

- Employers have a duty to set up a joint health and safety committee or health and safety representative if one is required by the *OHSA*. The employer must ensure that at least one worker member and one employer member of the JHSC become certified. The employer must pay for time spent by JHSC and HSR members while exercising their rights and duties under the *OHSA*.

The Occupational Health and Safety Act	
Part III: Duties of Employers and Other Persons	
Section	
23	Duties of Constructors
24	Duties of Licensees
25-26	Duties of Employers
25.1	Footwear
27	Duties of Supervisors
28	Duties of Workers
29	Duties of Owners
30	Duties of Project Owners
31	Duties of Suppliers
32	Duties of Directors and Officers of a Corporation

- Employers must prepare a written occupational health and safety policy and a program to implement that policy. A health and safety policy is the employer's statement of the principles that will guide health and safety in the workplace. The health and safety program is a set of procedures for implementing the policy. When the joint health and safety committee or health and safety representative is part of the employer's decision-making process, it is likely that the committee or HSR will be consulted in the development and review of the health and safety policy and program. The policy must be posted in the workplace and reviewed every year.

- Employers have a duty to provide pertinent information to JHSCs and HSRs. This includes information about workplace hazards, testing and training. Employers must respond in writing to recommendations from JHSCs or HSRs within 21 days.

- Employers have a general duty to make sure that their organization in compliance with *OHSA* and all regulations that apply to their workplace. All prescribed equipment, materials and protective devices must be provided and maintained. Prescribed measures and procedures must be carried out.

- Employers have a duty to take every precaution reasonable in the circumstances for the protection of workers. They must provide workers with information, instruction and supervision. The employer must appoint a competent person (as defined by the *OHSA*) as supervisor. A worker exposed to a hazardous material or physical agent must be given instruction and training prescribed by regulation. This training must be developed in consultation with the JHSC or the health and safety representative, if any.

- Employers have a duty to ensure that any hazardous material used in the workplace meets the requirements of the regulations concerning exposure limits, labeling, safety data sheets and worker instruction and training. Where so prescribed, the employer must make an assessment of all biological and chemical agents produced for use in the workplace to determine if they are hazardous. If there is anything in the workplace that causes, emits or produces a hazardous physical agent, the employer must post warnings as prescribed by the regulations.

Constructors – Section 23

- Constructors have the same general duties as employers.

- Constructors have a duty to ensure that all contractors and subcontractors on a project comply with the *OHSA*, and that the health and safety of all workers on the project is protected.

- Where so prescribed, constructors must also provide written notice to a director of the Ministry of Labour, Training and Skills Development when a project begins.

Supervisors – Section 27

- Supervisors have a duty to take "every precaution reasonable in the circumstances" for the protection of workers.
- Supervisors must ensure that workers comply with the *OHSA* and regulations and that they use protective devices and clothing as required by the employer.

- Supervisors have a duty to advise workers of actual or potential health and safety hazards including, in some cases, written instructions.

Workers – Section 28

- Workers have a duty to work in compliance with the *OHSA* and regulations.

- Worker must wear or use protective equipment or clothing provided by the employer and must not interfere with protective devices.

- Workers have a duty to report any violations of the *OHSA*, defective equipment or workplace hazards, of which they are aware, to a supervisor.

- Workers must not operate equipment in a way that may endanger themselves or any other worker, and are prohibited from engaging in contests, pranks, or boisterous conduct.

Owners – Section 29

- An owner of a workplace has a duty to ensure that the workplace and its facilities meet the regulations. Where required by regulation, they must provide workplace drawings, plans or specifications.

- An owner or employer can be required by regulation to file construction plans with the Ministry before any work is done. Owners of mines have a duty to update drawings and plans every six months.

- Owners must provide a list of designated substances that are on a project site to the constructor before entering into any contract for construction work. The constructor, in turn, must provide a copy of the list to contractors and sub-contractors.

Directors and Officers – Section 32

Directors and officers of a corporation shall take all reasonable care to ensure that a corporation complies with:

- the *OHSA* and regulations;

- orders and requirements of inspectors and Ministry directors; and

- orders of the Minister.

Suppliers – Section 31 (1)

Every person who supplies machines, devices, tools, or equipment under any form of rental or leasing agreement for use in a workplace shall ensure:

- that the machine, device, tool, or equipment is in good condition;

- that the machine device, tool, or thing complies with the *OHSA* and regulations; and

- if it is the person's responsibility under the agreement, that the machine, device, tool, or thing is maintained in good condition.

Architects and Engineers – Section 31 (2)

Professional architects and professional engineers must give competent and true advice. If they act negligently or incompetently, and a worker is endangered, they can be held accountable and charged under the *OHSA*.

Violence and Harassment

In 2009, Bill 168 added Violence and Harassment to the Occupational Health and Safety Act (Part III.0.1). Employers must develop and post policies and programs regarding workplace violence and harassment in the workplace. These are to be reviewed annually.

Codes of Practice

A Code of Practice as set out in Part III.1 is a set of documents that describes in detail, how a piece of legislation is to be followed. The Ministry of Labour, Training and Skills Development can approve all or parts of a code of practice as a means of compliance. Currently, there is only one Code of Practice in Ontario. It is the Code of practice to address workplace harassment.

Toxic Substances

Part IV of the *OHSA* deals with toxic substances. A toxic substance is a biological or chemical agent, or combination of such agents that may endanger the health of a worker. The *OHSA* also uses the terms hazardous materials and hazardous agents to describe toxic substances.

The *OHSA* deals with toxic substances in three ways. The first is by regulating the exposure to toxic substances during their use:

- There were 12 separate regulations (two regulations for asbestos) governing 11 hazardous substances designated under the *OHSA*. These regulations have been repealed and are now covered in Regulation 490/09 Designated Substances. To see the list of the 11 hazardous substances, please read Section 2 of Regulation 490/09.

- Ontario Regulation 833/90 regulates exposure to all hazardous or chemical agents and contains specific limits concerning such agents.

The Occupational Health and Safety Act	
Part III.0.1: Violence and Harassment	
Section	
32.0.1	Policies, Violence and Harassment
32.0.2	Program, Violence
32.0.3	Assessment of Risks of Violence
32.0.4	Domestic Violence
32.0.5	Duties re Violence
32.0.6	Program, Harassment
32.0.7	Duties, Harassment
32.0.8	Information and Instruction, Harassment

The Occupational Health and Safety Act	
Part III.1: Codes of Practice	
Section	
32.1	Definition
32.2	Approval of Code of Practice
32.3	Publication of Approval, etc.
32.4	Effect of Approved Code of Practice

The Occupational Health and Safety Act	
Part IV: Toxic Substances	
Section	
33	Orders of Director (regarding toxic substances)
34	Repealed
35	Designation of Substances
36	Repealed (Inventory of Hazardous Materials)
37	Hazardous Materials Identification and Data Sheets
38	Safety Data Sheets to be made available
39	Assessments for Hazardous Materials
40	Confidential Business Information
40.1	Information Privileged
41	Hazardous Physical Agents
42	Instruction and Training (Hazardous Materials)

- A Ministry of Labour, Training and Skills Development director can issue an order to an employer to prohibit or restrict the use of a toxic substance. These used to be referred to as "Section 20 Orders", but since *the OHSA* was amended in 1990 they are covered under Section 33. This power is rarely used.

The second way the *OHSA* deals with toxic substances is through the Workplace Hazardous Materials Information System (WHMIS). This is a nation-wide federal/provincial system, which is incorporated into the *OHSA* and regulations. The WHMIS regulation requires all hazardous materials in a workplace to be labeled, and safety data sheets to be available for each of them. Special WHMIS training is required for workers.

The hazardous material identification system known as 'GHS' an acronym for the Global Harmonized System of Classification and Labelling of Chemicals is an international agreement between most nations of the world to have one uniform labelling system. Canada's implementation is referred to as WHMIS 2015. Employers are required to educate and train workers about WHMIS 2015.

The third way the *OHSA* deals with toxic substances is by regulating the introduction of new substances into the workplace. A person who wants to manufacture, distribute or supply a new substance must notify a director of the Ministry in writing. The director may order an assessment of the substance.

The Right to Refuse or Stop Work

Part V of *the OHSA* gives workers the right to refuse to work or do particular work which they believe is likely to endanger them or another worker. At the first stage the worker simply has to have a subjective belief that the work is likely to endanger health and safety. If the worker continues to refuse after a supervisor has investigated, he or she must have "reasonable grounds". The right to refuse unsafe work is described in detail in Chapter 5.

The Occupational Health and Safety Act
Part V: Right to Refuse or Stop Work Where Health or Safety in Danger

Section

43	Procedure for Work Refusal
44	Definition of "Dangerous Circumstances"
45	Bilateral Work Stoppage
46	Application for Unilateral Work Stoppage Authority
47	Unilateral Work Stoppage
48	Investigation of Complaint by Certified Member
49	Filing of Complaint Against Certified Member

Procedures for stopping work under dangerous circumstances are also set out in Part V of the *OHSA*. A bilateral work stoppage occurs when a worker certified member and a management certified member agree that dangerous circumstances exist. A unilateral work stoppage can be initiated by a single certified member, under the following circumstances:

- Labour Relations Board has issued a declaration that the unilateral procedure is in effect; or

- An employer agrees to abide by the unilateral process. The right to stop work is described in detail in Chapter 5.

Reprisals by Employer Prohibited

Part VI has two sections. Section 50 prohibits employers from taking reprisals because a worker has acted in compliance with the *OHSA*. It also sets out procedures for dealing with complaints concerning reprisals.

The Occupational Health and Safety Act
Part VI: Reprisals by Employer Prohibited
Section
50   No Discipline, dismissal, etc. by Employer
50.1 Offices of the Worker and Employer Advisers

Section 50.1 explains that Office of the Worker Adviser shall provide representation to non-unionized workers and Office of the Employer Adviser shall provide representation to small employers with less than 100 employees on reprisal issues.

Notices

Part VII requires employers and constructors to immediately notify an inspector, the JHSC, health and safety representative and the union, if any, when a person is killed or critically injured at a workplace. Where a critical injury has occurred, the employer must also send a written report to the MLTSD within two days. Serious injuries or illnesses must be reported in writing within four days. Unexpected occurrences, sometimes called "near misses", must be reported if they occur at a construction site or mine.

The Occupational Health and Safety Act
Part VII: Notices
Section
51   Notice of Fatality or Critical Injury
52   Notice of Accident explosion, Fire or Violence causing injury.
53   Notice of Unexpected Occurrence in a Mine or Construction Site

Enforcement

The Ministry of Labour, Training and Skills Development has the authority to, and is charged with the responsibility of, enforcing the law. Part VIII of the *OHSA* gives inspectors broad powers and requires that employers, supervisors and workers assist in their investigations.

The Ministry of Labour, Training and skills Development. promotes the internal responsibility system. Health and safety issues should be handled by management and workers without intervention from government. Ideally, a problem or complaint is brought to the attention of JHSC members or a health and safety representative. These persons have knowledge of health and safety principles and the law and can suggest solutions. Most of the time, problems can be fixed by the supervisor without recourse to formal procedures under the *OHSA*. If this approach fails, however, the *OHSA* contains specific procedures for enforcement by Ministry of Labour, Training and Skills Development inspectors. There are also provisions for appealing the actions of inspectors to the Labour Relation Board.

The procedures for enforcing the *OHSA* include dealing with inspectors and the Labour Relations Officer and are explained in detail in Chapter 5.

Offences and Penalties

Part IX makes it an offence to contravene or fail to comply with the *OHSA* and its regulations. Fines of up to $100,000 for individuals ($1,500,000 for corporations) and jail terms of up to 12 months are set out. Procedures for presenting evidence and conducting trials are also set out in this part.

Regulations

Part X of the *OHSA* has only two sections. Section 70 empowers the Lieutenant Governor in Council (the Cabinet) to make regulations. Section 71 also empowers the Lieutenant Governor to make regulations for the taxi industry. The regulations are described in the following section of this chapter.

The Occupational Health and Safety Act
Part VIII: Enforcement

Section

54	Duties and Powers of an inspector
55	Order for Inspections
55.1	Order for Written Policies
55.2	Order for Written Assessment, etc.
55.3	Order for Workplace Harassment Investigation
56	Warrants – Investigative Techniques.
56.1	Power of inspector to Seize
57	Order by Inspectors where No Compliance
58	Entry into Barricaded Area
59	Notice of Compliance
60	Injunction Proceedings
61	Appeals from Order of an Inspector
62	Obstruction of Inspector
63	Information Confidential
64	Copies of Reports
65	Immunity

The Occupational Health and Safety Act
Part IX: Offences and Penalties

Section

66	Penalties
67	Evidence for Prosecutions
68	Trials
68.1	Publication re:conviction
69	Time Limit for Prosecution

The Occupational Health and Safety Act
Part X: Regulations

Section

70	Regulations
71	Regulations, Taxi Industry

The *OHSA* expresses the principles or intent of the law. The regulations state how *the OHSA* will be applied. For this reason, Section 70 sets out 56 specific areas where the Cabinet may make regulations. It also provides a general authority to make regulations that are "advisable for the health and safety of persons in or about a workplace." Regulations are enforceable under the *OHSA*.

There are four major types of regulations:

1. the Workplace Hazardous Materials Information System (WHMIS) regulation;

2. separate sector regulations for industrial establishments, mining, healthcare, farming and construction;

3. the designated substance regulation;

4. the Regulation Respecting Control of Exposure to Biological or Chemical Agents.

There are also a number of other regulations. They establish definitions, or regulate safety in specific areas.

The Workplace Hazardous Materials Information System

The Workplace Hazardous Materials Information System is usually referred to as WHMIS (pronounced whim-iss). This is a Canada-wide system, which was developed in consultation with management and labour. Separate packages of legislation were passed by the federal government and by all the provinces and territories. Thus, the same system applies in every Canadian workplace.

WHMIS provides information about hazardous materials in three ways:

1. labels on the containers of hazardous materials;

2. safety data sheets (SDS); and

3. worker education and training.

These three components work together to give practical meaning to the worker's right to know about toxic substances. Hazardous materials include substances that are toxic as well as those that present other hazards such as fire or explosion.

Federal WHMIS Legislation

The *Hazardous Products Act* places duties on suppliers who sell or import a hazardous material for use in a Canadian workplace. They must label their products and provide material safety data sheets to their customers.

The Controlled Products Regulations under the *Hazardous Products Act* define certain hazardous materials as controlled products, which are subject to the WHMIS requirements. The regulation also sets out the information the supplier is obliged to provide on the label and on the SDS.

Ontario WHMIS Legislation

Part IV of the *OHSA* requires employers to ensure, subject to the regulations, that all hazardous materials are labeled and to ensure that SDSs are available. Employers are required to develop training programs, in consultation with the joint health and safety committee. The employer also has a duty to ensure that no hazardous material is used, handled or stored in a workplace unless the WHMIS regulation has been met. The WHMIS regulation (Ontario Regulation 860/90) sets out in detail the requirements concerning labels, SDS's and worker training programs.

WHMIS Labels

Supplier labels and workplace labels are the first part of the WHMIS information delivery system. Controlled products used in a workplace must bear a WHMIS label.

Full information supplier labels are required for most hazardous materials. The regulations provide for special labels for small containers, laboratories and laboratory supply houses. There are detailed requirements for the label design. In the case of bulk shipments, only the outer container needs a label, provided that arrangements have been made for full labeling at the workplace.

Workplace labels are required when a controlled product is produced in the workplace, or when the product is transferred from the supplier container to workplace containers. Workplace labels do not require as much information as supplier labels. Only the product name, safe handling instructions and an SDS statement need be shown.

WHMIS Hazard Symbols (2015)

Pictogram	Description	Types of Hazards
	Gas Cylinder	• Gas Under Pressure
	Flame	• Flammables • Self-Reactive • Pyrophoric • Self-Heating • In Contact with Water, Emits Flammable Gases • Organic Peroxides
	Flame Over Circle	• Oxidizer
	Skull and Crossbones	• Acute Toxicity (fatal or toxic)
	Health Hazard	• Carcinogenicity • Respiratory Sensitization • Reproductive Toxicity • Specific Target Organ Toxicity • Germ Cell Mutagenicity • Aspiration Hazard
	Exclamation Mark	• Irritation (skin or eyes) • Skin Sensitization • Acute Toxicity (harmful) • Specific Target Organ Toxicity (respiratory irritation, drowsiness, or dizziness)
	Corrosion	• Serious Eye Damage • Skin Corrosion • Corrosive to Metals
	Exploding Bomb	• Self Reactive • Organic Peroxide
	Biohazardous	• Biohazardous Infectious Materials

Safety Data Sheets (SDSs)

Safety data sheets are the second part of the WHMIS information delivery system. The SDS is a technical document which summarizes the health and safety information available about a controlled product.

The SDS must be readily available at the worksite for use by workers who may be exposed to the hazardous material. It must also be provided to members of the joint health and safety committee and health and safety representatives.

In the Globally Harmonized System, Safety Data Sheets (SDSs) have 16 sections with specific information requirements. They are required in English and French. They will be updated when significant new information becomes available. Suppliers must provide this new information to their customers at the time of sale.

Worker Education and Training

The third part of the WHMIS information delivery system is worker education and training. To protect themselves and ensure proper handling, workers need to know how to use the information on labels and SDSs.

All workers who work with, or "in proximity" to, a controlled product must be informed about the hazard information provided by the supplier of a controlled product. In addition, they must be advised about any other hazard information of which the employer is aware or should reasonably be aware.

Worker training programs must be developed, implemented and reviewed at least once a year in consultation with the joint health and safety committee or health and safety representative. Reviewing the status of the WHMIS program does not necessarily mean that training must happen each year. Training will be required more or less frequently, depending on each workplace.

A supplier label needs the following elements:

❶ **Product Identifier** - name of the product
❷ **Pictogram(s)** – the symbol that represents the hazard class. In some cases, no pictogram is required.
❸ **Signal Word** – a word used to alert the reader to a potential hazard and to indicate the severity of the hazard.
❹ **Hazard Statement(s)** – an assigned statement that describes the hazard(s).
❺ **Precautionary Statements** – standardized phrases that describe measures to be taken to minimize or prevent adverse effects resulting from exposure to a hazardous product or resulting from improper handling or storage of a hazardous product.
❻ **Initial Supplier Identifier** – the name, address and telephone number of either the Canadian manufacturer or the Canadian importer.
Hazardous ingredients may or may not be listed on the label. Suppliers have this choice.

WHMIS 2015 Supplier Label

Methanol
Flammable – do not use near an open flame or near processes that generate sparks.

Avoid inhaling vapours.

Read the Material Safety Data Sheet before using this compound.

Workplace Label

Applying WHMIS in the Workplace
WHMIS is the principle method by which workers are informed about toxic substances in the workplace. The regulations for labeling and providing SDSs place very specific duties on the employer. The practical implementation of WHMIS in the workplace also involves the joint health and safety committee and health and safety representative. The first priority is to ensure that all of the controlled products in the workplace are identified. Next, every worker who is likely to be exposed to a controlled product must be identified. And finally, a training program must be carried out, to give each worker information about the safe use of these substances.

Sector Regulations
The following Sector Regulations apply to specific types of workplaces:

- Construction Projects – Ontario Regulation 213/91
- Health Care and Residential Facilities – Ontario Regulation 67/93
- Industrial Establishments – Ontario Regulation 851
- Farming Operations – Ontario Regulation 414/05
- Mines and Mining Plants – Ontario Regulation 854

Designated Substance Regulations
The *OHSA* includes regulations governing the use of designated substances. The fact that they are designated means that their use must be assessed and controlled. In certain cases, the use of such substances may be prohibited by regulation.

Previously there was a separate "green book" for each of the 11 designated substances. Those regulations have been revoked and the designated substances are now covered in Ontario Regulation 490/09. Ontario Regulation 278/05 also covers Asbestos in Construction.

Certified members need to be thoroughly familiar with the regulations covering any designated substances present in their workplace.

The regulation contains specific requirements for exposure limits, assessment methods, control programs, personal protective equipment and, where prescribed, medical surveillance procedures.

An assessment should be conducted for each designated substance present in a workplace. The assessment, and any control program found necessary by the assessment, must be developed in consultation with the joint health and safety committee or health and safety representative. The committee or health and safety representative must be given copies of both the assessment and the proposed control program, and must be provided with the results of air sampling tests. A worker member of the JHSC or the HSR may be present at the beginning of any such testing.

Control of Exposure to Biological or Chemical Agents

- The Regulation Respecting Control of Exposure to Biological or Chemical Agents (Ontario Regulation 833/90) requires employers to limit a worker's daily and weekly exposure to any of the approximately 725 specified hazardous substances. The regulation includes a schedule of biological and chemical agents for which exposure limits have been set. This regulation did not previously apply to the construction sector. As of July 1, 2016, codes of practice relating to exposure of workers to biological or chemical agents that have been approved by the MLTSD will be posted on their website.

The schedule of exposure values attached to the regulation includes three types of occupational exposure limits:

- **Time-weighted average limit** (TWA) to which a worker is exposed in a workday or work week (usually 8-hour day or 40 hours a week)

- **Short-term exposure limit** (STEL) exposed in any 15-minute interval no more than four times during an 8-hour work shift, and within at least one hour between exposures

- **Ceiling limit** (C) maximum exposure at any time

The regulation generally requires that worker exposure be kept below these exposure values without the use of personal protective equipment. The employer must also pay for medical examinations of workers who are exposed to the substance. Such examinations are voluntary on the part of the worker.

Other Health and Safety Legislation

The *OHSA* is known as a "comprehensive" act. This means that it has very broad coverage. With few exceptions, it applies to almost all Ontario workplaces. In fact, some of its provisions cover self-employed individuals. Moreover, it overrides any contrary provisions of other Acts that regulate health and safety.

At the same time, the *OHSA* incorporates, by reference, certain provisions of regulations (codes) under other Acts. This means that if a referenced Act such as the *Building Code Act* or its regulations, is amended, any changes to these provisions will automatically have force under the *OHSA*.

There are many Acts in this category, and certified members and health and safety representatives should be aware of those which might apply in their workplace. Only the most important of them are discussed here.

The Building Code Act

The *OHSA* incorporates regulations (codes) of the *Building Code Act* by reference. This includes, for example, the duty of the employer to ensure that a floor, roof, wall or pillar be capable of supporting loads. A Ministry of Labour, Training and Skills Development inspector has the right to obtain the report of a professional engineer as proof.

Coroner's Act

The *Coroner's Act* provides that a coroner may order an inquest into the death of a worker (compulsory in the death of a mine or construction worker). Such an inquest does not replace the investigation required under the *OHSA*. A member of the joint health and safety committee or health and safety representative who has a direct interest in the inquest may ask the coroner for permission to participate.

Employment Standards Act

The *Employment Standards Act* defines the standard hours of work. Employers can apply for variations to these standards.

Fire Protection and Prevention Act

The *Fire Protection and Prevention Act* provides special powers to fire marshals to enter workplaces and inspect the precautions that have been taken to protect life and property, and to make orders for improvements.

Health Protection and Promotion Act

The powers and responsibilities of Medical Officers of Health (MHO) are established by the *Health Protection and Promotion Act*. Under this Act, laboratories that examine human specimens must be licensed and must report their findings concerning reportable diseases to the MHO. Public Health Boards also get their authority to inspect food service establishments under this Act.

Labour Relations Act

The *Labour Relations Act* governs the certification of trade unions as bargaining agents and the practice of collective bargaining. It establishes the Ontario Labour Relations Board (OLRB). The *OHSA* empowers the OLRB to enquire into any complaint of reprisals under Part VI of the *OHSA*. A person delegated by the Minister to hear appeals under the Toxic Substances sections of the *OHSA* is given the powers of the chair of a board of arbitration under the *Labour Relations Act*.

Ministry of Labour Act

The *Ministry of Labour Act* gives the Ministry the authority it needs to carry out its powers and functions. This includes part of the authority for Ministry inspectors to enforce and implement the *OHSA*.

Provincial Offences Act

The *Provincial Offences Act* includes procedures for the prosecution of offences under provincial statutes, including offences under the *OHSA*. It also establishes procedures whereby inspectors may obtain a search warrant to enter a dwelling used as a workplace to make inspections under the *OHSA*.

Smoke-Free Ontario Act, 2017

The *Smoke-free Ontario Act* prohibits smoking of tobacco, the use of electronic cigarettes to vape any substance, and the smoking of cannabis (medical and recreational) in enclosed workplaces and enclosed public places.

Transportation of Dangerous Goods Act

The requirements for handling and transporting dangerous goods are uniform across Canada because all provinces have adopted this federal law. It outlines a system of dangerous goods labels and placards for use when such goods are being moved by road, rail or boat. This Act also requires special training, renewable every three years, for the persons involved according to the type of goods they handle.

Workplace Safety and Insurance Act

The *Workplace Safety and Insurance Act* provides for a type of "no-fault" insurance to pay for worker claims for compensation for occupational injuries and illnesses. This Act contains a number of regulations that affect health and safety in the workplace. These include Regulation 1101 concerning first aid equipment and training requirements. They also require that procedures to be followed in case of injury be prominently posted in the workplace. The *OHSA* requires the WSIB to send, on request from a worker, employer, committee, health and safety representative or union, a summary of claims data relating to the employer.

Highway Traffic Act

The *Highway Traffic Act* provides for the rules of the road and drivers' hours of work and is referenced in the regulations of the *OHSA*.

Review

This chapter introduces the laws that govern health and safety in Ontario workplaces. Principal among them is the *OHSA*. When it was passed in 1978, it became the first comprehensive health and safety law in Ontario. It applies to most workplaces in the province, regardless of the industries or occupations involved.

The *OHSA* places rights and duties on employers, workers, supervisors and others in the workplace. Individual workers are given **three** essential rights:

- the right to **know**;
- the right to **participate**; and
- the right to **refuse**.

The *OHSA* also establishes a number of processes that encourage joint participation in health and safety matters. Most importantly, it requires the formation of joint health and safety committees, or the selection of an occupational health and safety representative in many work places. These JHSCs are the focal point of joint action involving employers and workers. The *OHSA* supports these activities by placing a duty on employers to provide joint health and safety committees and health and safety representatives with a wide range of information.

Amendments made to the *OHSA* in 1990 had the effect of broadening the scope of joint consultation on health and safety. The *OHSA* now requires the selection and training of certified members of JHSCs. These certified members have special rights, duties and responsibilities under the *OHSA*.

This chapter also explains the structure of the *OHSA*. The *OHSA* is divided into 13 Parts. Several of these Parts concern administrative and enforcement issues. Others establish JHSCs and HSRs, assign rights and duties, and establish the right to refuse or stop work.

The last part of the *OHSA* empowers the government to make regulations which have the force of law. There are four major types of regulations under the *OHSA*:

- WHMIS (Reg. 860)
- Industrial establishments (Reg. 851); mining (Reg. 854); health care (Reg. 67); farming (Reg. 414); and construction (Reg. 213)
- Designated substance regulations (Reg. 490 and Asbestos in Construction Reg. 278).
- Biological or Chemical Agents (Reg. 833).

Finally, this chapter briefly reviews a number of other Acts that are relevant to occupational health and safety. Parts of some of these Acts, such as the *Building Code Act*, are incorporated by reference in the *OHSA*. Others, such as the *Health Protection and Promotion Act*, govern activities that may be of interest to the workplace parties.

Chapter 3

Understanding the Law

- The Legislative Process

- How a Bill Becomes Law

- How to Read the Law

- Keeping Track of Laws and Amendments

- Using the Law

- Review

Understanding the Law

For certified members of JHSCs and HSRs to fully understand the *OHSA*, they must first be able
to read it. The technical language and complex wording of laws can sometimes seem impossible
to understand. In fact, laws are written this way to ensure clarity. The more detailed and
precise they are on paper, the more effective they should be in practice. Fortunately, it isn't
necessary to become a lawyer to be able to read and understand the *OHSA* or law.

This chapter begins with a basic outline of how laws are made. A later section describes how to
read the law.

Laws have a vocabulary, grammar and structure all their own. Once the reader has learned to
recognize these, understanding a law's meaning becomes easier. An introduction to legal
terminology provides the basic tools. Their use can make the law understandable to everyone
in the workplace.

Finally, it is important to realize that statutes, and the regulations enacted under them, seldom
stand still. Amendments take place over time. To accurately interpret and apply the law, the
certified member and health and safety representative must be aware of those changes – and
know where to find them. The sources of that information are also provided here.

Legislative Process

The law-making or legislative process has an ordered, specific number of steps. However, there
are many forces affecting how those steps are taken and when. It is important to remember
that law-making is a political process, and therefore very much influenced by the elected men
and women involved.

Political Parties

Canadian government, both federal and provincial, works on a multi-party system with
democratic elections. The party that wins the most parliamentary seats in a general election
forms the government for up to four years. The party with the next highest number of seats
forms the official opposition. If no party wins a clear majority, the party with the most seats
may form a coalition with another party or function as a minority government.

Federal elected representatives are called Members of Parliament (MPs). Their provincial
counterparts in Ontario are known as Members of Provincial Parliament (MPPs).

Before its four-year term is over, the government must call a general election. An election must
also be called if opposition members win a vote on a formal motion of non-confidence, or if
major legislation proposed by the government fails to pass.

The Government

Both provincial and federal governments have the power to enact laws, usually called Acts or Statutes. According to the Canadian Constitution, employment law, including occupational health and safety, is a provincial jurisdiction, except where it affects employees of the federal government and inter-provincial or federally chartered corporations (such as communications, transportation and atomic energy).

A new government's election platform reflects the way the governing party feels the country or province should be run. It is usually also the blueprint for any legislation the government proposes. That legislation may not always be universally popular. If the opposition or any other group can successfully sway public opinion against government policy, it may have to be changed or abandoned.

Standing Committees

Government and opposition parties appoint MPPs to standing committees of the Legislature. Standing, or permanent, committees are made up of elected members assigned by each party at the beginning of a new session of the Legislature. The number of members from each party depends on that party's representation in the Legislature.

To assist in the development and fine-tuning of potential Ontario legislation, standing committees cover a variety of broad subject areas. These include Justice, Social Policy, General Government, Regulations and Private Bills, and Finance and Economic Affairs.

How a Bill Becomes Law

In Ontario, before the legislative process can begin, a Bill — or draft of a new law — must be created. Bills can be presented to the Legislature or House by the government or by an individual member. This chapter will focus on the most common kind, a government Bill. Before it reaches the House, a Bill will go through several stages to increase its chances of being passed or adopted.

Advance Consultation

To measure support for its policies, the government sometimes presents them to the public and relevant interest groups before actually drafting a Bill. Green papers are published, outlining policy options. Feedback may then be incorporated into final proposals in a white paper. Discussion papers contain both options and proposals. Either way, floating ideas in public can radically change a Bill's content and sometimes stop it from being drafted at all.

Development and Cabinet Approval

With or without advance consultation, a Bill's first draft is prepared by staff of the Ministry of the Attorney General. Once the Minister has approved the draft, he or she will present it to the other Ministers in the Cabinet. In Cabinet, the Bill is discussed in complete secrecy. Changes may be made to win the collective support of the other Ministers. Once the draft Bill has Cabinet approval, it is presented to the House for the first of three Readings or debates.

First Reading
First Reading represents introduction or tabling of a Bill. The Minister introduces the Bill to the House, sometimes giving a short statement on its contents. The Bill is then numbered according to its order of introduction in the calendar year. The Bill can then go to Second Reading. Sometimes, the government invites public input before proceeding to Second Reading.

Second Reading
At Second Reading, the principle of the Bill is debated. Members can speak as long as they want, but only once. The more controversial the Bill, the greater the number of opposition members likely to speak. At the end of the debate, a vote determines whether the Bill will pass or fail. Bills are usually approved in principle at Second Reading because opposition members don't have much detailed information at that reading.

If the House votes unanimously to accept it, the Bill can go directly to the Third, and final, Reading. If even one member wants further discussion of any clause, the Bill is sent to Committee Stage.

Committee Stage
Now the debate moves from general principle to specific detail. The goal is to amend the Bill to make it more acceptable to the House, either in Committee of the Whole House or at a Committee of the House (also known as a standing committee).

Committee of the Whole House
If a Bill is non-controversial or of little public interest, the debate takes place in the House itself, where members become the Committee of the Whole House. Members can speak as often as they wish on each clause to propose amendments. Votes must be held on each amendment, but this is usually done all at once at the end of the day, rather than after each debate. After the voting, the Bill can go to Third Reading.

Standing Committee
If the Bill is a controversial one, it will be sent to a standing committee, at the request of at least 20 MPPs.

The members of the standing committee usually cooperate to avoid taking up too much time. Party differences may be temporarily set aside, and members may even vote independent of their party. Various groups, including industries, labour organizations and interested individuals, are invited to present their views on the Bill. Committee members may also travel to different parts of the province for more feedback.

When all submissions have been heard, the Committee suggests amendments and votes on them before reporting or sending the Bill back to the House. There, the amended Bill will be debated and voted on, clause by clause, until it can go to Third Reading.

Third Reading

At the final Reading, there is usually no more debate unless the standing committee has introduced new concepts. The Bill is put directly to a vote. If it fails at this stage, it cannot be brought forward again until the next sitting of the House.

Royal Assent

At a convenient time in the House agenda, the Lieutenant Governor enters the House and ceremonially signs the Bill from the Speaker's Chair. The Bill is now an Act of the Legislature. But it may not be in force.

Proclamation

The *Act* is proclaimed law on a date chosen by Cabinet, but that proclamation is often delayed until detailed regulations of the *Act* are available in written form. Regulations are explained in a later section of this chapter. The *Act* can now be changed only by introducing a new Bill into the Legislature.

How to Read the Law

Laws are constructed very carefully to ensure they cover every possible interpretation. What is clear in legal terms, however, may be confusing to a lay person. To be able to interpret and use the law correctly, certified members and others should become familiar with the way laws are written.

Definitions

At the beginning of each Act, "Section 1" contains definitions of key words used in that Act, listed alphabetically. In the case of the *OHSA*, relevant words include employer, owner, workplace and project. Each has a precise meaning in the Act.

Divisions

All Acts are organized into several elements. These divisions ensure nothing is left out, and help break down a complex idea into more manageable components. This in turn makes it easier to identify a specific duty or provision.

Even though Acts are, by necessity, long and detailed, there is a short cut to reading or referring to them. The numbering and lettering of an Act's divisions is very precise. With practice, it is possible to identify a specific passage simply by its letter or number reference.

Margin Titles

In the margin of an Act, opposite each sub-section, a short title or explanation of that sub-section's contents appears in small print. If a sub-section has the same title as the one above it, the Latin word *idem* (which means "the same") will appear. It is best to check an Act's index, as well, when searching for a specific sub-section.

Margin References

If an *Act* makes mention of another Act, such as the *Education Act* or the *Fire Marshalls Act*, a special reference tells the reader where to find the text of that *Act* by citing the Revised Statutes of Ontario (RSO) as a source. The RSOs are described later in this chapter.

Punctuation

Periods, commas, semicolons and other punctuation are carefully positioned to further clarify a law's meaning.

DIVISIONS OF AN ACT

SECTIONS contain a main idea or subject heading, such as Joint health and Safety Committees.

PARTS group together sections covering the same subject area in particularly long acts.

HEADINGS describe the contents of a Part more precisely.

SUB-SECTIONS expand on the main theme of the section — e.g., a description of the functions and powers of joint health and safety committees.

CLAUSES divide the sub-section with related information, such as a list of the functions and powers of joint health and safety committees.

SUB-CLAUSES expand on any points made in the clause
— a detailed explanation of a specific function or power of joint health and safety committees, for example.

PARAGRAPHS further divide a sub-clause into more elements or provide additional detail.

NEWLY ADDED SECTIONS, SUB-SECTIONS AND

CLAUSES, once passed, are inserted into an act just after an existing section, sub-section or clause that covers the same subject matter.

Period (.) at the end of each section or sub-section. Periods indicate that these are full sentences, regardless of the number of clauses or sub-clauses they contain. A period also means that these are complete thoughts, unrelated to the section or sub-section before or after.

Comma (,) at the end of each sub-clause. Since sub-clauses are usually closely related in idea and content, the comma gives each one equal weight or importance.

Semicolon (;) at the end of each clause. The semicolon implies that each clause has equal weight, but the ideas within it are quite different from those in the clause before or after.

Colon (:) at the end of a clause if the clause is followed by a number of sub- clauses.

Use of "And" and "Or"

Either "and" or "or" will always appear at the end of the second-last clause or sub-clause in every sub-section. Neither word will be written out at the end of the preceding clause or sub-clause; they are "understood" to be there.

In this way,

"32.0.1 – (1) An employer shall,
    a) prepare…;
    b) prepare…; and
    c) review…..

is interpreted to mean that an employer must prepare a violence and harassment policy and review each of them annually, as a minimum.

"And" tells the reader that the contents of each clause/sub-clause are equal, and that all the directions they contain must be taken. "Or" offers a choice between the directions found in the clauses/sub-clauses, since only one must be taken.

Numbering and Lettering	
Part =	Part IX *(capital letters and large Roman numerals)*
heading =	Offences and Penalties *(capital letters)*
Section =	1,2,3 *(numbered consecutively in bold type)*
Newly added Section =	1a, 2b, 3c *(bold lower case letter added to number)*
Sub-Section =	(1) (2) (3) *(indented, numbered consecutively in brackets, non-bold)* *(not numbered at all if only one in Section)*
Newly added Sub-Section =	(1a) (2b) (3c) *(lower case letter added to number in bracket)*
Clause =	(a) (b) (c) *(lower case letters in brackets)* *(if there are more clauses than letters in the alphabet, then numbered consecutively instead)*
Newly added Clause =	(aa) (ab) (ba) (bb) *(lower case letter added to letter in bracket)*
Sub-Clause =	(i) (ii) (iii) *(small Roman numerals in brackets)*
Sub-Sub-Clause =	a., B., C. *(capital letters)*

Use of "Shall", "May" and "Will"

The choice of one of these words changes the force of an instruction from compulsory to discretionary to possible. "Shall" means the action must be taken; "will" expresses a future possibility of it being taken; and "may" offers a choice of whether or not to take it at all.

Use of "Prescribed"

The use or meaning of "prescribed" depends on whether it is defined. If it is defined in the Act, the phrase "as prescribed" simply means "as dictated or laid out by" the regulations of the Act.

Repetition

Quite often, the same phrase will be repeated several times within the same sub-section, for example, "agent or combination of such agents". This repetition ensures that each separate requirement or direction of the sub-section refers to every single agent or combination of agents — not just an agent in one case and a combination of agents in another. Again, this helps eliminate any doubt as to intent in the reader's mind.

Keeping Track of Laws and Amendments

Information on all laws or statutes is available from various government sources. Some are more up-to-date than others. For complete accuracy, it is advisable to check them all.

Revised Statutes of Ontario

Every 10 years, the government publishes an official, bound record of all statutes still in effect, including any and all amendments made to laws up to and including the tenth year. This is called the Revised Statutes of Ontario (RSO). Each law becomes a chapter in the RSO. Between 1980 and 1990, the *Occupational Health and Safety Act* of 1978 was known as "RSO 1980, c.321".

Statutes of Ontario

Every year, new laws and amendments passed since the previous year are officially consolidated into the Statutes of Ontario (SO). Again, each law represents one chapter. Ten years' worth of statutes will then be combined into the next RSO.

The Ontario Gazette

This bimonthly, official government publication contains all government announcements, including the proclamation of new laws and amendments to existing laws. It is the most current source of information available.

Regulations

Regulations take an Act from theory to practice by providing detailed instructions on how the principles of that Act are to be carried out. They are the part of the law most often referred to besides the Act itself. Regulations can go only as far as the Act allows. For example, if the Act requires that an employer make sure the workplace complies with regulations, the regulations will set out in detail what the employer must do.

The Act itself empowers Cabinet to make regulations, which are usually written by Ministry staff after a Bill has passed. They are adopted by Cabinet without public debate.

Because Acts are not amended frequently, changes to regulations are what keep the law up to date. A certified member or health and safety representative can check regulation amendments in the annual Statutes of Ontario or the Ontario Gazette. Regulations and their amendments do not appear in the RSO, but are available in the revised Regulations of Ontario (RRO), consolidated every 10 years like the RSO.

Office Consolidations

Acts that are in public demand -– like the *Occupational Health and Safety Act* -– are often printed and issued as "green books". The green books are pocket-sized. They are also convenient because they include the regulations and all amendments made to that *OHSA* up to the time of printing. The more recent the printing, the less need there is to check the RSOs, SOs or Ontario Gazette. Office consolidations also include helpful tables of contents and indexes to both the *OHSA* and the regulations.

e-Laws

e-laws can be accessed at ontario.ca. Here one has access to official copies of Ontario's statutes and regulations. When one browses "O" under consolidated laws, the reader will find Occupational Health and Safety Act. Upon choosing the *OHSA*, the reader can access current regulations under the Act as well as Revoked Regulation under the *OHSA*. By clicking on the tab to the right, which says "Regulations under this Act", the certified member or joint health and safety representative has access to all the regulations made under the authority of the *OHSA*.

Using the Law

As mentioned earlier, it is possible to refer to an Act in a letter or oral or written report without including lengthy quotes. Specific number/letter references are easily looked up by the reader in the Act itself or in the RSO.

Using a Citation from an Act

If a section of an Act is referred to, there is no need to quote the whole section. Simply use the section, sub-section, and clause numbers to allow the reader, if required, to find the complete text of the law. Although the main point could be in the clause itself, the reader will need the full reference (section, sub-section and clause) to be able to read that point in relation to the surrounding language.

If more than one Act is involved in a report, it is helpful to identify which one is meant by starting the citation with an Act's RSO reference, for example, "RSO 1990, c.o.1". In this case, c. stands for chapter. If an Act has been amended since the last RSO, the reference can read either "RSO 1990, c.o.1, as amended" or include the specific amendment reference ("1991, c.o.1, s.24.-(1)").

This chapter introduces the main players in the law-making process, including political parties, the government, and standing committees. It establishes Bills as the starting point of all new legislation.

Once a policy is approved, a Bill is prepared and presented to Cabinet. Amendments may be made to win Cabinet approval before the Bill is introduced by the Minister concerned in the House.

A series of "readings" or debates among Members takes place to determine whether the Bill will pass or fail. Most Bills pass First Reading without debate because the House is only concerned with tabling or introducing the Bill at this stage.

At Second Reading, Members discuss the Bill's principle. If the Bill is not passed unanimously, it goes to Committee Stage, where the debate shifts to fine detail. If non-controversial, each clause of the Bill will be debated in the Committee of the Whole House. If controversial, it may be "sent out" to a standing committee. After hearing submissions from interest groups and individuals, the Committee makes and votes on amendments to each clause before sending the Bill back to the House for Third Reading.

If the Bill fails at Third Reading, it cannot be brought forward again until the next sitting of the House. If passed, it becomes an Act of the Legislature after receiving Royal Assent from the Lieutenant Governor. The Act is then proclaimed law by Cabinet. An Act may come into force on Royal Assent, or on a past date (retroactive), or on some future date.

The second part of this chapter deals with reading the law. Since laws are structured extremely carefully, they can seem complex unless the reader is familiar with the system used to organize them.

The final section of this chapter discusses ways of keeping track of laws and amendments, using the following sources:

- Revised Statutes of Ontario;
- Revised Regulations of Ontario (published every 10 years);
- Statutes of Ontario;
- Ontario Gazette;
- Regulations;
- Office Consolidations; and
- e-Laws

The chapter closes with a method for referring to a piece of the Act in letters or written reports by simply writing out a short number/letter reference rather than quoting entire sections. Called writing a "citation", this requires familiarity with the numbering and lettering systems used in an Act, the RSO or the SO.

Chapter 4
Joint Health and Safety Committees

- JHSC Functions

- When is a Committee Needed?

- JHSC Procedures

- JHSC Activities

- Making the JHSC Work

- Review

Joint Health and Safety Committees

The joint health and safety committee is a forum where employer and worker members can act together to identify, assess, control, and evaluate health and safety hazard controls. It is therefore an essential part of the internal responsibility system.

Certified members will work closely with other JHSC members. Because of their duties and responsibilities under the *OHSA*, they will have a special relationship with their counterpart certified member. Although they may interact less formally with other members of the JHSC, their training will make them a valued resource for committee activities. They will also be responsible to the employer or worker group they represent. It is essential that certified members have a good understanding of the functions, duties, rights and authority of the JHSC. The *OHSA* sets out several very specific functions for JHSCs. They add up to an overall objective of identifying and evaluating hazards and recommending action on health and safety issues. To do its job, the committee needs the full commitment of both workplace parties to the spirit as well as the letter of the law. It is especially important that the employer's health and safety policy and programs recognize a key role for the JHSC.

To carry out its functions, the committee engages in a wide range of activities. It conducts meetings, inspects the workplace, participates and makes recommendations in developing health and safety programs, and communicates with both workers and management.

The committee provides an opportunity for those affected by health and safety hazards to use their first-hand knowledge of the workplace to identify hazards and make recommendations to control them.

A JHSC is not a substitute for enforcement of the law, and it doesn't have to wait for a violation before making recommendations. The committee's work should emphasize prevention by anticipating problems before they occur.

This chapter examines the rights, duties and responsibilities placed on JHSCs and individual members by the *OHSA*. It also explains their structure and operation, and describes several practical methods for making JHSCs work.

When is a Committee Needed?

A joint health and safety committee is required in any workplace which regularly employs 20 or more workers. This includes full and part-time employees. A JHSC is also needed on a construction projects where 20 or more workers are regularly employed and is expected to last at least three months. If a designated substance applies (other than on a construction project), a committee must be formed. If a Ministry of Labour, Training and Skills Development inspector issues an order to convene a JHSC, then the employer must comply.

In farming, a JHSC is required if the farming operation has 20 or more workers who are regularly employed and those 20 or more workers have duties that include performing work related to mushroom, greenhouse, dairy, hog, cattle or poultry farming.

JHSC Functions

The functions of JHSCs are specified in the *OHSA*. The *OHSA* also gives JHSCs certain duties and powers to carry out their functions.

Most of these functions, powers and duties relate directly to the three major tasks of identifying, assessing, recommending action to control health and safety hazards, and evaluating hazard controls. A few others deal specifically with committee procedures. To provide a better understanding of the purpose and application of the *OHSA*, the descriptions in the following sections are presented in plain language. The *OHSA* contains the exact wording, and should be consulted when precise interpretations are needed.

Identifying Health and Safety Hazards

For a JHSC to make recommendations, it must first be aware of any hazards in the workplace. For this reason, the *OHSA* places a broad duty on committees "to identify sources of danger or hazards in the workplace". A wide variety of techniques are involved, including workplace inspections, hazard assessments, monitoring, and reviews of written records.

Committees are empowered to carry out these activities by several rights set out in the *OHSA*. In particular, JHSCs have the right to obtain information from employers or constructors, and the worker members have the right to designate members to conduct inspections of the workplace.

- JHSC has the right to obtain information on actual or potential hazards of materials, processes or equipment.

- JHSC has the right to be furnished by the employer with updated copies of all safety data sheets for materials used in the workplace.

- JHSC has the right to obtain an annual summary of employer-specific claims information from the Workplace Safety and Insurance Board. This summary includes data on injuries, fatalities, lost work-days, cases that required medical aid and the incidence of occupational illnesses. The Board must supply this information.

- JHSC has the right to information on health and safety experience and standards that the constructor or employer is aware of in other industries.

- The worker members must designate a member (if possible a certified member) to inspect the workplace at least once a month. Where this is not practical, part of the workplace must be inspected at least once per month according to a schedule determined by the JHSC. The entire workplace must be inspected at least once a year.

Worker Members of JHSCs

The *OHSA* sets out special rights and duties for the members of JHSCs who represent workers. These are in addition to the rights and duties that apply to the entire committee.

A worker designated member must be given the opportunity to conduct workplace inspections. If possible, the designated member shall be the certified member.

A worker designated member has a right to accompany an inspector during Ministry of Labour, Training and Skills Development inspections of the workplace.

A worker designated member has a right to assist in resolving matters when a worker refuses work because they believe that it endangers health or safety. A designated worker member shall also be present when a Ministry of Labour, Training and Skills Development inspector investigates a work refusal.

A worker designated member has a right to investigate serious incidents.

A worker designated member has a right to be present at the beginning of testing.

- JHSC shall set out an inspection schedule, and the member (or members) conducting the inspection has a duty to report hazards or potential hazards to the committee, which must consider this information within a reasonable period of time.

- A worker member of the committee shall be given an opportunity to accompany a Ministry inspector when a workplace inspection is conducted.

Assessing Health and Safety Hazards

When a hazard has been identified, the extent and severity of the hazard must be assessed. JHSCs, and in particular the worker members, have the right to participate in these procedures.

- JHSC has the right to obtain information about health and safety testing.

- JHSC has the right to be consulted prior to tests of equipment, machines or the work environment. The worker members have the right to designate a worker member to be present at the beginning of such testing.

- JHSC has the right to be consulted about proposed industrial hygiene testing strategies. The worker members have the right to designate a worker member to be present at the beginning of such testing.

- JHSC has the right to receive copies of assessment reports and to be consulted about assessment methods for designated substances.

- The worker members must designate a worker member to investigate incidents that result in critical injuries or fatalities.

Recommending Action to Control Health and Safety Hazards

The *OHSA* gives the JHSC the right to make recommendations, and it places a duty on the employer or constructor to reply.

- JHSC has the right to make recommendations regarding control programs for designated substances.

- JHSC has the right to make written recommendations for the improvement of the health and safety of workers.

- A reply from the employer or constructor must be given in writing within 21 days, with either a schedule for implementation or a statement of reasons for disagreement.

- JHSC has the right to be consulted about the development of worker training and instruction concerning exposure to hazardous material or hazardous physical agents, and to participate in an annual review of these training programs.

Evaluating Hazard Controls

Members of the joint health and safety committee evaluate hazard controls during monthly inspections, while speaking to fellow workers, and by monitoring the control measures put in place by the employer. At times this is done formally. For example, if a ventilation system has been upgraded to clear high carbon monoxide levels, the joint health and safety committee members expect to see a second set of indoor air quality tests to verify that the carbon monoxide levels are within safe levels.

Expanded Functions

The *OHSA* places specific duties and responsibilities on the JHSC, and gives it the right to obtain the information it needs to carry them out.

The *OHSA* also endeavours to establish the JHSC as a forum for broader consultation between the workplace parties on health and safety issues. Ideally the committee will assist in the development of health and safety programs in the workplace.

Examples of Expanded JHSC Functions

- Promoting acceptance of health and safety policy
- Assisting in developing health and safety rules and standards
- Job safety analysis
- Assessing the safety potential of new equipment, procedures and materials
- Assisting in the investigation of incidents and occupational illnesses
- Recommending worker health and safety training

JHSC Procedures

Selection of Members

The provisions of the *OHSA* respecting the selection of worker JHSC members are fairly clear in the case of workplaces with one union. Where there is more than one union in a workplace, the unions should work together to ensure the interests of all workers are represented by the committee.

Where there is no union representing the workers, the *OHSA* states that the constructor or employer shall cause a joint health and safety committee to be established and maintained and that the worker members shall be selected by the workers they are to represent.

The members of the committee who represent management are selected by the constructor or employer. The *OHSA* requires that these members be chosen from among persons who exercise "managerial functions" and who "to the extent possible" are employed at the workplace. While this may not be practical in every case, the intent of the *OHSA* is to ensure JHSC members are familiar with workplace problems and are readily available.

Meetings

The *OHSA* is silent on how meetings are called, agendas set and meetings conducted. It is up to the members to decide how they will conduct their meetings. The JHSC may decide to set a schedule of regular meetings for a year in advance. Members can then reserve these dates and schedule their other activities around them.

The committee should determine a method of scheduling that is flexible enough to accommodate changing conditions in the workplace.

The *OHSA* requires that members be paid for one hour or such longer period of time as the committee determines is necessary to prepare for each committee meeting.

Co-Chairs

The *OHSA* requires that meetings be co-chaired by worker and management members. This sharing of the authority of the chair demonstrates the cooperation and equal status of the workplace parties and provides for agreement on such matters as agendas and the length of meetings. One approach is to alternate the chairing of meetings between the two chairs. Alternately, the worker and manager co-chairs can share the responsibility at each meeting. The two co-chairs can also serve as spokespersons for their respective constituents.

Quorum

Each committee will need to agree on how many members need to be present for the JHSC to have an official meeting. This is called a quorum. There must never be more managers than workers at a meeting. Regardless of the minimum that is agreed to, the emphasis should always be on full attendance.

Consensus

One method of decision making is a formal vote, where committee members indicate their individual agreement or disagreement with a proposed course of action, and the majority of votes decides the issue. An alternative is to base decisions on consensus. Consensus means that each committee member is prepared to support a compromise — even though it may not be their first choice — in order to reach an agreement that the whole committee will support. This is the preferred method of conducting JHSC business.

Non-Consensus

It is the goal of the committee to reach consensus. If, however, the committee fails to reach consensus despite good faith attempts, either co-chair, worker or manager, can make recommendations to the employer

Confidentiality

The *OHSA* requires that JHSC members keep confidential any trade secrets or personal medical information they receive in their work. This will require strict attention to the contents of minutes and the security of the committee records.

Confidentiality is more than a legal principle. JHSC cannot operate effectively unless all parties are confident that no improper use can be made of the information they receive. Without this confidence and trust the committee will find it difficult or impossible to obtain the information it needs. Some committees choose to have each member sign an Oath of Confidentiality upon becoming a JHSC member.

Agenda

The purpose of an agenda is to provide a plan for the meeting. It organizes the discussion and ensures that important business is not overlooked. Proposed agenda items should be given to the co-chairs in advance. Certain items such as workplace inspection reports will be routinely placed on the agenda. The agenda should be circulated by the co-chairs about a week in advance of the meeting, so that members have time to prepare for a full discussion.

The committee should also be involved in reviewing proposals for new processes, equipment or materials. Such changes affect all parties in the workplace, and the involvement of the JHSC at an early stage can eliminate potential problems.

Typical JHSC Agenda
JOINT HEALTH AND SAFETY COMMITTEE MEETING

Date   Time   Place

1. Roll Call

2. Minutes of the Last Meeting

3. Unfinished Business:
   a. Employer response to recommendation
   b. Results of Investigations

4. Regular Reports:
   a. Workplace Inspections and Recommendations
   b. Reports of Members and Subcommittees
   c. Update on Incidents / First Aid
   d. Reports on Implementation and Development of Health and Safety Program

5. New Business

6. Date of the Next Meeting

7. Adjournment

Records

The *OHSA* requires that minutes be taken at each meeting of the committee and if requested made available to a Ministry of Labour, Training and Skills Development inspector. The minutes should record the disposition of each issue discussed by the committee. They should be circulated to committee members, together with any copies of reports and briefs presented at the meeting. Before the minutes are circulated, the committee co-chairs should review them and sign them to authorize distribution.

Checklist for a JHSC Meeting

- Notice of Meeting
- Agenda
- Minutes of Previous Meeting
- Written Material to be Discussed
- Meeting Room Booked
- Appropriate Furniture
- White Board / Flip Charts
- Audio-visual Materials

It is also useful to post minutes in the workplace, so that everyone can see the progress of the committee. Minutes must be kept as a permanent record of the activity of the committee and for future reference. Minutes can also help JHSC members to assess the effectiveness of their committee, and see how health and safety issues are being handled. The preparation of minutes is discussed later in this chapter.

Various other records may also have to be maintained by the JHSC. These include committee correspondence, briefs and reports considered by JHSC monitoring and test results and records of worker training. In addition, a wide variety of other material relevant to workplace hazards may be maintained.

JHSC Activities

To successfully carry out its functions and duties, the JHSC must engage in a number of activities. Although they may be implied by the *OHSA* and regulations, they are not described there in detail. These committee activities can be grouped into several categories.

Gathering Information

The employer or constructor is the normal source of most information required by the JHSC – especially data that originates in the workplace. For example, access to first aid reports, specifications of the equipment used in the workplace, and safety data sheets on workplace materials will normally be provided to the JHSC by the employer.

The committee receives such documents as:

- workplace monitoring reports;

- worker health and safety surveys or questionnaires;

- inspection or assessment reports;

- Workplace Safety and Insurance Board reports; and

- Ministry of Labour, Training and Skills Development bulletins and circulars.

Much valuable information is also available from technical and medical journals, industry prevention associations, labour and business organizations, and other occupational health and safety agencies. Most organizations and agencies have websites with easily accessed resources. Some examples of such organizations and agencies are:

- Canadian Centre for Occupational Health and Safety
  www.ccohs.ca

- Infrastructure Health and Safety Association
  www.ihsa.ca

- Public Services Health and Safety Association
  www.pshsa.ca

- Workplace Safety North
  www.workplacesafetynorth.ca

- Workplace Safety & Prevention Services
  www.wsps.ca

- Workers Health and Safety Centre
  www.whsc.on.ca

- Ministry of Labour, Training and Skills Development
  www.ontario.ca

- Ontario Federation of Labour
  www.ofl.ca

- Occupational Health Clinics for Ontario Workers
  www.ohcow.on.ca

Numerous employer, trade associations, trade unions, and private consultants can also supplement occupational health and safety information.

The JHSC may have regular access to much of this information because the employer or constructor or local trade union is on a membership or subscription list. Some large multi-workplace employers operate regular internal distribution systems for such data. Valuable information may also be derived from "networking" with other JHSCs.

Inspecting the Workplace

Workplace inspection is a JHSC function described by the *OHSA*, but it also involves a great number of activities that are not described there. Useful inspections depend on advance planning by the JHSC. Careful planning ensures that thorough preparations, including the gathering of background information, are made before the actual inspection is carried out, and that the physical inspection itself is properly conducted.

Workplace inspections are described in detail in Chapter 17 of this reference guide.

Identifying Hazards

Workers have a duty to report health and safety hazards to their supervisors. Hazard identification is a vital function of JHSCs. The committee activities connected with this function are described in some detail in Section Two of this reference guide.

Assessing Changes in Equipment and Work Procedures

Changes in workplace equipment and procedures may be implemented in response to health and safety recommendations or as a means of increasing efficiency or productivity. Often, the changes may produce improvements in both areas of concern. Either type of change may also create unintended new hazards.

Careful assessments of new and changed methods by everyone concerned, including the JHSC, will help to ensure that unwanted side effects are avoided or eliminated.

Participating in Workplace Testing

Workplace testing for health and safety purposes may involve a variety of sampling techniques and testing equipment. The usual goals of testing are to detect and measure a suspected workplace hazard or to evaluate the effectiveness of hazard controls. Equipment can include such things as gas detectors and other devices that measure the presence and amount of hazardous substances in the air. Radiation and noise metres are other examples.

The JHSC may recommend testing based on the findings of an inspection, on reports from workers, or as a follow-up to the installation of a new hazard control. The committee is therefore likely to be a source of advice about the nature of observed hazard effects and about the appropriate locations for testing.

The *OHSA* says that the JHSC should be consulted about testing, and that a worker member may be present at the beginning of testing. This gives the worker member an opportunity to verify that the methods, procedures and equipment are appropriate.

The *OHSA* also requires that test results be given to the JHSC. It is a duty of the committee to make recommendations to the employer for the control of hazards. Knowledge of test results is essential to the committee's ability to carry out this duty.

Following up on Action Plans and Work Orders

Installation or repair of a hazard control may result from an employer initiative, a JHSC recommendation, or a work order issued by a Ministry inspector. Verification that the action has been effective is an important activity of the JHSC. Typically, this will require an inspection and possibly further testing. Where the JHSC finds that the control is not effective, it should, if possible, make further recommendations to the employer. The procedures to be followed when work orders have been issued are discussed in greater detail in Chapter 7.

Taking Part in Incident Investigations

The *OHSA* gives specific duties to worker members of JHSCs with respect to incident investigations.

Effective investigations require special training and are the subject of Chapter 18.

Investigations may involve the occurrence of a fatality, a critical injury, or an occupational disease. Investigations usually take place after the damage has been done. Nonetheless, a thorough investigation is a vital stage in preventing further harm to workers. The causes of incidents must be analyzed and effective preventative measures implemented.

Members of JHSCs may also participate in the investigation of health and safety incidents in the workplace that could have resulted in harm to persons or property if circumstances had been slightly different. They are sometimes called "near misses". All incidents that resulted, or could have resulted in harm, should be investigated because they may reveal causes which could lead to an occupational injury or disease.

Communicating with Workers and Management

JHSC recommendations for the elimination or control of hazards cannot be effective unless they are communicated accurately to those affected, including the constituents that JHSC members represent. This includes management, workers and the union, if any. Action is rarely accomplished without good communication.

All workplace parties need regular information about the ongoing activities of the JHSC. This includes not only recommendations to the employer, but also information the committee has gathered, concerns it has raised, and details of other work in progress.

Recommending Health and Safety Improvements

Making recommendations for improvements is a specific duty given to JHSCs by the *OHSA*. Careful work in other JHSC activities provides the basis for practical recommendations to achieve health and safety objectives. These recommendations relate to the requirements of the *OHSA* and its regulations, as well as to the employer's health and safety policy and programs.

Developing Training Programs

The *OHSA* gives JHSC members the right to participate in the development, design and regular upgrading of worker health and safety training for workers exposed or likely to be exposed to a hazardous material or to a hazardous physical agent. Training can achieve its objectives only if it is designed to deal with the unique hazards and special needs of the individual workplace.

Making the JHSC Work

Although not required under the *OHSA*, the following are suggested guidelines for making the JHSC work.

Terms of Reference

An essential element in any effective JHSC is an agreement between the parties that sets out exactly what the JHSC is supposed to do. A written statement of the functions and operating procedures of the JHSC is usually called the terms of reference.

The terms of reference should be consistent with the *OHSA* and should be established by a consensus of the workplace parties. The JHSC should have a role in the employer's overall health and safety program.

The terms of reference specify the functions of the committee, the responsibilities of committee members, the rules for calling and conducting meetings, and the records to be kept. A copy of the terms of reference should be provided to each member of the committee and should be available at every meeting. New or replacement members should review the terms of reference as part of their orientation.

Effective Meetings

Effective meetings are absolutely critical for the efficient operation of a JHSC. It is here that views are shared and proposals developed.

The importance of a formal agenda has already been noted. The responsibility for circulating the agenda, and then conducting the meeting in accordance with the agenda, falls mainly on the co-chairs. The *OHSA* requires meetings to be co-chaired by worker and management nominees, and the job may, by agreement, alternate between the two.

It is normal that there will be disagreements between JHSC members on some issues. This should not be seen as a negative situation. The process of discussing and overcoming disagreements leads to new ideas, and ultimately, progress on health and safety issues. This requires skill, knowledge, and a willingness to find common ground for the betterment of the workplace.

Planning

Part of the job of planning a meeting is to make sure that all documents, reports and other material to be discussed have been distributed in advance. The co-chairs should consult with committee members and communicate a week or so before the meeting to discuss any agenda items that might be particularly difficult to deal with. This ensures that adequate time is allotted to key issues, and may also signal the need for extra preparation by committee members.

An understanding of each side's concerns about a particular agenda item can help the co-chairs to keep the meeting focused and minimize unnecessary discussion or other distractions. If everyone involved shares the same understanding about the purpose of the meeting, committee time can be used effectively.

Conducting a Meeting

A typical JHSC meeting proceeds as follows.

When enough members are present to constitute a quorum, the meeting is called to order by the chair and the names of members present are recorded in the minutes. Next, the agenda is reviewed. If a member wishes to alter it, the chair will consider the views of the other members, and may allow the change.

Once the agenda has been agreed to, the items are addressed in sequence and committee business gets underway. It is usual for the first item to be a review of the minutes of the previous meeting. It is expected that committee will have read the previous minutes and this is simply a check-in to ensure that the minutes are accurate.

A good co-chair concentrates on helping the committee to reach a decision rather than attempting to impose her or his own views. Normal practice is for the co-chair to allow discussion, ask for clarification and to summarize the points being made. As committee members, the co-chairs can offer their views, but they normally wait until others have had a chance to speak. Committee decisions are usually made by consensus rather than by formal votes. If the JHSC is unable to reach a consensus, recommendations can be made by either co-chair to the employer. When the agenda has been exhausted the co-chair will adjourn the meeting. The members may agree to place unfinished business on the agenda of the next meeting.

Minutes

The accuracy and completeness of the minutes are the responsibility of the chair. They can be very brief, but they should include all the important facts. Some committees identify "who said what", others simply record the item and the substance of the discussion.

The minutes ensure that important discussions and decisions are not later forgotten, altered or misunderstood. All committee recommendations should be recorded. Any action items are documented and assigned to an individual with special attention given to a completion date. Minutes are required under the *OHSA*, and must be made available to a Ministry inspector if requested.

Minutes should be recorded by one of the committee members unless the committee agrees to have someone else prepare them. Some workplaces have an individual attend meetings exclusively to take and distribute meeting minutes. This person does not vote and is often also available to assist the co-chairs in logistics associated with setting up meetings, preparing agendas, and distributing the minutes.

Communicating JHSC Decisions

The effectiveness of a joint health and safety committee depends on cooperation and respect from everyone in the workplace. If the JHSC is to contribute to improved health and safety, it must communicate with workers, supervisors, managers, inspectors and everyone else who is concerned with eliminating hazards. An obvious way to communicate JHSC activities is to circulate or post JHSC minutes. There are other effective techniques for highlighting important developments, such as a special notice distributed to each employee.

Existing Communication Networks

Management and workers have access to internal systems such as board meetings, management meetings, employee meetings, newsletters, and, if applicable, union meetings. These vehicles can be useful in sharing JHSC information.

Reviewing Data and Trends

Many workplaces are using technology to gather and analyze information. Computerized systems can make the data more accessible and assist with analytics. Joint health and safety committee members and health and safety representatives can review occupational health and safety trends to enhance worker safety.

Annual JHSC Report

An annual report of JHSC activities is another vehicle for communicating results. It provides a summary of action taken by the JHSC throughout the year, and can be used to build confidence in the committee within the workplace. If the JHSC has not had many major issues to deal with over the year, the members may feel that they haven't accomplished much. However, when all the little items are added up, the real picture of the committee's activities can create a much different impression. If there is a Board at the workplace, the Board of Directors should receive a copy of the annual JHSC report.

This chapter explains that the main functions of a JHSC are to identify, assess and recommend ways of eliminating or controlling health and safety hazards. Once controls have been implemented, JHSCs are involved in evaluating hazard controls. Specific rights and duties associated with each of these functions are listed. In particular, the JHSC has the right under the *OHSA* to receive specific kinds of information from the employer.

A broad range of activities is used by JHSCs to carry out their functions. These activities include information gathering as well as participation in inspections, assessments, investigations, and testing. JHSCs also communicate with workers and others in the workplace. The JHSC makes recommendations to the employer based on these activities.

The chapter describes the procedural requirements of the *OHSA* and reviews a number of techniques that have proven effective in keeping committee meetings on track. The need for orderly procedures, including terms of reference, agendas and minutes, is stressed.

Several ideas are suggested for making JHSCs effective. The most important is that the terms of reference provide the committee with a key role in implementing the employer's health and safety program. Both parties should appoint members to the committee who have the knowledge, competence and authority to take action on committee decisions.

The importance of careful planning of JHSC meetings is emphasized. This includes preparing agendas, consultation between co-chairs and circulating background material in advance. JHSC time is used most effectively when committee discussions concentrate on items that the members have prepared for in advance.

Finally, the chapter highlights that the committee will be most successful when it communicates its activities effectively to others in the workplace, including workers, managers, and supervisors. Several possible communication vehicles are suggested. Because of their training and experience, certified members have a special role to play in all JHSC activities. Chapter 5 deals with the rights, duties and responsibilities of certified members in more detail.

Chapter 5

Certified Members

- The Right to Refuse Unsafe Work

- The Right to Stop Work

- Complaints Concerning Dangerous Circumstances

- Dealing with Inspectors

- Dealing with the Labour Relations Board

- Communications

- Training

- Review

Certified Members

Certified members of joint health and safety committees play an essential role in workplace health and safety. The status of certified members was established by amendments to the *OHSA* that were passed in 1990. It was at this point that the right to stop unsafe work was added to other rights set out in the *OHSA*. The legislation's intention was to restrict the stop-work authority to committee members who had the training to use the power appropriately. For this reason, the *OHSA* assigns the rights and duties connected with this authority only to certified members. The Labour Relations Officer can revoke the certification of a JHSC member who handles a stop-work situation "recklessly" or "in bad faith".

The *OHSA* gave the authority for certification to the Workplace Safety and Insurance Board. The Board set standards for certification and administered the certification process. As of April 1, 2012 this authority moved to the Chief Prevention Office at the Ministry of Labour, Training and Skills Development.

Only *designated* certified members of a JHSC can exercise stop-work authority. The workplace parties designate one or more certified members to carry out this function by the same process used to appoint members to the JHSC in the first place. At least one certified member must represent workers and at least one must represent the employer. They are often referred to as the *worker certified member* and the *employer certified member.*

Certified members have other responsibilities and duties. They have the right to investigate complaints that dangerous circumstances exist. The *OHSA* specifies that "if possible" certain other duties of worker JHSC members should be assigned to worker certified members. They include inspecting the workplace and assisting in the investigation of a work refusal.

Certified members may be asked to be involved with other duties by the employer or workers they represent. These include such things as incident investigations, being present at the beginning of workplace tests, and reviewing employer compliance with inspector's orders. Certified members from either the worker or employer side are more likely to be given additional duties because of their training and knowledge.

This chapter concentrates on the provisions of the law that concern certified members. A certified member has the right to investigate complaints and initiate stop-work procedures if a dangerous circumstance exists.

The *OHSA* gives individual workers the right to refuse work if they have reason to believe that it may endanger them or another worker, or that they are in danger from workplace violence. Some workers such as nurses, firefighters, and police officers cannot refuse work if the danger is a normal part of their job or if refusing work would endanger someone else. See Section 43(1)(2) of the *OHSA* for more details.

A work refusal is initiated by an individual worker. The *OHSA* requires an investigation to take place in the presence of a worker member of the JHSC or another worker representative. This may be a certified member. If the employer reassigns the refused work, the *OHSA* states that the reasons for the refusal must be explained to the worker in the presence of a worker member of the JHSC (if possible a certified member), or another worker representative.

A work refusal begins when a worker reports the circumstances of the refusal to the supervisor (or employer). The supervisor must investigate "forthwith" in the presence of the worker and a worker representative. This representative may be a worker certified member. The employer has a duty to make the committee member available, and the member has a duty to attend "without delay".

The first priority is to verify that a work refusal is in progress and to find out why the worker has refused. The worker representative then accompanies the supervisor who must conduct an investigation. Ideally, the supervisor will listen carefully to the complaint and take whatever steps are required to remove the danger. In this case, the supervisor will advise the worker that the problem has been corrected and it is safe to return to work. The worker, however, may still believe that a danger exists.

If the supervisor does not agree that an unsafe condition exists, or continues to exist, and the worker continues to refuse, one of the parties must call a Ministry inspector.

What the Law Says
Required Duties of Certified Members

Section 45-48 of the *Occupational Health and Safety Act* sets out duties that are required of certified members who have been designated by the workplace party they represent. These duties are:

- To investigate any complaint from anyone in the workplace that a dangerous circumstance exists;
- To initiate and assist in the investigation of a bilateral work stoppage;
- To initiate a unilateral work stoppage in prescribed circumstances.

What the Law Says
Possible Other Duties of Certified Members

Section 9 of the *Occupational Health and Safety Act* states that a worker member must be designated to perform the following duties, and that "if possible" the designated member should be a certified member:

- Conducting workplace inspections;
- Assisting in the investigation of a work refusal.

While the inspector's investigation is in progress, the employer may assign the refused work to another person. No worker may be assigned the refused work without first being informed that a refusal is in progress, and of the reasons for the refusal. The supervisor or employer must give this advice in the presence of a worker representative who, if possible, is a certified member. The assigned worker has the option to accept or refuse the work.

The worker and the worker representative are both entitled to be present when the inspector investigates. The inspector must provide the workplace parties with a written decision as soon as practicable. The inspector's decision may be appealed to the Ontario Labour Relations Board, as described later in this chapter.

Section 43 of the *Occupational Health and Safety Act* gives workers the right to refuse to work or do particular work, if they have reason to believe that any of the following conditions exist:

- Any equipment, machine, device or thing they are to use or operate is likely to endanger them or another worker;
- The physical condition of the workplace, or the part of the workplace in which they work, or are to work, is likely to endanger them;
- Workplace violence is likely to endanger them;
- Any equipment, machine, device or thing they are to use or operate or the physical condition of the workplace or the part of the workplace in which they work or are to work is in contravention of the *OHSA* or the regulations and such contravention is likely to endanger them or another worker.

Following the initial investigation and action (if any) by the supervisor, workers may continue to refuse the work only if they have reasonable grounds to believe that any of these conditions continue to exist.

The right of refusal does not apply in certain circumstances. For specific exclusions, see Section 43 (1) and (2) of the *OHSA*.

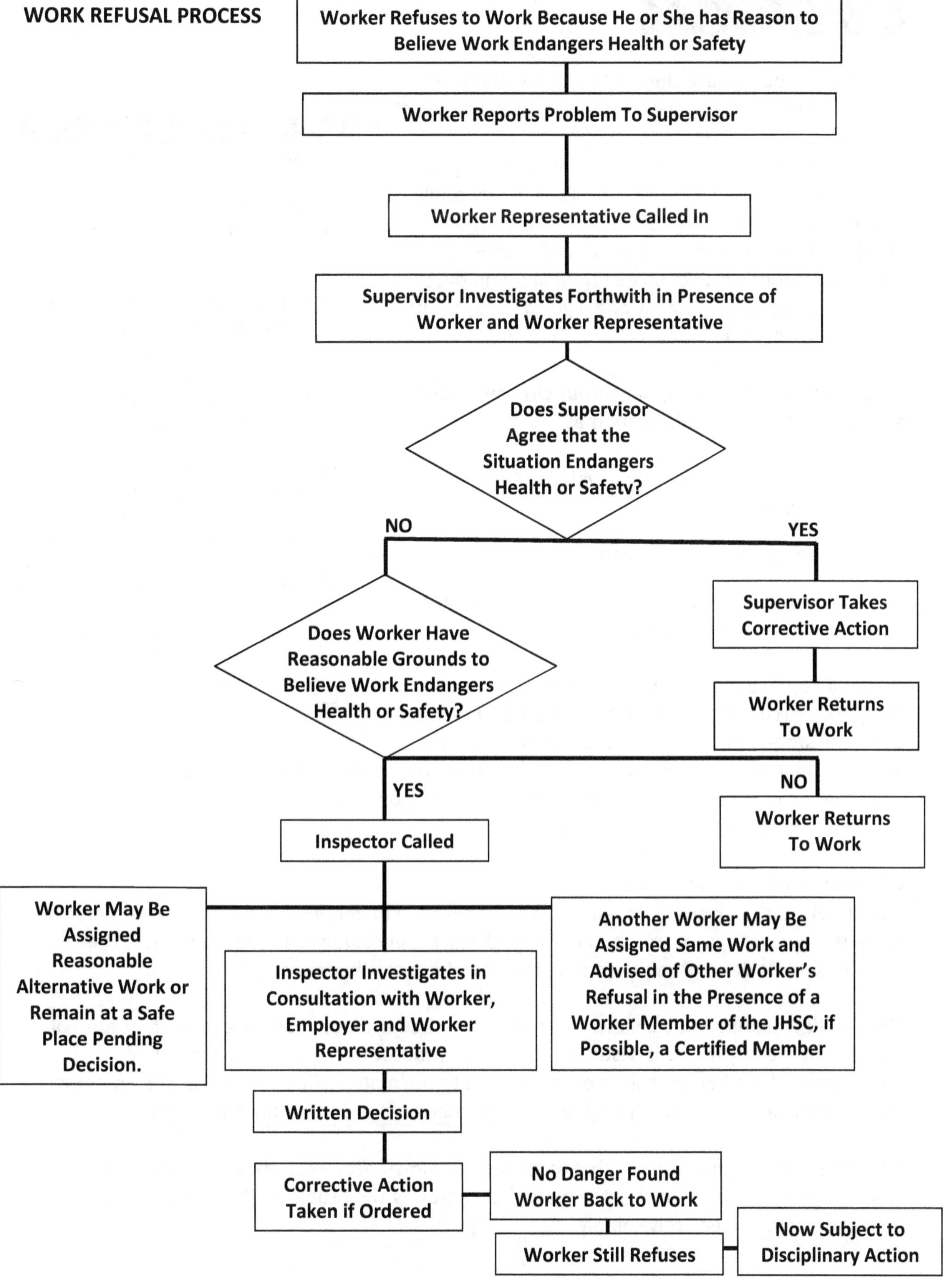

WORK REFUSAL PROCESS
Worker Refuses to Work Because He or She has Reason to Believe Work Endangers Health or Safety
Worker Reports Problem To Supervisor
Worker Representative Called In
Supervisor Investigates Forthwith in Presence of Worker and Worker Representative
Does Supervisor Agree that the Situation Endangers Health or Safety?
NO
YES
Supervisor Takes Corrective Action
Worker Returns To Work
Does Worker Have Reasonable Grounds to Believe Work Endangers Health or Safety?
YES
NO
Worker Returns To Work
Inspector Called
Worker May Be Assigned Reasonable Alternative Work or Remain at a Safe Place Pending Decision.
Inspector Investigates in Consultation with Worker, Employer and Worker Representative
Another Worker May Be Assigned Same Work and Advised of Other Worker's Refusal in the Presence of a Worker Member of the JHSC, if Possible, a Certified Member
Written Decision
Corrective Action Taken if Ordered
No Danger Found Worker Back to Work
Worker Still Refuses
Now Subject to Disciplinary Action

Certified members have the right to stop work when they find that dangerous circumstances exist. Section 45 of the *Occupational Health and Safety Act* sets out specific circumstances under which this right may be exercised. The work stoppage provisions do not apply to a workplace at which workers described in Section 43 (2) (a), (b) or (c) are employed or a workplace at which workers described in Section 43 (2) (d) are employed if a work stoppage would directly endanger the life, health or safety of another person.

In Section 44 of the *OHSA*, dangerous circumstances exist where three conditions are met:

- there is failure to comply with the *OHSA* or regulations;

- it poses a hazard to a worker; and

- any delay in controlling the danger or hazard may seriously endanger a worker.

Where a certified member has reason to believe that dangerous circumstances exist, he or she has the right to begin the stop-work process. The certified member may learn of dangerous circumstances during an inspection, an incident investigation, or the investigation of a work refusal or a worker complaint. Supervisors or others in the workplace may also report dangerous circumstances.

> **What the Law Says**
> **During a Work Refusal Investigation**
>
> Section 43 of the *Occupational Health and Safety Act* requires that a refusing worker:
>
> - Be present when a supervisor or an inspector is investigating the workplace;
> - Be in a safe place;
> - Be near the work station (during normal working hours).
>
> While an inspector is investigating a continuing work refusal, the employer has the right to assign the worker to "reasonable alternative work", or to give other directions, subject to the provisions of a collective agreement if any.
>
> The employer's right to give other directions to the worker is subject to Section 50, which prohibits reprisals against a worker for a work refusal.

Bilateral Stop-Work Procedure

A bilateral stop-work procedure begins when a certified member advises a supervisor that dangerous circumstances exist and requests that a supervisor investigate the matter. The supervisor must do so promptly in the presence of the certified member.

The certified member may believe that dangerous circumstances continue to exist, in spite of any action taken by the supervisor. He or she may request that the certified member representing the other workplace party investigate the matter. That second certified member must investigate the matter promptly in the presence of the first certified member.

If both certified members agree that dangerous circumstances exist, they may direct the constructor or employer to stop the work that is causing the problem. The constructor or employer must immediately comply.

BILATERAL WORK STOPPAGE

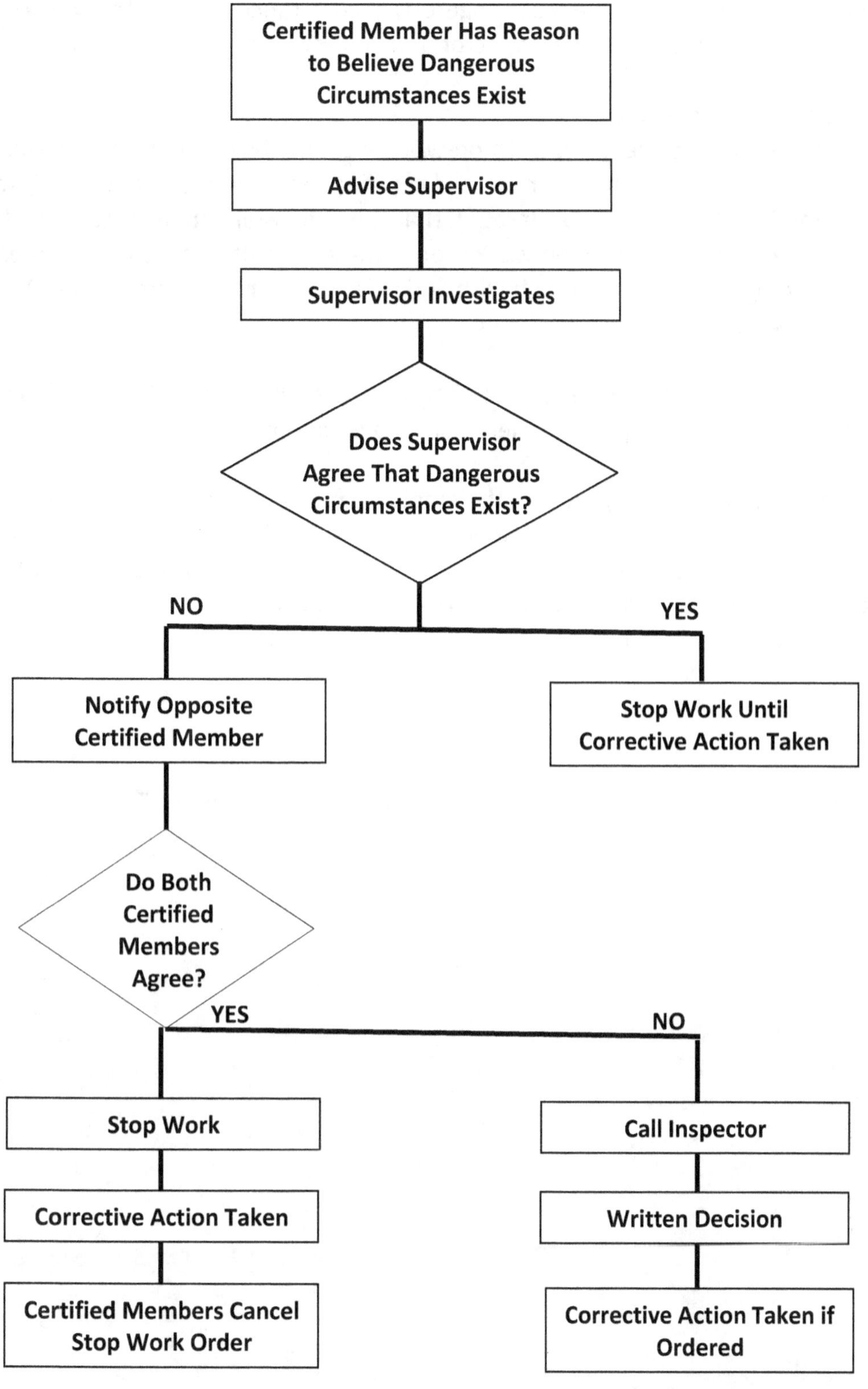

When action has been taken to correct the problem, either the certified members or an inspector may cancel the stop-work direction.

If the certified members can't agree that dangerous circumstances exist, either one of them can call in an inspector to investigate. The inspector must investigate and issue a written decision.

Unilateral Stop-Work Procedure
Certified members may acquire unilateral stop-work authority by two means. The employer may advise the JHSC in writing that an individual certified member has this right. Alternately, a Labour Relations Board can make a declaration that the unilateral right applies, if the Labour Relations Board finds the bilateral stop-work procedure is not sufficient to protect workers at the workplace from serious risk to their health and safety. The criteria used by the OLRB can be found in O. Reg 243/95.

Where the unilateral work stoppage right has been granted, an individual certified member may direct the employer to stop work where dangerous circumstances exist.

After taking steps to correct the problem, the employer may request that the certified member or an inspector cancel the stop-work direction. Where the certified member and employer do not agree that dangerous circumstances exist or continue to exist, an inspector may be called in to investigate and provide a written decision, which may specify corrective action or cancel the stop-work direction.

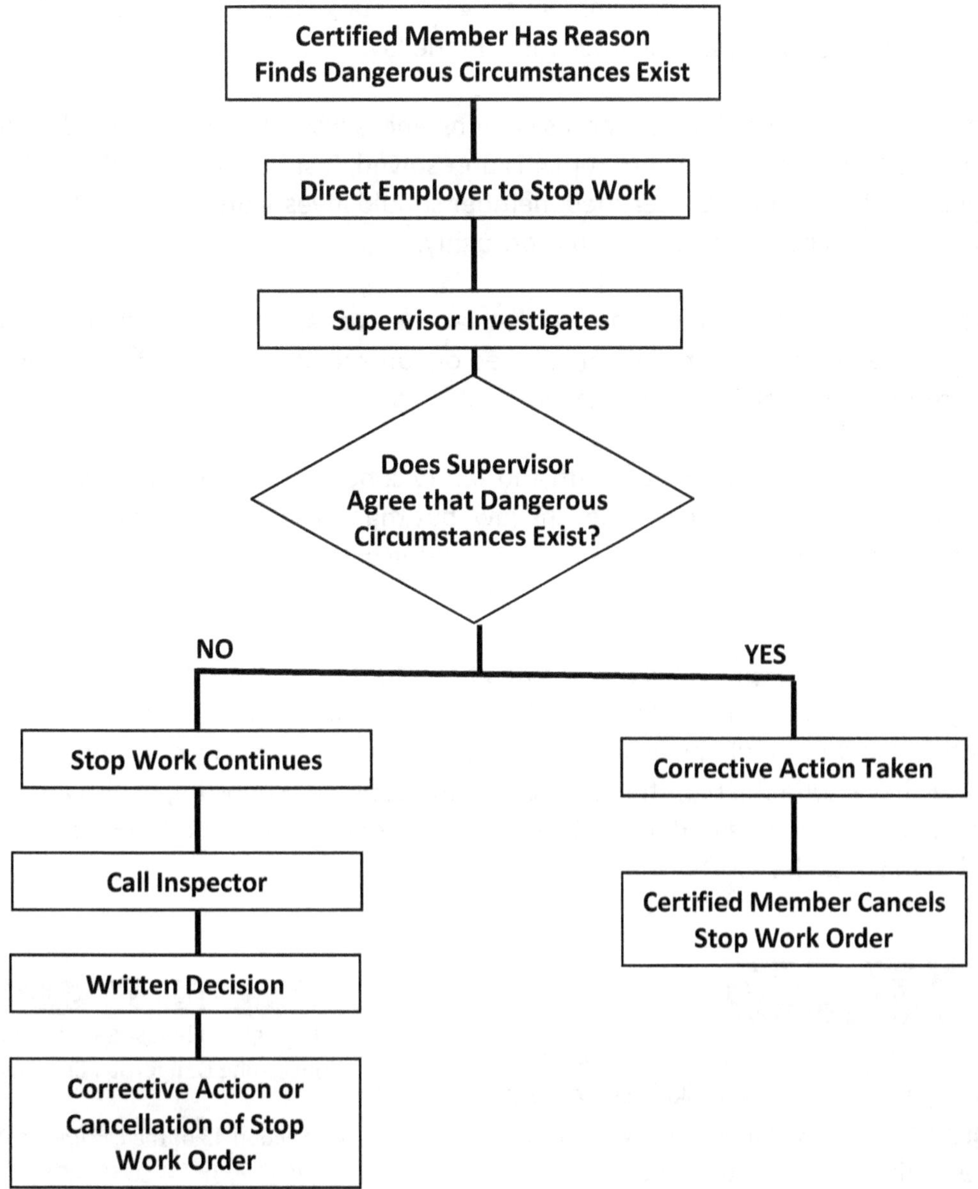

Certified Member Has Reason
Finds Dangerous Circumstances Exist
Direct Employer to Stop Work
Supervisor Investigates
Does Supervisor Agree that Dangerous Circumstances Exist?
NO
YES
Stop Work Continues
Corrective Action Taken
Call Inspector
Certified Member Cancels Stop Work Order
Written Decision
Corrective Action or Cancellation of Stop Work Order

The *OHSA* gives certified members the authority to investigate complaints concerning dangerous circumstances. At the complaint investigation stage, problems can often be fixed quickly without relying on the formal procedures in the law.

A complaint from any person that dangerous circumstances exist should be immediately reported to a supervisor. If the concern remains unresolved, it should be brought to the attention of a certified member. A certified member should investigate any complaint of dangerous circumstances immediately and thoroughly.

The first step is to determine if dangerous circumstances exist as defined by the *OHSA*. Where they do exist, it is essential that they be eliminated or controlled. It is up to the supervisor to see that appropriate corrective action is taken.

The certified member may find that a health and safety concern reported by a worker does not constitute dangerous circumstances under the law, but that it is hazardous nevertheless. In this case, the certified member should attempt, by consulting with the supervisor, to get the concern investigated and resolved.

When someone in the workplace has raised a health and safety concern and if, after investigating, the certified member decides that dangerous circumstances do not exist, the reasons for this decision should be explained to the worker. It is important for the worker to know that they have done the right thing by raising the concern. Reporting health and safety concerns is a duty of everyone under the *OHSA* and everyone in the workplace should be encouraged to make such reports.

Dealing with Inspectors

The preceding sections have described the role of Ministry of Labour, Training and Skills Development (MLTSD) inspectors in investigations, work stoppages and work refusals. There are further situations when the JHSC worker members, including certified worker members, may be expected to deal with inspectors:

- MLTSD workplace inspections;

- MLTSD investigations;

- MLTSD investigations of critical injury or fatalities; and

- MLTSD orders.

What the Law Says
The Right to Investigate Complaints Concerning Dangerous Circumstances

- Section 48 of the *Occupational Health and Safety Act* gives certified members the right to investigate a complaint from anyone in the workplace that dangerous circumstances exist.
- The *OHSA* also provides that certified members shall be paid at the appropriate regular or premium rate for time spent exercising this right.

Worker members who accompany the inspector can explain any hazards they have identified and corrective actions that have been taken. The inspector may want explanations of items listed in the JHSC minutes and may request other assistance or information.

A JHSC member shall be present when a Ministry inspector investigates a critical injury or fatality. The inspector has broad powers to gather information and may ask questions and request documents. The worker members may be asked for their notes or other background information about the workplace.

Section 44 of the *Occupational Health and Safety Act* defines dangerous circumstances as follows:

- A provision of the *OHSA* is being violated;
- The violation poses a danger or a hazard to a worker; **and**
- The danger or hazard is such that any delay in controlling it may seriously endanger a worker.

All three of these conditions must simultaneously exist before there are dangerous circumstances.

Dealing with the Ontario Labour Relations Board

The Labour Relations Board is an independent decision-maker appointed under the *Labour Relations Act* (1995) to handle disputes under a number of different pieces of legislation including the *OHSA*.

The Labour Relations Board may:

- issue a declaration or make a recommendation to the Minister of Labour, Training and Skills Development.

- hear appeals of an inspector's decision or order; and

- hear complaints that a certified member at the workplace, recklessly or in bad faith, exercised or failed to exercise a power under the stop-work provisions of the *Act*.

These procedures are described in Chapter 7.

Communications

The importance of good communications between the JHSC and others in the workplace is discussed in Chapter 22. Certified members have communication needs related to their special duties and powers under the *OHSA*. The worker and employer certified members should work out procedures for promptly responding to concerns, work stoppages and other differences of opinion.

Workers and supervisors need to know who the certified members are and how to contact them. Names and work locations of certified workers must be posted.

Supervisors of certified members will have to make provisions for relieving them of their regular work while they are performing their health and safety duties.

Every certified member should have a list of the names, addresses, phone numbers, and email address of people who may have to be contacted. This includes the Ministry of Labour, Training and Skills Development inspector, the appropriate Ministry director, the Labour Relations Board, key employer and worker representatives, and emergency personnel.

Another aspect of communications is keeping records. Certified members should keep their own records noting the times and dates of their actions and the responses of other workplace parties. Written material received should be retained, along with a record of the time and date they were received. These records will help the certified member to make accurate reports to the JHSC, and may be essential if there are further complaints or appeals.

Training

The certified member plays a fundamental role in the operation of the joint health and safety committee. It follows that certified members should continually seek to upgrade their skills. This means learning more about health and safety issues, and keeping up with new knowledge and other developments in the field.

The following information is found in Appendix B of the Program standard for joint health and safety committee training.

Section 22.3 of the Occupational Health and Safety Act (*OHSA*) provides that the Minister of Labour, Training and Skills Development shall appoint a Chief Prevention Officer (CPO) to establish requirements for certification of persons for the purposes of the *OHSA* and to certify persons under section 7.6 who meet those requirements.

Specifically, pursuant to section 7.6 of the *OHSA*, the CPO has the authority to establish training and other requirements a joint health and safety committee member shall fulfill in order to become a certified member, and to certify a committee member who fulfils those requirements.

On April 1, 2012, the CPO established the standards set out in the Workplace Safety and Insurance Board (WSIB) document entitled "Certification Standards for Joint Health and Safety Committees, May 1996" updated January 2007 ("1996 JHSC Certification Training Standards") as the training requirements that committee members must meet in order to become certified. These standards continued to be in effect until February 29, 2016.

Committee members who successfully completed Part One and Part Two training under the 1996 JHSC Certification Standards prior to March 1, 2016 were considered for certification by the CPO pursuant to the training and other requirements established by the CPO on April 1, 2012. In other words, certified members were grandfathered in, under the 1996 JHSC Certification Training Standards.

In accordance with the authority set out in section 7.6 of the *OHSA*, and effective May 1, 2020, the CPO is establishing the following training and other requirements a committee member must fulfill in order to become a certified member.

As of May 1, 2020, the CPO may certify committee members who fulfill the training and other requirements set out in either Part A or Part B:

A. General training and other requirements for committee members seeking certification

The committee member must meet the requirements set out in paragraphs A1-3:

1. Complete a JHSC Certification Part One Training Program that:

    i. is approved by the CPO under subsection 7.1(2) of the Act as meeting the Ministry of Labour, Training and Skills Development Joint Health and Safety Committee Certification Program Standard, dated October 1, 2015 or May 1, 2020

    ii. is delivered by a training provider approved by the CPO under subsection 7.2(2) of the Act as meeting the Ministry of Labour, Training and Skills Development Joint Health and Safety Committee Certification Provider Standard, dated October 1, 2015 or May 1, 2020.

2. Complete a JHSC Certification Part Two Training Program that:

    i. is approved by the CPO under subsection 7.1(2) of the Act as meeting the Ministry of Labour, Training and Skills Development Joint Health and Safety Committee Certification Program Standard, dated October 1, 2015 or May 1 2020

    ii. is delivered by a training provider approved by the CPO under subsection 7.2(2) of the Act as meeting the Ministry of Labour, Training and Skills Development Joint Health and Safety Committee Certification Provider Standard, dated May 1, 2020 or October 1, 2015

    iii. provides training in a minimum of 6 hazards relevant to the committee member's workplace

iv.   is completed within 12 months of the date that the committee member
       completed a JHSC Certification Part One Training Program that met the
       requirements of paragraph A1

3. Take Refresher Training in accordance with the requirements and timeframes set out in
   Part C to maintain their certification.

**B.   Training and other requirements for committee members who have only completed
       Part One training under the 1996 JHSC Certification Training Standards prior to
       March 1, 2016.**

Committee members who have successfully completed Part One training under the 1996 JHSC
Certification Training Standards prior to March 1, 2016 may submit proof of successful
completion of that training, and in addition, must meet the training and other requirements set
out in paragraphs B1 -2:

1   Complete a JHSC Certification Part Two Training Program that:

   i.   is approved by the CPO under subsection 7.1(2) of the Act as meeting the
         Ministry of Labour, Training and Skills Development Joint Health and Safety
         Committee Certification Program Standard, dated May 1, 2020 as amended or
         October 1, 2015

   ii.   is delivered by a training provider approved by the CPO under subsection 7.2(2)
         of the Act as meeting the Ministry of Labour, Training and Skills Development
         Joint Health and Safety Committee Certification Provider Standard, dated May 1,
         2020 as amended or October 1, 2015

   iii. Provides training in a minimum of 6 hazards relevant to the committee
         member's workplace.

2   Take Refresher Training in accordance with the requirements and timeframes set out
     in Part C to maintain their certification.

C.   **REFRESHER TRAINING REQUIREMENT FOR ALL COMMITTEE MEMBERS CERTIFIED UNDER THE TRAINING AND OTHER REQUIREMENTS ESTABLISHED BY THE CPO, effective March 1, 2016 and May 1, 2020.**

Committee members who have been certified by the CPO pursuant to the training and other requirements set out in Part A or B above, must take Refresher Training in accordance with the following requirements and timeframes to maintain their certification:

1   Subject to paragraphs C2-5, a certified member must complete a JHSC Certification Refresher Training Program within three years of being certified by the CPO; and thereafter, within three years of the date of successfully completing a JHSC Certification Refresher Training Program, that is:

   i.   approved by the CPO under subsection 7.1(2) of the Act as meeting the Ministry of Labour, Training and Skills Development Joint Health and Safety Committee Certification Program Standard, dated October 1, 2015 or May 1, 2020 as amended

   ii. is delivered by a training provider approved by the CPO under subsection 7.2(2) of the Act as meeting the Ministry of Labour, Training and Skills Development Joint Health and Safety Committee Certification Provider Standard, dated October 1, 2015 or May 1, 2020 as amended

2   The member may apply for an exemption pursuant to paragraph C3 from the CPO, from the requirement to take JHSC Certification Refresher Training in accordance with paragraph C1, within 3 years of one of the following dates, as applicable:

   i.   the date that the committee member became certified; or

   ii. the date that the committee member last completed a JHSC Certification Refresher Training Program after becoming certified.

3   The CPO may grant an exemption from JHSC Certification Refresher Training to a certified member:

   i.   who has applied for the exemption in accordance with paragraph C2; and

   ii. who has served as a committee member within 12 months of applying; and

   iii. who has not previously been granted an exemption by the CPO for Refresher JHSC Certification Training.

4   If an exemption is granted under paragraph C3, the certified member must complete a JHSC Certification Refresher Training Program that meets the requirements of paragraphs C1 i-ii within 6 years of one of the following dates, as applicable:

   i.   the date that the committee member became certified

   ii.   the date that the committee member last completed a JHSC Certification Refresher Training Program after becoming certified.

5   At the time the CPO denies a certified member an exemption, the CPO may allow the certified member to complete a JHSC Certification Refresher Training Program within a specified period.

6   Failure to complete the JHSC Certification Refresher Training requirements within the timeframes specified in paragraphs C1, C4 and C5 will result in the member no longer being certified.

Review

Certified members have the right, under certain circumstances, to order the employer to stop work where dangerous circumstances exist.

This chapter explains the circumstances under which a certified member may deal with an inspector or the Labour Relations Board. It also briefly describes the special communications and record-keeping needs of certified members and points out methods they can use to keep their knowledge and skills up to date. This chapter discusses the role of certified members of joint health and safety committees. Certified members were established in 1990 and they play a broad role in health and safety in the workplace.

In particular, certified members may be involved in assisting in the resolution of work refusals. In this case, the worker certified member or another worker member of the joint health and safety committee must be present during the investigation. Certified members are also involved in the investigation of complaints concerning dangerous circumstances.

The JHSC Certification Provider Standards changed in October 2015 and were amended in May 2020. Certified members under the current standards require 19.5 hours of Basic Certification Training Part I, and 13 hours of hazard training covering a minimum of six hazards. The second part of the training must be completed within one year of Part I training. Refresher training must be completed within three years of completing Part II training.

Chapter 6
Health and Safety Representatives

- HSR Training

- HSR Functions

- Review

Health and Safety Representatives

Health and safety representatives are required under the *OHSA*, in any workplaces that employ six to 19 workers, at a construction site that employs more than 20 workers but where work will be completed in under three months, and in a farming operation which regularly exceeds five workers and no JHSC is required.

The HSR is chosen by the workers, or the union if there is one, and do not exercise managerial function.

It is essential that health and safety representatives have a good understanding of the functions, duties, rights and authority of the HSR. The *OHSA* sets out several very specific functions for HSRs. They add up to an overall objective of identifying and evaluating hazards and recommending action on health and safety issues. To do his or her job, the health and safety representative needs the full commitment of the employer. It is especially important that the employer's health and safety policy and programs recognize a key role for the HSR.

To carry out the functions, the health and safety representative engages in a wide range of activities. He or she inspects the workplace, participates and makes recommendations, and communicates with both workers and management. The health and safety representative uses first-hand knowledge of the workplace to identify hazards and make recommendations to control them.

Health and safety representatives are paid at their regular rate or premium rate, whichever applies, for the time they spend carrying out their duties under the *OSHA*. This includes inspections, investigating a work refusal, or investigating incidents.

This chapter examines the rights, duties and responsibilities placed on HSRs by the *OHSA*.

Unlike certified members of joint health and safety committees, there is no legislated training for health and safety representatives. Section 8 (5.1) in the *OHSA* states that a HSR "receives training to enable him or her to effectively exercise the powers and perform the duties of a health and safety representative." This section, however, is not currently in effect. The Ministry of Labour, Training, and Skills Development has issued a Health and Safety Representative Basic Training Program Guideline as well as a provider guideline. The four health and safety associations provide this training. Alternately, HSRs take Basic Certification Training for health and safety committees. Basic Certification Training meets the voluntary standards as set out by the MLTSD.

HSR Functions

The functions of health and safety representatives are specified in the *OHSA*. The *OHSA* also gives HSRs certain duties and powers to carry out their functions.

Just like joint health and safety committees, these functions, powers and duties relate directly to the four major tasks of identifying, assessing, recommending action to control health and safety hazards, and evaluating hazard controls once they have been implemented.

Identifying Health and Safety Hazards
A health and safety representative may make recommendations directly to the employer. There is no group or opposite member with which to discuss ideas. The HSR, therefore, needs to be well versed in all hazards in the workplace. The *OHSA* places a broad duty on committees "to identify sources of danger or hazards in the workplace". A wide variety of techniques are involved, including workplace inspections, hazard assessments, monitoring, and reviews of written records.

Health and safety representatives are empowered to carry out these activities by several rights set out in the *OHSA*. HSRs have the right to obtain information from employers or constructors, and conduct inspections of the workplace.

- HSR has the right to obtain information on actual or potential hazards of materials, processes or equipment.

- HSR has the right to be furnished by the employer with updated copies of all safety data sheets for materials used in the workplace.

- HSR has the right to obtain an annual summary of employer-specific claims information from the Workplace Safety and Insurance Board. This summary includes data on injuries, fatalities, lost work-days, cases that required medical aid and the incidence of occupational illnesses. The Board must supply this information.

- HSR has the right to information on health and safety experience and standards that the constructor or employer is aware of in other industries.

- HSR is to inspect the workplace at least once a month. Where this is not practical, part of the workplace must be inspected at least once per month according to a schedule agreed upon by the representative and the employer. The entire workplace must be inspected at least once a year.

- HSR shall be given an opportunity to accompany a Ministry inspector when a workplace inspection is conducted.

Assessing Health and Safety Hazards

When a hazard has been identified, the extent and severity of the hazard must be assessed. HSRs have the right to participate in these procedures.

- HSR has the right to obtain information about health and safety testing.

- HSR has the right to be consulted prior to tests of equipment, machines or the work environment and to be present at the beginning of such testing.

- HSR has the right to be consulted about proposed industrial hygiene testing strategies and to be present at the beginning of such testing.

- HSR has the right to receive copies of assessment reports and to be consulted about assessment methods for designated substances.

- HSR investigates incidents that result in critical injuries or fatalities.

Recommending Action to Control Health and Safety Hazards

The *OHSA* gives the HSR the right to make recommendations, and it places a duty on the employer or constructor to reply.

- HSR has the right to make recommendations regarding control programs for designated substances.

- HSR has the right to make written recommendations for the improvement of the health and safety of workers.

- A reply from the employer or constructor must be given in writing within 21 days, with either a schedule for implementation or a statement of reasons for disagreement.

- HSR has the right to be consulted about the development of worker training and instruction concerning exposure to hazardous material or hazardous physical agents, and to participate in an annual review of these training programs.

Evaluating Hazard Controls

Health and safety representatives evaluate hazard controls. At times this is done formally. For example, if the employer has a noise evaluation done, and the industrial hygienist recommends isolating noisy equipment in a sound-proof room, the health and safety representative expects to see a post-control evaluation. The results should show less noise exposure for the workers after the control measure is put in place.

Confidentiality

Like the JHSC members, the HSR must keep any trade secrets or personal medical information confidential. The HSR gains trust from the workers and the employer when personal and business information is highly respected.

Inspecting the Workplace

Workplace inspection a is function of the HSR.

Workplace inspections are described in detail in Chapter 17 of this reference guide.

Taking Part in Incident Investigations

The *OHSA* gives specific duties to HSRs with respect to incident investigations.

Effective investigations require special training and are the subject of Chapter 18.

Recommending Health and Safety Improvements

Making recommendations for improvements is a specific duty given to HSRs by the *OHSA*. HSR recommendations for the elimination or control of hazards are communicated directly to management. There is no counterpart or committee with which to discuss ideas. The HSR needs to be fully supported in the workplace to be effective.

Developing Training Programs

The *OHSA* gives HSR the right to participate in the development, design and regular upgrading of worker health and safety training for workers exposed or likely to be exposed to a hazardous material or to a hazardous physical agent. Training can achieve its objectives only if it is designed to deal with the unique hazards and special needs of the individual workplace.

This chapter explains that the main functions of the HSR is to identify, assess and recommend ways of eliminating or controlling health and safety hazards. Once controls have been implemented, HSRs are involved in evaluating hazard controls. Specific rights and duties associated with each of these functions are listed. The HSR has the right under the *OHSA* to receive specific kinds of information from the employer.

The activities used by HSRs to carry out their functions are the same as the JHSC's. These activities include information gathering as well as participation in inspections, assessments, investigations, and testing. HSRs communicate with workers and others in the workplace and make recommendations to the employer based on these activities.

Chapter 7

Administration and Enforcement of the *OHSA*

- Inspectors

- The Ontario Labour Relations Board

- Offences and Penalties

- Interpretations

- Review

Administration and Enforcement of the *OHSA*

Under the *OHSA,* employers and supervisors are required to take every reasonable precaution in the circumstances for the protection of a worker. Workers are required to report any violations of the *OHSA*, as well as any defective equipment or workplace of which they are aware, to their supervisor or employer. The joint health and safety committee or health and safety representative identify and evaluate hazards and make recommendations to the employer. They are not, however, a substitute for enforcement of the *OHSA*. If, after the duties and responsibilities of the workplace parties have been carried out and anyone in the workplace continues to believe that the *OHSA* is being contravened, the Ministry of Labour, Training and Skills Development may be asked to investigate. The Ministry of Labour, Training and Skills Development has a responsibility under the *OHSA* to enforce the law.

Joint health and safety committees or health and safety representatives will normally consider many health and safety concerns which do not involve a work refusal or a stop-work procedure. They can be identified during a workplace inspection or by someone in the workplace reporting a concern. Committee members or health and safety representatives may not be able to agree on a solution or a recommendation, or the employer may not act on the recommendation. In these unusual cases, anyone who believes the *OHSA* is being contravened may report the facts to the Ministry. All Ministry of Labour, Training and Skills Development health and safety enquiries and notifications can be made to a single, province-wide health and safety contact centre by calling 1-877-202-0008. The addresses and phone numbers of the Ministry's offices are provided in the back of each *Occupational Health and Safety Act* book.

The *OHSA* provides three ways of dealing with complaints:

- The Ministry of Labour, Training and Skills Development can send an inspector to investigate the situation. The inspector may or may not issue an order depending on whether or not corrective action is required.

- Any of the parties to the complaint who disagree with the decision of the inspector can appeal to the Labour Relations Board. In addition, the Labour Relations Board hears applications to apply the unilateral stop-work procedure or appoint an inspector to a workplace. A complaint about the conduct of a certified member is also heard by the Labour Relations Board.

- The Ministry may prosecute persons who commit offences under the *OHSA*. Those convicted are liable for fines and/or imprisonment. This procedure is normally used only for serious offences.

This chapter describes the roles of inspectors and the Labour Relations Board in greater detail and summarizes the conditions under which the Ministry may conduct a prosecution. It also describes sources of information about interpretations or decisions that have been made under the *OHSA*.

Inspectors

Inspectors are the primary enforcement officers of the *OHSA*. The Ministry assigns an inspector to investigate most complaints. In addition, inspectors conduct investigations of serious incidents and may inspect a workplace on their own initiative. Inspectors have many powers under the *OHSA*, including the right to enter any workplace at any time without notice. Anyone in the workplace can call the Ministry of Labour, Training and Skills Development to request that an inspector be sent to the workplace.

Inspectors have a duty to enforce the *OHSA*. They are also expected to maintain contact with joint health and safety committees and health and safety representatives.

JHSC members, especially certified members, are likely to be involved when an inspector is at the workplace. Worker-designated JHSC members, if possible the certified member, have the right to be present during workplace inspections and investigations. Inspectors may wish to speak with the JHSC members to obtain information about the workplace including any health and safety hazards. In smaller workplaces employing 6-19 workers, a ministry inspector will seek out the health and safety representative.

Inspector's Orders
Inspectors use orders to enforce the *OHSA* and regulations. An order is an instruction to an owner, constructor, employer, supervisor, supplier, or worker to stop violating the *OHSA* or regulations. The most common type of order is a compliance order which specifies corrective action to be taken and sets a deadline for compliance.

Another type of order is the stop-work order which specifies that work is not to proceed, or equipment is not to be used, until a problem is fixed. The inspector may order that the area be cleared of all workers who are not involved in carrying out the order. Stop-work orders remain in effect until they are expressly withdrawn by an inspector in accordance with the provisions of Section 59 of the *OHSA*.

An order may be given orally, but it must be confirmed in writing before the inspector leaves the workplace. Copies of an order must be given to the employer, to the JHSC or HSR, and to an individual who has complained.

Orders must also be posted in a place most likely to be seen by workers, for example, on a piece of equipment or in the vicinity of the problem. If the inspector does not post the notice personally, the employer must do so. It is an offence under the *OHSA* to remove or interfere with an inspector's order or notice.

Another approach to enforcing the *OHSA* is 'ticketing.' Ticketing allows Ministry of Labour, Training and Skills Development inspectors to issue on-the-spot offence notices for certain violations under the *OHSA* and regulations. Tickets can be issued to individual workers, supervisors and/or employers. The violations are obvious and have potential for serious hazards to workers (for example, a worker working on a construction site not wearing a hard hat). They are evident to inspectors, and do not raise complex or confusing legal or factual issues. The fines range from $250 to $650 under the auspices of Ontario Provincial Offences.

Money collected from the fine(s) goes to the offence location municipality and the province's Victims Justice Fund Account. While some believe the fine amounts should be raised to act as a further deterrent to non-compliance or to account for inflation, others would like to see more fines covering a broader range of offences.

Legal Enforcement of Inspector's Orders

Where an inspector's order concerning a stop-work situation is not complied with, the Ministry of Labour, Training and Skills Development may apply to a judge for a court order. The court can grant the application without notice to the violator, but such cases are rare. If the violation continues despite the court order, the court may order a fine or imprisonment for contempt of court.

The Ontario Labour Relations Board

The Ontario Labour Relations Board is an independent decision-maker appointed under the *Labour Relations Act*, 1995. The Labour Relations Board has three main functions under the Act. The first is to conduct appeals of an inspector's orders. The second is to decide on applications by either a certified member of the workplace or an inspector to have the unilateral stop-work procedure applied to a workplace, or to recommend the appointment of an inspector to oversee the workplace's health and safety practices. If an inspector is appointed, the employer must pay the costs associated with the inspector. The third function of the Labour Relations Board is to hear complaints about the conduct of a certified member related to the stop-work authority.

Appeals of Inspector's Orders
Any worker, worker's representative or employer can appeal a decision of an inspector. The appeal may concern an order, a failure to issue an order, or any term or condition imposed by an inspector's decision. The appeal must be directed to the Labour Relations Board within 30 days of making the order. The appeal may be made in writing, in person, or by telephone. The grounds for the appeal may be required in writing before the appeal is heard.

There is one exception to this procedure. An appeal of an order by a director, made under the toxic substances part of the *OHSA*, must be made directly to the Minister of Labour, Training and Skills Development in accordance with the provisions of Section 33 of the *OHSA*.

Mediation
The Labour Relations Board may authorize a labour relations officer to inquire into an appeal and attempt to resolve it. A report of the findings will be sent to the Labour Relations Board.

Hearings
If an appeal of an inspector's order cannot be resolved by the Labour Relations Officer, a formal hearing is held. The hearing reviews the facts of the situation or incident that gave rise to the inspector's action. Labour Relations Board consultations are not subject to the provisions of the *Statutory Powers Procedures Act*.

The Labour Relations Board hears the presentations and receives evidence and may also visit the workplace. The Ministry is represented by legal counsel at these hearings. Other parties to the appeal may also seek external advice and be represented by legal counsel or advisors at the hearing.

To be successful, an appeal will have to set out clear and persuasive reasons why the decision should be overturned. These reasons may include errors of fact or errors of interpretation.

A review of previous orders of the Labour Relations Board can provide a useful guide to the principles that should guide an appeal.

The Labour Relations Board may decide to delay the application of the inspector's order pending the outcome of the appeal. Otherwise, the order remains in effect during the appeal process.

Decisions

The decision of the Labour Relations Board may take one of three forms. It may:

- confirm the order or decision;

- cancel the order or decision; or

- make a new order or decision.

The *OHSA* states that the decision of the Labour Relations Board is final. However, a decision might still be challenged in the courts on narrow legal grounds.

Applications to the Ontario Labour Relations Board

A certified member may believe that the bilateral work stoppage procedure is not adequate to prevent serious risk to the health or safety of workers. The certified member may apply for a declaration or a recommendation by the Labour Relations Board. An inspector may also apply for such a declaration or recommendation.

A *declaration* is a notification by the Labour Relations Board to the employer that the workplace will be subject to the unilateral work stoppage procedure for a specified period.

A *recommendation* is a proposal from the Labour Relations Board to the Minister of Labour that an inspector be assigned on either a full-time or part-time basis to oversee health and safety practices at a workplace for a specified period. If the Minister approves a Labour Relations Board recommendation to appoint an inspector to oversee the workplace's health and safety practices, the associated costs must be paid by the workplace employer.

The Minister may appoint an inspector to meet with the workplace parties and try to mediate a settlement of the issues raised by the application.

Using prescribed criteria, if the Labour Relations Board agrees with the application, the Labour Relations Board may issue a declaration or a recommendation or both. The specified period can be a fixed period of time, or whatever time is needed to satisfy a set of conditions defined by the Labour Relations Board.

Complaints to the Ontario Labour Relations Board

Anyone in the workplace, including the employer, a worker or a union representing the workers, if any, may lodge a complaint with the Labour Relations Board that a certified member has acted "recklessly" or "in bad faith" in exercising or failing to exercise the stop-work authority.

The complaint must be filed with the Labour Relations Board within 30 days of the incident to which the complaint applies.

The Minister of Labour is entitled to be a party to a proceeding before the Labour Relations Board.

The Labour Relations Board can make an order to decertify the certified member, or take other action that the Labour Relations Board thinks is appropriate.

For information on the Ontario Labour Relations Board, see their website at: www.olrb.gov.on.ca

Offences and Penalties

A person who contravenes or fails to comply with the *OHSA*, the regulations, or a Ministry order is guilty of an offence under the *OHSA*. Part IX of the *OHSA* sets out offences and penalties. A person who is convicted of an offence under the *OHSA* may be fined or imprisoned. The maximum fine is $100,000 for an individual and $1,500,000 for a corporation.

In considering whether to prosecute under the *OHSA*, the Ministry will consider such factors as: fatalities or critical injuries;

- high risk of causing a fatal or critical injury;

- conscious or gross disregard for the *OHSA*;

- contravention of a designated substance regulation, and no satisfactory compliance;

- failure to comply with orders, or a history of similar orders; or

- failure to advise and to take reasonable precautions to protect the health or safety of a worker.

In reaching a decision about a possible prosecution, Ministry officials may interview members of joint health and safety committees, health and safety representatives as well as other witnesses.

Over the years many provisions of the *OHSA* have been interpreted through decisions by the Director of Appeals or the Adjudicator. Certified members and health and safety representatives may be guided by these previous Ministry decisions. These decisions are, in

effect, interpretations of what the law means and they provide a guide to how the *OHSA* has been interpreted in the past. The Director of Appeals and Adjudicator have now been replaced by the Labour Relations Board.

As decisions of the Labour Relations Board accumulate, they will provide a growing understanding of how the law will be applied. The conditions under which the Labour Relations Board may implement the unilateral work stoppage provisions will become clearer when applications have heard. Similarly, the criteria to be used for assessing complaints about the way that certified members have exercised or failed to exercise their stop-work authority under the *OHSA*, will evolve over time.

Anyone in the workplace can complain to the Ministry that the *OHSA* is being contravened.

The Ministry has three main ways of dealing with complaints. Depending on the nature of the complaint, the Ministry may send an inspector to investigate. The inspector's decision can be appealed to the Labour Relations Board. An application can also be made to the Labour Relations Board to implement the unilateral stop-work procedure, or to recommend appointment of a special inspector to a workplace. The Ministry may also prosecute offences under the *OHSA* through the courts.

Most complaints are settled by inspectors. They have broad powers to enter and inspect the workplace and determine whether a contravention of the *OHSA* or regulations has taken place.

They have the authority to issue orders requiring employers, constructors, supervisors, suppliers or workers to take corrective action. If necessary, they can order the work to be stopped.

In addition to hearing appeals against inspectors' orders, the Labour Relations Board considers applications to implement the unilateral stop-work procedure in a workplace for a specific period.

The Labour Relations Board may recommend to the Minister of Labour, Training and Skills Development the appointment of an inspector to a workplace. If the MLTSD approves the appointment of an inspector to oversee the workplace's health and safety practices, the associated costs must be paid by the employer.

When determining whether to prosecute under the statute, the Ministry considers such factors as whether there has been a fatality or critical injury, or whether the situation might have led to a fatality or critical injury, as well as the overall record of the employer or constructor in complying with the *OHSA*.
Joint health and safety committee members and health and safety representatives may be uncertain about the application of some of the *OHSA*'s provisions and can learn about interpretations of the law from previous decisions made by the Adjudicator or decisions of the Labour Relations Board who has replaced the Adjudicator.

Chapter 8
The Body and the Workplace

- Routes of Entry

- The Human body

- Review

The Body and the Workplace

This chapter is about the body and the effects that hazards in the workplace may have on it. Workplace hazards affect the body in many ways. Sometimes the effect is obvious. Incidents result in trauma injuries that are felt immediately. If the body is injured from contact with a moving object, the exact nature of the injury will be important mainly for treatment purposes. From the point of view of preventing future occurrences, it is the circumstances of the contact that matter most.

The effects of health hazards on the body are not always readily apparent. Health effects can be subtle, and may not even be noticed until considerable damage has been done. Chemical and biological agents can enter the body in more than one way. The damage they do is often related to the route of entry involved. For these reasons, effective control of health hazards depends, to some extent, on an understanding of how the body works, and how it is affected by hazardous agents in the workplace.

The Body and the Workplace

Routes of Entry

Substances, toxic or otherwise, can enter the body in four main ways, often called routes of entry:

- Some toxic substances can enter by inhalation, which means they are breathed through the nose, down the windpipe and into the lungs. Some substances may be absorbed through the mucous membranes of the nose and sinuses. This is the major route of entry for most toxic substances. An adult at rest breathes about five litres of air per minute. Agents in the form of dusts, fumes, gases, and vapours or mists which are in the air may be inhaled along with the air. Some substances, such as fibres, may directly injure the lung. Others are absorbed into the bloodstream and transported to other parts of the body.

- Some substances can enter by absorption through the skin, through cuts or abrasions or, less commonly through the mucous membranes of the eyes. Some liquids may be absorbed through the skin, especially through the hands, the face, and the scrotum. They pass through the skin into the small blood vessels.

- Some substances can enter by ingestion, which means they are swallowed. This can happen from eating contaminated food, or from eating with contaminated hands or in a contaminated environment. Airborne substances may also be ingested when they are breathed in and become mixed with mucous from the nose, mouth, throat, and airways. The toxic substance follows the same route as food does. It moves down the esophagus, into the stomach and through the intestines where it may be absorbed into the bloodstream.

- A less common route of entry for substances is injection which includes puncture of the skin. This could result from a needle-stick injury from a used contaminated needle such as a puncture after treating a patient with an infectious disease. It can also be the result of an insect bite from a mosquito that is a carrier of West Nile virus. When a substance has entered the body, it often finds its way into the bloodstream and is circulated throughout the body. If it is toxic, it can then cause damage to other body systems and organs.

The Human Body

The human body is a complex organism. Its functions are carried out by dozens of separate organs. While each organ performs a specific function, it is also linked with other organs to make up the body's different systems. These systems are interdependent. Damage to any of the organs can interfere with the functions of the whole system.

For example, the circulatory system consists of the heart, the blood and a vast network of blood vessels. The heart acts as a pump causing blood to circulate through the system. The blood delivers nutrients to every cell in the body and removes waste products. Excessive exposure to carbon monoxide can indirectly damage the heart, even though its direct effect results in replacement of oxygen in the blood.

Other body systems that are susceptible to workplace hazards include the digestive system, the nervous system, the respiratory system, and the reproductive system.

In many cases, a malfunction of an organ or system caused by a workplace hazard is part of the body's normal defensive reactions. For example, scarring of lung tissue caused by the inhalation of asbestos fibres is part of the body's attempt to enclose and isolate the invading substance.

In spite of this interdependence, it is convenient to discuss health effects according to the site of the damage. This section describes some of the body systems and organs that are most susceptible to occupational health hazards.

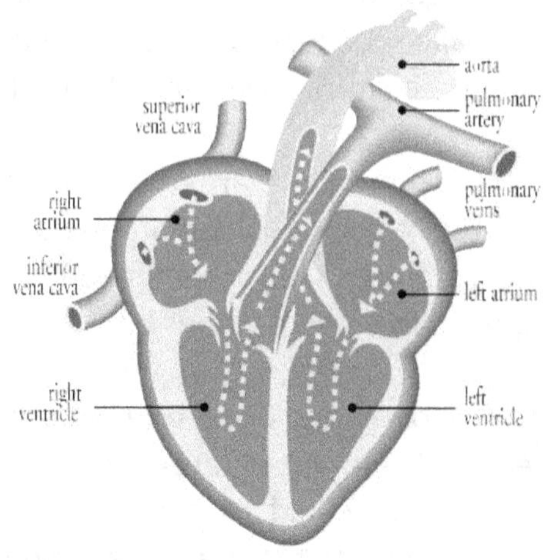

The Heart

The heart is the pump which circulates blood throughout the body. It is part of the circulatory system. It is divided into four chambers. Each time the heart contracts, the left side forces blood out into the arteries.

At the same time, the right side receives blood from the veins. A system of valves prevents the blood from flowing backwards when the heart relaxes. The contraction and relaxation of the heart are controlled by electrical impulses from the central nervous system.

The arteries and veins are referred to as blood vessels. They branch out like a tree, becoming smaller and smaller as they reach the outer extremities. The smallest blood vessels, called capillaries, deliver nutrients to every cell in the body. The heart, blood and blood vessels comprise the circulatory system.

The Blood

Blood is made up of red blood cells and white blood cells and forms part of the circulatory system. Red blood cells transport oxygen throughout the body and carry away wastes in the form of carbon dioxide. White blood cells protect against invasion of the body by attacking infectious agents such as viruses and bacteria. The red blood cells contain a protein called hemoglobin, which binds to oxygen. Oxygen is delivered to every cell in the body where, as a result of oxidation of nutrients, energy is produced. Red blood cells are manufactured in the marrow inside bones. This process can malfunction, leading to a shortage of red blood cells. This is called anemia.

If carbon monoxide is present in the air in excessive concentrations, it can interfere with the blood's ability to transport oxygen. This happens because carbon monoxide binds to hemoglobin much more readily than does oxygen.

In the course of transporting nutrients and waste products the blood can also carry hazardous agents throughout the body. When certain infectious agents are involved, this can result in the blood itself becoming a hazardous agent. One example is Human Immunodeficiency Virus (HIV). HIV, which can lead to Acquired Immune Deficiency Syndrome (AIDS). HIV attacks the body's immune system, making it vulnerable to many other infections or infection-related cancer.

HIV is commonly regarded as a sexually transmitted infection. The virus may be spread through exposure to blood, blood products or other body fluids but this mode of transmission is very rare. Although AIDS is not spread by casual contact, caution must be exercised when a worker is exposed to blood or other body fluids.

In any workplace, blood-borne hazards are controlled by placing a barrier, usually latex and frequently non-latex (latex can cause allergic reactions) gloves, between the worker and the blood or body fluid. In some workplaces, such as those in the health care sector, additional controls may be required. These precautions provide protection against all blood-borne infections, including HIV, the hepatitis B virus (HBV), and hepatitis C virus (HCV).

The Liver

The liver performs several functions. It is a purification plant, a chemical factory, and a chemical storehouse. Liver cells contain enzymes that can convert one substance into another. The liver manufactures chemicals that the body needs from nutrients in food. Some of these chemicals are stored in the liver until they are needed. The liver also breaks down toxic substances absorbed by the body into water-soluble substances that can be excreted.

The liver can be damaged in the process of breaking down toxic substances if the absorbed dose exceeds the liver's threshold for detoxification. It may become inflamed, a condition known as hepatitis. Repeated exposure to toxic substances can lead to scarring, called cirrhosis of the liver.

The Kidneys

The two kidneys are part of the body's waste disposal system. Tiny filters in each kidney remove impurities from the blood so they can be excreted as urine. The kidneys also play a role in maintaining the body's delicate chemical balance. They regulate the amount of water in the body as well as the levels of acid and salt.

The kidneys may be damaged by toxic substances which they filter from the blood. This damage may disrupt the functions of the kidneys and upset the chemical balance of other body systems. The kidneys are also susceptible to external physical damage.

Urine from the kidneys is stored before excretion in another organ, the bladder. Toxic substances in the urine may also cause damage to the bladder.

The Digestive System

The digestive system breaks down food into the basic nutrients the body needs. The system does its work by means of enzymes and acids secreted in the stomach. The digestive tract begins at the mouth and ends at the anus. In the mouth, food is chewed and mixed with an enzyme in the saliva. It passes down the esophagus to the stomach.

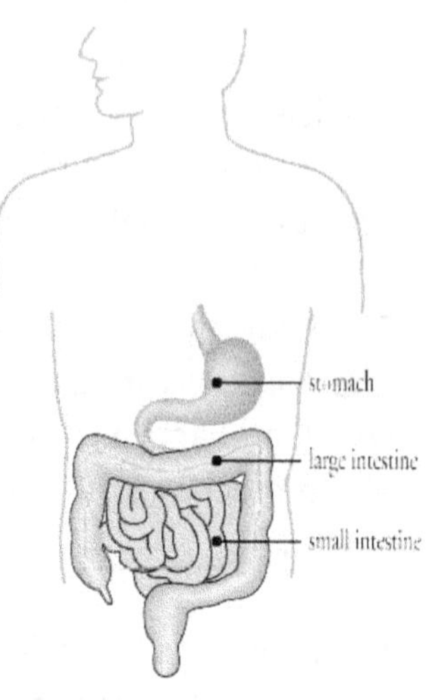

The stomach contains acid and enzymes that further break down the food into its basic components, which are protein, carbohydrates, and fat. From the stomach, food passes to the duodenum which breaks up the basic components even further. It moves on to the small intestine and then the large intestine. The intestines transfer the nutrients to the circulatory system and remove water. Bacteria in the large intestine help to decompose waste material and remove the last of the usable substances before the waste is excreted.

When a person swallows something contaminated with a toxic substance, there are sites along the digestive system, such as at the small intestine, where the toxic material may cause damage. The greatest long-term potential for damage to health comes after the system has treated the material. At this stage it may pass through the lining of the digestive system and into the bloodstream. The blood can then circulate it to other organs.

The digestive tract is, for the most part, self-regulating. The stomach is controlled by a complex system of nerves. This system is vulnerable to malfunction. The overproduction of acid in the stomach can contribute to the development of ulcers of the stomach or duodenum. The mechanisms that create ulcers are not fully understood. Stress has been identified as a contributing factor.

The Lungs

The lungs are part of the respiratory system that also includes the nose and windpipe, or trachea. The lungs remove oxygen from the air and transfer it to the blood. They then remove waste carbon dioxide from the blood and exhale it into the air.

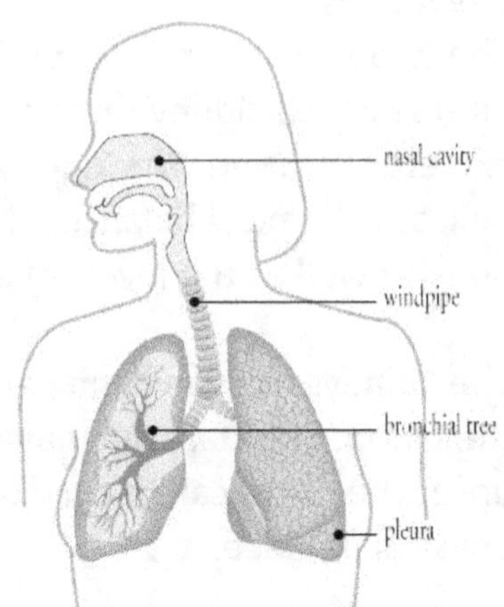

Air enters the lungs through the nose and windpipe and is divided into two passages called bronchi, which lead to the right and left lungs. In the lungs, the bronchi divide into smaller and smaller passages called bronchioles, and end up in a cluster of air sacs called alveoli. This is where the oxygen is transferred to the blood and the carbon dioxide is released. The rate of respiration (breathing) is regulated by nerve impulses which signal changes in the body's carbon dioxide levels. The lungs are covered by a delicate membrane known as the pleura, which protects the lung tissues.

Damage to the lungs can be caused by particles suspended in the air that is breathed. Larger particles are removed by the nose, or by the mucous membranes in the bronchi, but very small particles can reach the air sacs and cause considerable damage. The damage may be scarring of the lung tissue. Some particles cause allergic reactions or irritation. Cancer of the lungs can result from inhalation of particles or gases.

The Nose

The nose performs two functions. It operates the body's sense of smell, and acts as a kind of air conditioner. The sense of smell is an alarm mechanism. It can alert a worker to the presence of a toxic material.

The air conditioning function of the nose is elaborate. The small hairs in the nostrils filter out dust and other particles. The mucous membranes also trap particles which are later blown out or swallowed. The nose also adjusts the temperature of the air it breathes to 35 degrees centigrade, even in freezing cold weather. Wet mucous tissues regulate the moisture of the air.

Both the warming and air-conditioning operations of the nose can be damaged by certain chemical agents. The sense of smell can be reduced in sensitivity or destroyed altogether. The nose may become sensitized to the point of allergic reaction to some chemicals. It can also become the site of a cancer.

The Eyes

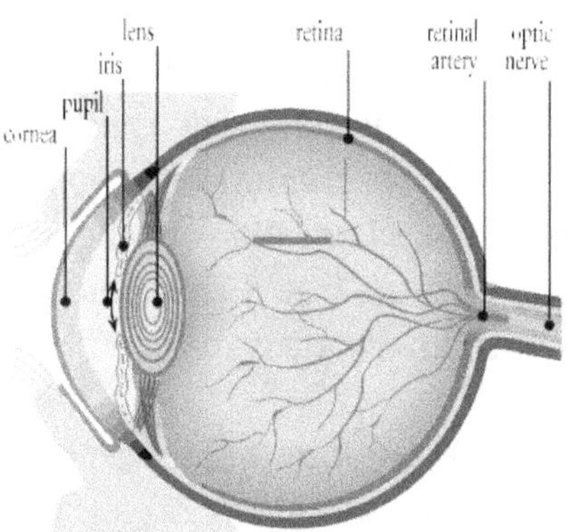

The function of the eyes is to catch light and convert it into electrical impulses which can be "seen" as images by the brain. Light enters the eye through the cornea and passes through the pupil. The pupil adjusts its size to regulate the amount of light admitted. The light is focused by the lens onto the retina which has special photoreceptor cells for converting the light into electrical impulses. The ciliary muscles change the shape of the lens to focus on objects at varying distances. The electrical impulses are transferred by the optic nerve to the brain, where they are interpreted as images. Fluids around the eyes provide lubrication and protection against particles in the air.

The eyes are very complex and sensitive organs that are highly vulnerable to damage from physical, chemical, or biohazardous agents. They can be a route of entry for certain toxic substances which can become dissolved in the eye fluids. The eyes can also be damaged by the action of radiation on cells and tissues. For example, infrared and ultraviolet light from welding without protection, can harm the eye.

The Ear

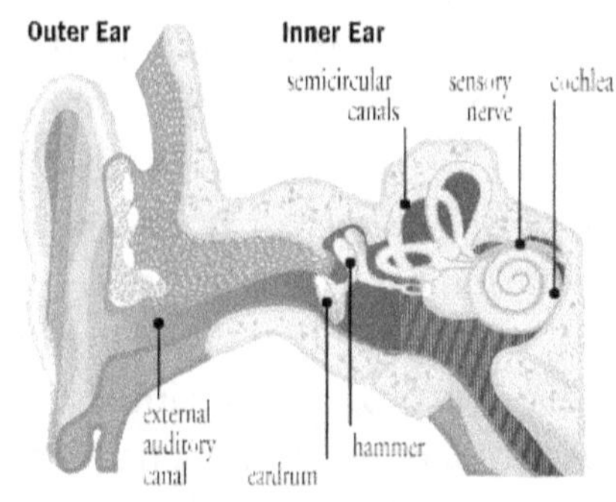

The ear performs two important functions. It translates pressure waves in the air into sounds that can be registered by the brain. It also controls the body's sense of balance. The waves produced by a source of sound are funneled by the outer ear onto the eardrum which passes these vibrations into the inner ear. There, a series of sensitive and delicate mechanisms transforms the vibrations into nerve impulses. These impulses are then transmitted along the auditory nerve to the brain which interprets the message.

The ear can be damaged by workplace hazards. Hearing loss can result from a powerful sound that ruptures the eardrum, but more often develops over time from regular and prolonged exposure to noise. Noise is sound whose intensity or frequency may cause damage to hearing. Damage to the balance organ itself is rare, but the part of the brain that analyzes balance signals can be damaged or impaired by some chemical agents.

The Nervous System

The nervous system consists of the central nervous system, the peripheral nervous system and the autonomic nervous system.

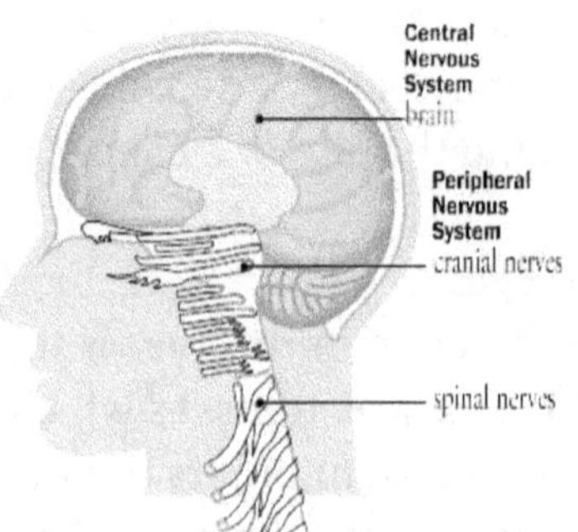

The central nervous system is the most complex of the body's systems. It has been compared to computer communications systems. The human brain is indeed a powerful computer, but it is much more than that. It shapes every aspect of human life, from ideas and emotions to the most basic mechanical functions of the body. The brain and the spinal cord make up the central nervous system.

The central nervous system exchanges information back and forth with the peripheral nervous system which serves the organs and limbs of the body. This two-way communications system relies on specialized cells called receptors. The receptors convert data from the body parts into electrical signals that are sent to the brain along a network of nerves. The brain quickly analyzes this information and sends out instructions to the muscles and organs along the same network.

The brain performs these actions in response to conscious thoughts in some cases. The brain does much of its work automatically as well, through the autonomic nervous system. Examples are breathing and the pumping of the heart.

The cells in the peripheral nervous system can normally restore themselves after an injury, but those in the central nervous system cannot heal or regenerate. Harm done to the central nervous system is permanent. The health effects can range from a minor trembling of the hands, to occasional loss of memory, to crippling disability or death.

The Musculoskeletal System

The musculoskeletal system is the complex network of muscles, joints and bones that allow the body to move. The movement of the body is produced by interaction of muscles and bones. Muscles operate in pairs, helping each other or opposing each other to produce the desired motion. The muscles are connected to the bones of the skeleton by tough fibrous tissues called tendons.

The joints are the connections between the bones of the skeleton. They are protected by smooth coverings of cartilage between the bones and by a synovial membrane attached to the end surface of the bones.

The spine is a specialized arrangement of bones called vertebrae, cartilage in the form of shock-absorbing discs between the vertebrae, and muscles which twist and bend the spine. The spine connects the upper and lower parts of the skeleton and houses the spinal cord linking the brain to other body parts.

Almost every part of the musculoskeletal system is susceptible to damage. Repetitive strenuous motion can lead to progressive damage to the joints, muscles, tendons, and blood vessels as well as several kinds of back injuries. Some of these effects can be sudden and acute, like a torn muscle from heavy lifting, but most develop over time.

The Skin

The skin is a protective organ covering the entire body. The skin has an outer layer called the epidermis and an inner layer called the dermis. The epidermis itself consists of several layers, or strata.

Between the epidermis and the dermis there is another layer called the malpighian layer. It contains the colour pigment and is responsible for skin regeneration.

The dermis contains blood vessels, hair follicles, sebaceous glands, sweat glands, and nerves. Sebaceous glands produce an oil called sebum which flows out of the hair follicle onto the skin, helping it to reduce evaporation and making it less absorbent. Sweat glands release a fluid containing salt onto the skin. The sweat evaporates, cooling the body. The blood vessels in the dermis also play a role in body heat regulation. Nerves known as sensory receptors are located in the dermis. They are responsible for the sensations of pain, touch, pressure, cold, and heat.

The skin is susceptible to damage from a wide range of chemical, biological, and physical agents.

The Cell

The cell is the fundamental unit from which all living things are made. It is the basic building block of all of the body's tissues and organs. There are many kinds of specialized cells but they all have the same components. The cell has an outer shell called the membrane. The bulk of the cell is made up of cytoplasm. The cytoplasm includes a number of structures called organelles, which are the sites of various kinds of cell activity. This includes consumption of oxygen fuel, the handling of waste products, cell division, the production of proteins, and the secretion of cell products.

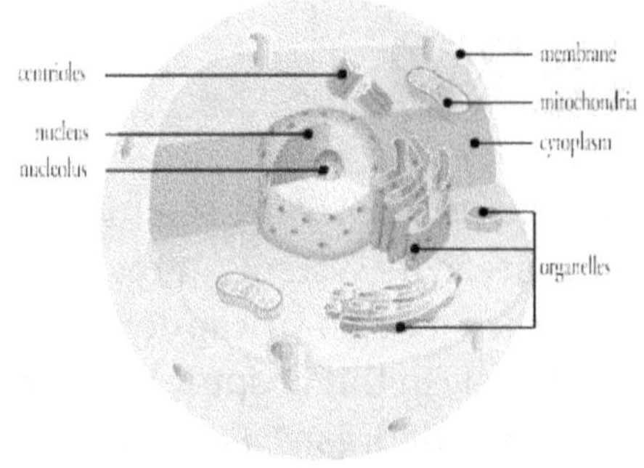

All of this activity is supervised by the nucleus. It contains DNA, a substance that holds the inherited codes instructing the cell how to operate. Most cells reproduce by division, a process called mitosis. Sometimes the process of mitosis, or cell division, malfunctions. A mutation can occur spontaneously, or as the result of exposure to radiation or a chemical.

When this happens, the daughter cells are not exact duplicates of the original cell. Whether a tumour ever develops from the altered cell depends on a variety of factors, such as the presence of other internal or external agents that promote or inhibit tumour development, and the effectiveness of the immune system.

A tumour is called benign if it is localized and self-contained. It can often be removed by surgery. In contrast, a malignant tumour is not contained and invades surrounding tissue. A malignant tumour sends out daughter cells that can spread throughout the body and invade any of the organs. Eventually, tumours can grow so large that they block the normal functioning of the body and deprive other cells of nutrients. The victim dies from failure of one or more body systems. Mutated cells do not necessarily grow into tumours. Even when they do, many cancers do not develop until many years after the first mutation.

A substance which can cause cell mutation is called a mutagen. A substance that causes cancer is called a carcinogen. These include some chemicals which are not themselves mutagens, but can be transformed into one when they are broken down by the body. Some substances, such as asbestos, interfere with cell division when their tiny fibres invade the cell. Some forms of radiation are also carcinogenic.

The Reproductive System

The human reproductive system combines genetic information from both parents. Some chemicals, known as reproductive toxins, can damage the reproductive system if they are mishandled. It is important that workers recognize this potential hazard and the specific chemicals which are associated. The fetus may also be harmed during the process of development, if the mother is exposed to toxic substances known as teratogens. The result of damaged egg or sperm cells, or the mother's exposure to a teratogen, may be a miscarriage or a birth defect.

Review

This chapter describes the routes of entry by which hazardous agents can enter the body and circulate in its systems. It reviews the principal functions of the body's organs and describes how they may be susceptible to damage by hazardous agents. The organs have been discussed separately in this chapter because they may be sites of damage. The body is more than a collection of organs. Each organ plays a role in one or more of the body's interrelated systems. As a consequence, the damage caused to one organ by a hazardous agent may harm the entire system.

2 HEALTH AND SAFETY HAZARDS

Chapter

Chapter 9

Recognition, Assessment, Control, and Evaluation of Hazard Controls

- Adverse Health Effects

- Recognizing Hazards

- Assessing Hazards

- Controlling Hazards

- Evaluating Hazard Controls

- Review

Recognition, Assessment, Control, and Evaluation of Hazard Controls

Hazards occur in every workplace. A hazard is defined as a potential source of harm to a worker. The harm can be in the form of a physical injury, illness, or have an adverse effect on the health of a worker (acute or chronic). A potential hazard exists when a person comes in contact with any agent or object, whose properties can cause harm to the body when excessive exposure takes place.

An occupational injury is any injury that leads to bodily harm, that was incurred by an employee in the performance of or in connection with his or her work.

An occupational illness is a condition that results from exposure in a workplace to a physical, chemical, or biological agent to the extent that the normal physiological mechanisms are affected, and the health of the worker is impaired. It includes an occupational disease for which a worker is entitled to receive benefits under the Workplace Safety and Insurance Act. Some examples include silicosis, pneumoconiosis, and asbestosis. There are a number of presumptive diseases for firefighters. More information can be found in the Workplace Safety and Insurance Act.

Dealing with health hazards in the workplace involves four key steps: recognition, assessment, control, and evaluation of the hazard controls. Recognizing the hazard means identifying equipment, process, substances and agents present in the workplace which have the potential to cause adverse health or safety effects. Assessing the hazard involves a process of identifying the actual or potential exposure of workers to the hazard and determining whether or not the exposure is hazardous. Controlling the hazard means limiting or preventing harmful exposure of workers to the hazard. Evaluating the hazard control includes evaluating the effectiveness of the controls put in place.

There are **six hazard categories**:

- **Physical**, which are forms of energy or force;

- **Chemical**, in the form of solids, liquids or gases;

- **Biological**, which include animals and insects as well as microorganisms in plant, animal or human tissue, or in materials derived from these sources;

- **Musculoskeletal**, including ergonomic hazards which affect the muscles and the skeletal systems;

- **Psychosocial**, including violence and stress; and

- **Safety**, which include tools, machinery, equipment, and slips, trips, and falls.

One or more hazard categories are likely present in any kind of workplace.

Adverse Health Effects

The illnesses, diseases and other conditions that can result from health hazards are often referred to collectively as health effects, or adverse health effects. Some health effects result from short-term exposure to a high concentration of a health hazard. Effects that are immediate and direct are called acute effects.

Symptoms of illnesses or diseases of long duration or frequent occurrence are called chronic effects. They develop slowly, sometimes from repeated exposures to low concentrations of a health hazard. The time it takes for a health effect to develop after first exposure to a hazard is called the latency period.

Some health effects are local while others are systemic. A local effect occurs at the place where the hazardous agent contacts the body. A systemic effect occurs at a location different from the point of exposure. Blood circulation and the digestive system are the principal routes by which hazardous agents travel from the point of exposure to other locations in the body. Adverse health effects include bodily injury, disease, chronic conditions, or a decrease in lifespan.

Recognizing Health and Safety Hazards

Recognition of health and safety hazards involves the identification of agents, workplace conditions, machinery, equipment, and processes that can cause adverse effects if exposure or overexposure occurs. Understanding the health and safety effects of hazardous agents, workplace conditions, machinery, equipment, and processes in the workplace is an essential part of determining whether workers are being exposed to hazards.

In order to recognize/identify hazards, one needs to know what processes are taking place within the facility. These processes may include maintenance, welding, office work, lift truck operation, cleaning and sanitation, or packaging. One also needs to know what type of tools and equipment are being used to complete the work.

In the case of toxic substances, knowledge of health effects may be gained from the safety data sheet (SDS) for each chemical or biological hazard. To properly interpret this information, it is useful to have an understanding of the routes that these substances take when they enter the body, and the way they affect the body's systems. This understanding is very important in the case of physical hazards, musculoskeletal, and psychosocial hazards where there is no equivalent to the SDS.

Inspecting the workplace is the most obvious way to identify hazards. An important purpose of an inspection is to observe the actual conditions in the workplace.

Warning Properties and Hazard Indicators
There are a number of hazard indicators and warning properties that can help to identify chemical and physical agents in the workplace. Some substances or physical agents can be detected with the senses. For example, ammonia has a characteristic smell. Others can be seen as a haze or a dust in the air or on surfaces. Abnormal tastes in the mouth are another way that substances can be detected. Some physical agents, like noise, vibration, heat and cold are easy to identify with the senses. A joint health and safety committee member or health and safety representative conducting an inspection should be alert for these warning properties, but should not rely only on the senses. Many substances are hazardous in concentrations too low to detect this way.

A process diagram, floor plan or other information should be developed to help locate possible hazard sources. Sensitive detection or measuring instruments may be necessary to reveal the presence of some chemical, physical, or biological agents. Ideally, all hazardous agents will be identified by means of labels or hazard indicators, such as colour-coded process pipes.

Those performing an inspection should also speak to workers and supervisors. They are most likely to notice irregularities in the workplace, or in the state of their own health, which could identify actual or potential hazards. Comments from workers or supervisors may be brought to committee members or health and safety representations at any time, not just during a formal inspection. They might include information about health and safety issues which are a concern to workers.

Supervisors, certified members, and health and safety representations must be careful observers of work design and the movements and exertions it demands from the individual worker. One or more physical agents, like excessive vibration or temperature, may contribute to an ergonomic hazard.

There are five factors which can lead to a health and safety hazard. These include:

- People factors;

- Equipment factors;

- Material factors;

- Environmental factors; and

- Process factors.

The acronym PEMEP is often used for these five factors.

People Factors
The actions that people take, or do not take, greatly affect what happens in the workplace. This is true for both management and workers. Employers have the authority and responsibility to control the way work is done. They select equipment, design the work, assign workers, and provide training and supervision. The workers' role is to actually perform the work. If they are to do this safely, they need well-defined safe work procedures and practices.

Designing safe work practices is the responsibility of management. Following these safe work practices is the responsibility of the worker. The joint health and safety committee or health and safety representations should be part of the design process. Everyone in the workplace has a responsibility to report health and safety concerns. Workers are required to report to the employer any contravention of the *OHSA* or regulations, defective equipment, or safety hazards of which they are aware. When all parties work together, the potential for controlling hazards is greatly improved.

Equipment Factors
Equipment refers to the tools, machines, facilities, vehicles, and other hardware used in the workplace. Equipment may be hazardous if a person is exposed to parts that move, spin, rotate or cut. Some equipment has the potential to release harmful physical agents such as heat, pressure, electricity or radiation. Equipment, if not properly maintained, is prone to failure which may cause an incident.

Material Factors
Many of the materials involved in producing goods and services in the workplace, including waste products, involve safety hazards. Material comes in different shapes and sizes. These hazards include risks from explosions, fires and unexpected traumatic exposure to highly toxic substances, such as acids. Incidents can occur because a control over a known hazard is not in place, or fails, particularly while the material is being moved or handled.

Environmental Factors

The workplace environment is the place where people, materials and equipment come together to get work done. There are many aspects of the environment that can affect or alter conditions adversely and contribute to safety hazards. Temperature, humidity, air quality, lighting quality, radiation, housekeeping, and noise level are examples. These factors may be controlled individually. Controls must also be effective in situations where two or more environmental factors combine to create a hazard.

Process Factors

A process is the sequence of actions used to transform materials and human skills into goods or services. It is the way work is designed. It includes the overall organization of the workplace as well as the individual workstation. Process factors include byproducts such as heat, noise, dust, vapours and fumes that may be created by the production process.

A properly designed process has a smooth flow of materials and activities. Hazards are identified, eliminated, controlled or isolated, and workers have well-defined tasks. Unforeseen circumstances can lead to the failure of a process. Members of the joint health and safety committee and health and safety representatives need to understand the process, in order to recognize the hazards present in the workplace.

Identifying Specific Hazards

Certified members apply the PEMEP principles when they conduct a workplace inspection, investigate a complaint that dangerous circumstances exist, or conduct an incident investigation. During an inspection, a checklist may be used to ensure that all known hazards have been considered.

Other sources of information that can be used to identify hazards include the following:

- Safety data sheets;

- Incident reports;

- WSIB claim reports;

- First aid statistical records;

- Joint health and safety committee minutes;

- Previous inspection reports;

- Job hazard analysis;

- Work procedures;

- Safety manuals; and

- Equipment manuals and maintenance records.

Assessing Hazards

Once a potential hazard has been recognized in the workplace, the next step is to assess it to determine if it is possible for a worker to be exposed and/or determine if exposure is at a harmful level. The exposure of workers to the agent must be evaluated to see if there is a risk of injury or illness. If so, a control will be needed.

Exposure Assessments
Exposure assessments are one example of an assessment method. Exposure means being in contact or exposed to a potentially hazardous agent for a determined period of time. Some agents can cause health effects even though the period of exposure is very short. Others are harmful only if exposure is for a prolonged or excessive period of time. In both cases, the higher the exposure level, the greater the potential for harm.

When an exposure level to a specific agent for a worker or group of workers has been determined, it can in some cases be compared with a standard or guideline to determine whether the exposure is within acceptable limits. There are many agents present in workplaces whose health effects are not fully understood. There are also many for which no legislated or recommended standard exists.

Exposure Limits
Exposure limits, sometimes called occupational exposure limits (OEL), are set out in Ontario Regulation 833/90 for more than 700 biological and chemical agents. The purpose of the limits is to provide standards for assessing the quality of the workplace air. Methods for calculating exposure values that conform to the requirements of the regulation are explained in Chapter 19. Monitoring results can be compared with these standards to ensure compliance with the regulations.

Substance Mixtures

The hazardous substances covered by the regulations are quite often present in the workplace in some combination. The exposure values, on the other hand, are based only on the health effects of a single agent in isolation. When a worker is simultaneously exposed to many substances, there are several possible ways for the components to interact:

- The health effects may be independent. This means that they have different effects on different body systems, and exposure to each substance can therefore be assessed independently.

- The health effects may be additive. In this case, the total health effect of the mixture is the total of the individual effects of the components.

- The health effects may be interactive or synergistic. This means that the total health effect of the mixture is greater than the sum of the individual hazards, but not additive.
- The health effects may be antagonistic, which means that the components of the mixture reduce each other's toxic effects like insulin and glucose.

It is common practice to assume that health effects are additive, unless there is evidence to the contrary.

Workplace Monitoring

Some hazardous agents can be detected by the human senses. But many others pose a risk in concentrations far too small to be detected without monitoring instruments or tests. For example, a radiation detector reveals a hazardous agent which cannot be identified with the senses. Similarly, a Mantoux skin test is a type of medical surveillance that may reveal the presence of tuberculosis infection in a person's body.

Monitoring in the workplace consists of sample testing to measure the presence and levels of a hazardous agent. The information gained from monitoring will help in assessing the need for controls. If action is necessary, these measurements will also help in the design and maintenance of controls used to reduce or prevent the exposure of workers.

Monitoring may be conducted for several reasons. For instance, the employer may wish to ensure compliance to the exposure limits in the various regulations. Monitoring may be conducted in response to a complaint of a health effect or a concern that a hazard might exist. Monitoring can be used to locate the source of a hazard and to test the effectiveness of controls. Sometimes monitoring is conducted as part of research. Monitoring can also be conducted to help determine the best ways to perform work to lower exposures.

When a serious hazard is known to exist, especially for a fast-acting agent, continuous monitoring may be employed. A monitoring device is placed at a fixed location in the workplace and operates all the time. It may be connected to an alarm system. For example, continuous monitoring may be used as a protective measure against carbon monoxide exposure in vehicle repair garages.

Different Hazards — Different Monitoring Methods

Monitoring for chemical and biological hazards normally involves sampling the air in the workplace. Physical hazards have different exposure guidelines and require different evaluation methods. Physical hazards include noise, vibration, temperature, pressure, and both ionizing and non-ionizing radiation.

Heat and cold exposures are measured with a variety of instruments which record temperature and humidity. These include thermometers and instruments for measuring humidity. Vibration hazards, such as whole-body vibration and hand-arm vibration are evaluated with a number of sophisticated instruments. Workplace noise levels are monitored with a noise or sound level meter.

Radiation of many types may be found in different workplaces. Each type has its own measurement methods and exposure standards.

Air Sampling

Monitoring for some substances in the workplace air involves a technique called sampling. An air sample is a small quantity of the workplace air that has been captured so that it can be analyzed. Some samples can be analyzed directly using portable equipment in the workplace, but in most cases, samples must be sent to a laboratory for analysis.

To provide an accurate estimate of a worker's true exposure, samples must be collected at the right place and at the right time. The proper method and instruments for the substance to be analyzed must be used. The number of samples to be taken must be adequate to reveal changes in the concentrations of hazardous agents over the work cycle. These are all elements of an efficient monitoring strategy. Monitoring strategies are discussed in Chapter 19.

The designated substance regulations include detailed rules about how monitoring is to be conducted. Regulation 833/90 says that the procedures must be in accordance with "recognized industrial hygiene practice". The joint health and safety committee or health and safety representatives has a right to be consulted about monitoring procedures, and a designated worker member or health and safety representative has the right to be present at the beginning of testing. It is important that the people who do the monitoring and those who analyze the samples are competent.

A wide variety of testing equipment is available to measure concentrations of toxic substances in the workplace air. Direct-reading instruments provide an immediate indication of the amount of the hazardous agent. They include sophisticated electronic instruments that can detect the presence of a specific substance or a range of substances.

Colorimetric tubes are another type of direct reading device. They consist of a pump which draws in a fixed quantity of air and exposes it to a chemical reagent in a transparent tube. Tubes are available for about two hundred different substances. A colour change in the tube indicates the presence of the substance. Colorimetric tubes are widely used because they are inexpensive and versatile, but they are not as accurate as other types of direct-reading instruments. They can have an error rate of plus or minus 25 per cent.

Job Hazard Analysis

Job hazard analysis is a technique used to assess health and safety hazards associated with particular jobs or tasks and to identify possible controls. There are many specific methods for doing this, each with its own terminology. This chapter describes the elements of job hazard analysis in general terms. Certified members and health and safety representatives should be familiar with any system of job hazard analysis used by their employer. Some of these systems have forms and checklists to ensure that every aspect of the analysis is complete.

A job hazard analysis systematically breaks down work into its basic components. This allows the hazards at each step to be thoroughly evaluated. A job hazard analysis leads to conclusions about procedures needed to eliminate or control the hazards.

The joint health and safety committee or health and safety representative has an obvious interest in participating in a job hazard analysis. They have a right to receive any report that concerns occupational health and safety. The report of a job hazard analysis may call attention to problems that JHSC members should consider during workplace inspections. The JHSC or HSR may make recommendations to the employer based on a job hazard analysis.

A job hazard analysis might reveal hazards specific to the use of that equipment in a particular workplace. In this case, customized procedures might be required. The equipment supplier might be consulted in the process.

Steps in a Job Hazard Analysis

A job consists of a number of tasks. A job hazard analysis is performed on an individual task. There are five steps.

1. Identify tasks and steps

Break each task down into steps. There may be only two or three steps in a task. If a task has a lot of steps, break it down into two smaller tasks and perform a job hazard analysis on each of them separately. Describe and list each task in sequence.

2. Identify the risk factors at each step

Beside each task, write down the materials, equipment, processes and environmental factors involved that could cause an incident or health effects. People factors and system factors may also be relevant.

3. Identify the hazards associated with each task/factor combination

Systematically go through every risk factor for every task, and consider what specific hazards might be involved. This may include the evaluation of worker exposure to one or more hazardous materials. Make a list of all the types of hazards that apply; physical, chemical, biological, musculoskeletal, psychosocial, and safety. This should include the time spent by the worker in various parts of the workplace.

4. Identify controls

Identify procedures or modifications needed to eliminate or control the hazards. This may require changes to people factors, equipment, materials, procedures, tools, systems, or processes.

5. Validate the analysis

Implement the needed controls, and then validate the analysis by observing the task in operation. Make sure that new hazards have not been introduced.

Other Laws, Standards, Guidelines
There are many laws, standards, guidelines, and codes that members of the joint health and safety committee and health and safety representatives may use to evaluate hazardous conditions. These include:

- *Occupational Health and Safety Act*;
- Regulations;
- Fire and Building Codes;
- Ministry of Labour, Training and Skills Development Guidelines;
- Workplace Policies and Procedures and
- Manufacturer and Supplier Manuals.

Once hazards have been identified and assessed, they must be controlled. Control means eliminating the hazard or reducing it to a level that protects workers from adverse effects. Effective controls should decrease the potential for injury or damage. To be effective, a control must satisfy four criteria. It must:

- adequately control the hazard to eliminate the danger to the worker;

- protect all workers who are likely to be exposed;

- not create a new hazard in the workplace; and

- not create an environmental hazard outside the workplace.

Hazards may be controlled at the source, along the path from the source to the worker, or at the worker.

Control at the Source
The best control is the total elimination of the hazard from the workplace. Lockout eliminates worker contact with various forms of energy such as electrical, pressurized, and pneumatic. Where the hazard is a vital component of the production process, elimination of the hazard may not be possible or practicable.

The next best alternative is substitution of a non-hazardous or less hazardous material or process. Where no acceptable substitute is available, enclosing or isolating the hazard can protect against exposure to the hazardous agent.
It may be possible to remove a hazardous gas or dust with a local ventilation system. Local ventilation can be seen at a welder's workstation, where a hood over the area removes welding fumes as they are generated.

An example of isolation is a control room in a refinery which completely separates workers from the process and therefore the source of the hazard. Another example is the negative pressure glove box used in laboratories where biological materials are handled.

Control Along the Path
Some processes, by their nature, cannot be enclosed or isolated. In these cases, the hazard may be controlled along the path between the source and the worker. Controls along the path do not remove the hazard. The blade on a saw cannot be eliminated, however, an engineered guard is an excellent control along the path, between the blade and the worker.

General dilution ventilation reduces the concentration of a substance by diluting the air with cleaner air from other parts of the workplace or from the outside. It is a suitable control only for certain materials which are not toxic. General ventilation cools air in the hot summer months and warms it in the colder months.

Other examples of control along the path are screens to prevent welding flash from reaching the eyes of nearby workers, and housekeeping.

Control at the Worker
Where neither control at the source nor control along the path are effective, control at the worker may be necessary. Types of controls at the worker include standard operating procedures, administrative controls, hygiene practices and facilities, and personal protective equipment. Controls at the worker are the least desirable and the least effective. There are too many variables. At times, workers do not wear personal protective equipment correctly. This type of control is difficult to enforce and monitor.

Hierarchy of Controls
In health and safety, the principle of hierarchy of controls is used to describe the order in which controls should be implemented. It takes into consideration the effectiveness of controls, within the hierarchy.

- Elimination (including substitution) – remove the hazard from the workplace or substitute it with less hazardous materials or machine

- Engineering controls – these include ventilation, barriers, and redesigning of processes that reduce the source of exposure

- Administrative Controls – change the way work is done, including work procedures, timing of work, policies, and training

- Personal Protective Equipment – is equipment that a worker wears.

	CONTROLS	EXAMPLES
Most Effective	1. Elimination (including substitution)	• Design to eliminate hazards, such as falls, hazardous materials, noise, confined spaces, and manual material handling. • Substitute for less hazardous material. • Reduce energy i.e., lower speed, force, amperage, pressure, temperature, and noise.
	2. Engineering Controls	• Ventilation systems • Machine guarding • Sound enclosures • Circuit breakers • Platforms and guard railing • Interlocks • Lift tables, conveyors, and balancers
	3. Administrative Controls	<u>Procedures</u> • Housekeeping • Safe job procedures • Rotation of workers • Preventative maintenance • Changing work schedule <u>Education and Training</u> • Hazard communication training • Confined space entry <u>Warnings</u> • Signs • Backup alarms • Beepers • Horns • Labels
Least Effective	4. Personal Protective Equipment	• Safety glasses • Hearing protection • Face shields • Safety harnesses and lanyards • Gloves • Respirators • Safety boots

Elimination

Elimination includes removing hazards from the workplace. It is the most effective way of controlling a hazard because it is no longer present in the workplace. Elimination should be used whenever possible. Substitution is a form of elimination. Examples of substitution include using water-detergent solutions in place of organic solvents or substituting a quiet piece of equipment in place of a noisy one.

Engineering

Engineering controls are built into the design of a plant or piece of equipment. They include ventilation systems (local and general dilution), machine guarding, lift table and conveyors, and sound enclosures. Some engineering controls are retrofitted, like a set of stairs built where a ladder cage existed. Engineering controls are very reliable but must be maintained.

Administrative Controls

Administrative controls are directed at the organization of the workplace or the work. They include such arrangements as job rotation and relief procedures to allow workers time away from certain work. They are intended to limit exposure to designated substances and other hazardous agents when other controls are not effective. Hazardous work, including maintenance, can be scheduled for off-peak periods when fewer workers are at risk.

Work Practices and Procedures are another form of administrative control. Proper work practices are a very important form of control at the worker. These include standardized work rules which ensure that every worker follows procedures that have been found to be safe. Regular maintenance of equipment can prevent leaks or other emissions of hazardous agents. Effective training programs help workers to fully understand the hazards in the workplace.

The use of written safe work procedures ensures that every worker who performs a task gets the same instructions. Preparing these procedures often starts with an equipment manufacturer's standard instructions. The new work procedures would ensure that safe practices were followed and that the machine was operated properly.

For example, a task might involve unloading cylinders of welding gas and moving them to a workstation. The procedure would describe each step, such as removing the tanks from a truck, checking their WHMIS labels, placing them on a hand truck, moving them to the workstation and transferring them to a specific location. One of the principles involved would be to ensure that the cylinders were always upright and secured with straps to the hand truck or to a rack in the workstation.

An associated work rule might be "no smoking within 10 feet of a compressed gas cylinder". Work procedures should be reviewed regularly to take account of new factors that may have been introduced into the work process. Written work procedures can be useful in training programs and new employee orientation. They are also helpful during workplace inspections or incident investigations.

Written procedures to be used in emergencies like chemical spills, fires and other such unplanned incidents should be established and readily available. Workers should be given training and practice in these procedures – and in the use of emergency equipment – at regular intervals. Where appropriate, special response teams may be trained to deal with emergency situations.

Developing written safe work procedures can be time consuming. It requires a commitment from management and the full cooperation of the workers who do the job. Both parties need to see the connection between the analysis and the creation of safer working conditions.

Preparing written procedures is a management responsibility, usually involving both workers and supervisors. It is important that the workers who actually perform the task also have an opportunity to contribute their ideas. They may have first-hand knowledge about how the job can be done better. Their participation will help them to understand the importance of following safe work procedures.

Joint health and safety committees and health and safety representatives have a role to play in developing safe work procedures. During workplace inspections or the investigation of complaints, JHSC members and HSRs may learn of hazards that are not adequately controlled by an existing procedure. A written procedure facilitates discussion of the issue and helps the committee or HSR to focus on the problem and make very specific recommendations to the employer.

Personal Hygiene Practices reduce the chance of toxic substances being absorbed or ingested into the body. They may also prevent hazardous agents from being carried outside the workplace. Workers should avoid touching any part of their body with contaminated hands. Eating, drinking, and smoking should take place only in designated areas which are isolated from contaminated areas and have been designed for this purpose.

Workers exposed to contaminated air should wash hands, arms, face, and nails before entering these designated areas. If work clothing may be contaminated with toxic substances, locker facilities should be provided to keep it separate from street clothes. Protective clothing should be removed before entering designated clean areas or leaving the workplace.
All of the same precautions should be taken before leaving work. Hygiene practices work best when workers are given appropriate training and adequate time and facilities for changing clothes and washing or showering. Hygiene practices should be enforced by formal work rules.

Housekeeping is another effective control. It prevents the accumulation of hazardous or toxic substances such as dust, and also prevents slips, trips, and falls in the workplace.

Education and Training are also considered administrative controls. Training is critical to ensure that workers know how to safely do their jobs to minimize risk. The effectiveness and application of training needs to be monitored in the field. It is simply not enough to sit a worker in front of a computer, or in a classroom and expect that they have understood and can apply all that they learned in the training program.

Personal Protective Equipment
Personal protective equipment (PPE) describes articles of protective clothing and other personal equipment. The term includes safety boots, gloves, overalls, safety glasses, and hard hats. It also includes fall arrest harnesses and respirators, as well as personal hearing protection devices.

Personal protective equipment may be necessary where other controls are not possible or practicable or where the PPE is needed as additional protection. It may be needed in emergencies, while engineering controls are being repaired or installed, or where it is not possible to provide other controls. PPE is also commonly used during maintenance or for work in confined spaces. It may be mandatory at all times in some work areas.

Personal protective equipment should be fitted individually, and employees should be trained in its use, storage and maintenance.

After controls have been put in place, it is necessary to reassess the hazard measures in place to determine if the hazard has been eliminated or adequately controlled. An effective control should decrease the potential for injury or damage. It is also important to communicate the control measures to workers and ensure that they have the tools, training, and knowledge to implement all of the control measures.

If future actions have been identified, it is imperative to put interim control measures in place to protect workers. For example, if it has been decided that a permanent guard rail will be built to prevent a fall, it may not be able to be completed until next year. In the interim, components of a fall restricting system will be purchased and put into place until such time as the guard rail can be constructed. Remember that workers need to be trained in the fall protection system used at the workplace.

The individuals evaluating the hazard controls need to be certain that the controls have solved the original problem. Are all the hazards dealt with in a manner that is agreeable to the joint health and safety committee or health and safety representative? Are the risks originally identified now contained? At times, new hazards are created, when control measures are put in place. It is necessary to identify the new hazards, and control those as well. For example, in replacing a noisy piece of equipment, there may be new lockout procedures that need to be followed. It is imperative that the workers are trained prior to using the new equipment. Orientation programs need to include the new control measures as well.

It is reasonable to expect different air monitoring results, when certain types of control measures are implemented. For example, if a ventilation system is improved, the employer should make plans to take dust samples post implementation and compare the results to those prior to the control measures being put into place. If the results have not improved as expected, the ventilation may need to be adjusted, and more tests taken.

Evaluation is ongoing. With any control measures that are implemented, members of the joint health and safety committee or health and safety representatives have an opportunity to talk to workers about the new control measures during a workplace inspection. If workers are involved in investigating work refusals, complaints, or incidents, issues may be evident. Any concerns should be noted, and discussed with recommendations made to the employer, if necessary.

This chapter introduces the concept of health and safety hazards and the methods used for recognizing, assessing, controlling, and evaluating them. It identifies six categories of hazards:

- Physical;
- Chemical;
- Biological;
- Musculoskeletal;
- Psychosocial; and
- Safety.

Hazards can be controlled at the source of the hazard, along the path between the hazard and the worker or at the worker. The first priority is to eliminate the hazard from the work process entirely, or to control it at its source. Controlling the hazard before it reaches the worker is the next most preferred method. Control at the worker is used where the hazard cannot be eliminated or blocked.

This chapter describes a generalized system for assessing the hazards to which individual workers are exposed. This chapter also discusses the Hierarchy of Controls, and how to evaluate the hazard controls. Members of joint health and safety committees and health and safety representatives are encouraged to be a part of hazard management at their workplaces.

Chapter 10
Physical Hazards

- Electricity

- Noise

- Vibration

- Temperature

- Radiation

- Review

Physical Hazards

A physical hazard is a type of occupational hazard that involves environmental hazards that can cause harm with or without contact. Physical agents are forms of energy that can harm the body when exposure takes place. Physical hazards include electricity, noise hazards, vibration hazards, heat and cold stress, and radiation. Engineering controls are often used to mitigate physical hazards.

Electricity, when handled improperly, can injure or kill. Electrical injuries can range from shock to severe burns. Electricity can also "jump" through the air, which is known as arcing. Arc flashes can occur when there is an electrical fault and energized conductors are short-circuited or grounded. Arc flash burns are the most common electrical injury. Arc flashes can kill at a distance of three meters.

Excessive noise levels may be hazardous. Loud or prolonged noise can damage the sensitive nervous tissue in the ear, resulting in temporary or permanent hearing loss. Vibration may affect the whole body, but more frequently this hazard involves hand-arm vibration from using hand-held power tools. Some types of vibration may damage the small blood vessels and nerves in the hands, while others can cause back pain.

Temperature is considered extreme when it falls outside the range where the human body can easily maintain its normal internal temperature. Workers may be exposed to extreme temperatures when working outside, near furnaces or stoves, in refrigerated workspaces, or in loading areas with open doors. Extreme temperatures put the body under stress as it struggles to maintain its normal internal temperature.

Radiation is electromagnetic energy which radiates in waves. Radiation may damage the skin or the eyes, as well as damage the cells and cause cancer.

Each of these physical hazards has specific health effects. The methods of exposure assessment, types of control, and evaluation are also specific to each hazard. This chapter discusses each of them separately.

Electricity

Electricity is the most versatile form of energy. When used properly, it is safe and reliable, but like any form of energy, its misuse can be harmful to those exposed. Electrical hazards are often difficult to detect because they give no warning signs. Electricity is often referred to as the "silent killer". Members of the joint health and safety committee and health and safety representatives can play an important role in recognizing, assessing, controlling, and evaluating electrical hazards. However, they will need to understand some basic electrical terms and concepts.

Volts

Electrical "pressure" is measured in units known as volts. To make electricity flow, there must be a higher pressure level at the source than at the point of use. Voltage is the electrical equivalent of water pressure. It pushes electricity through the power lines.

Amperes

The strength of the electrical current is measured in amperes, better known as "amps". Amperage is the rate of flow of electrons through a wire or other conductor. It is this characteristic of electricity which actually makes a light bulb glow, heats an oven, or runs a television set. Current is the actual cause of health effects in workers that receive electrical shocks.

The amount of current used to perform these and other tasks ranges from one milliamp, or 1/1000 of one amp to *fault* currents exceeding 70,000 amps. A fault current is the maximum current produced when an electrical system is short-circuited. A short-circuit happens when the normal flow of current is disrupted. This is caused by contact with the ground or with someone or something which is in touch with the ground. A short circuit is usually caused contacting ground but can be caused by any two different potentials shorting. This is more common on three phase systems at larger sites.

The amount of fault current in the electrical system can range from 15 amps on a small distribution panel to over 70,000 amps on some high-voltage installations. Breaker ratings such as 15A in a distribution panel is the continuous current rating. The actual fault current at any given point on a circuit is around 20 times that. The fault current is determined by how much current the system can supply and what the resistance of the circuit is. The full fault current is present at the outlet for a short amount of time before the breaker will trip. Breakers and fuses have a 'trip' curve that is an inverse curve relating the current to time. The higher the current the faster the trip. Interestingly, this can make higher fault current (to a degree) safer as the breaker will trip almost instantaneously. A fault with less current may take longer (0.5 - 1 seconds) to trip. Even though the current is less, due to the exposure time, the risk may be greater.

Ohms

Resistance to the flow of electricity is measured in ohms. Resistance means opposition to the flow of current. Any component of an electrical circuit which decreases the flow of current is said to provide resistance or to be a resistor. Copper and aluminum wires allow current to flow easily. They have "low resistance" and are "good conductors". Porcelain is an example of a material that does not allow current to flow. It provides "high resistance" or is a "non-conductor". A more common term is "insulator".

Common Electrical Hazards

Electric shock is caused by electric current passing through the body. In some cases, electric shock can cause injuries that are not evident and the symptoms may be delayed. For this reason, all electric shock victims should seek medical attention.

The breakdown or deterioration of insulation is a common electrical hazard. Insulation can deteriorate as a result of daily wear and tear. Any breakdown in insulation can result in uncontrolled energy flow.

Workers sometimes work near low-voltage overhead lines. They may be working on buildings such as houses which receive low-voltage electricity from overhead distribution lines. When first installed, the insulation level is 1-5 times the voltage rating of the line but insulation always deteriorates over time (especially due to UV rays) and even if you can read the rated insulation voltage it cannot be trusted.

Workers using a ladder may come in contact with low-voltage lines when painting or window washing. These lines are not insulated well enough for a person to touch them safety. They are energized and dangerous.

Contact between equipment such as cranes or boom trucks and high-voltage overhead lines must be avoided. This type of contact will cause current to flow through the crane or truck to the ground. The ground itself will be charged with high voltage in the vicinity of the equipment and with progressively lower voltage at distances away from the source. This effect, like ripples created by a stone thrown into the water is called the potential gradient. A worker standing on the ground and touching the crane can receive a severe shock.

Arc flash hazards are a growing concern in industry. They are due to a sustained arcing fault between two potentials; they produce a rapid release of energy, and depending on the current, can extend quite far. They have the ability to injure workers who aren't directly working on or operating the equipment. They can be caused by a worker causing a short (i.e. dropped tool) or equipment deterioration.

Another characteristic of potential gradient is known as step potential. A person standing on the charged ground near the machine may try to move away. A person with one foot on highly charged ground may put the other foot down on the ground with much lower charge. This differential or potential gradient will cause current to flow through the person's body from the high charge to the low charge area. The result is likely to be a severe life-threatening shock. Electric shock may also affect anyone on or in a machine in contact with the ground.

Poorly maintained or poorly constructed grounding equipment can increase the risk of shock as well as other hazards such as fires. Electrical systems must be grounded to prevent the occurrence of excessive voltages from lightning, inadvertent contact with higher voltage lines and other sources. Electrical systems and metallic enclosures are grounded to cause overcurrent devices to operate in the event of a fault occurring from insulation failure. When the insulation on conductors fail within ungrounded metal enclosures, the enclosures are raised to line voltage. Workers coming into contact may suffer shock which can prove fatal.

Workers have been electrocuted or badly burned as a result of contact with damaged extension cords. Electrical cords are often left unprotected and stretched across the ground in the path of machinery. Portable electrical equipment must be effectively grounded unless it has double insulation or equivalent protection.

Some batteries have a high level of stored energy (battery-powered vehicles or large banks of storage batteries). Short-circuiting by a ring or wristwatch bracelet can cause severe burns, even if no shock hazard exists. The voltage of some battery banks, however, may be high enough to be a shock hazard.

Uncontrolled energy flow can be caused by over voltages from lightning strikes hitting electrical equipment, or voltage surges due to switching operations. Any breakdown in an electricity barrier can cause undesired energy flow.

Health Effects of Electrical Injuries

Most electrical injuries can be classified as burns, electric shock injuries, or eye injuries. Other associated injuries can be as a result of being thrown or falling, after an electrical injury. The worker may suffer fractures, spinal injuries, or internal injuries.

Burns are the most common electrical injury. Workers may suffer flash burns, arcing burns, flame burns, contact burns, or electrical burns. Health effects include first- to third-degree burns, damage to nerves, blood vessels, muscles, organs, and eyes.

Electric shock is caused by electric current passing through the body. The symptoms can range from a small tingle to immediate heart stoppage. As a result of the electric shock, workers can suffer electrical burns as well as internal bleeding, unconsciousness, respiratory paralysis, and cardiac disorders. Some injuries may not be evident immediately, and may appear later. For this reason, any worker who suffers an electric shock needs to be taken to the hospital for observation.

The extent of possible eye injury depends on the nature of the electrical contact. A worker can suffer a surface burn to the cornea or permanent retinal damage. If there is a fire, the eyelids are frequently burned. In the event of any eye injury, both eyes should be covered with sterile bandages and left to be examined by a health care professional.

Controlling Electricity

The most effective control of electrical hazards is to eliminate them. This is an at the source control measure.

Lockout Procedures

Lockout procedures are a principal means of controlling energy hazards. A lockout procedure is a set of safe work practices and rules that makes it impossible for a worker to come into contact with an uncontrolled energy source.

The first step in designing a lockout procedure is to identify all sources of energy that affect the work. The second step includes taking action to neutralize, redirect, or stop the energy from performing its normal function, before workers enter the area to make adjustments or perform maintenance. The third step is to verify that a zero-energy state has been achieved.

This means that there is no energy available to cause a hazard. The final step is to physically prevent re-energizing the system until the work is completed and every worker is in a safe place.

This last step often involves placing padlocks on equipment controls, which is the origin of the "lockout" term. For example, there might be five workers involved in a maintenance procedure. Each of them might have a colour-coded lock. Each lock will have its own key. All five locks could be placed on an electrical switch, preventing the power from being turned back on until all of the workers have removed their locks. Many lockout systems use other types of seals rather than padlocks. Most also use tags to identify lockout equipment.

Achieving a zero-energy state is often more complex than the simple example given above. Energy sources are not always obvious. Equipment is often initially powered by electricity. But this "main" energy source may be converted into other forms of energy as part of the operation of the machine. For example, a punch press might use electricity to power a pump, creating hydraulic pressure to operate the punch. The hydraulic pressure remains stored in the system even when the electricity is turned off. Gravity and momentum can be stored in a stationary machine by springs or counterweights. The term zero-energy state means that all of these energy sources have been controlled.

Capacitance is also a major issue and some form of capacitance is present in most electrical devices. A capacitor has the ability to store electrical energy even after it has been turned off. Temporary grounds as mentioned on the following page is one of the ways to bleed off this stored energy.

One evaluates the effectiveness of the controls by testing to ensure that all of the equipment has reached the zero-energy state.

Lockout Policy and Safe Work Procedures

Every workplace where workers could come into contact with energy sources should have written safe work procedures that implement a lockout policy. In some large workplaces, a lockout subcommittee of the joint health and safety committee is formed to advise the employer on lockout procedures. Job hazard analyses will be required. Training programs need to be designed. Responsibility for specific lockout procedures must be assigned to individuals by the employer.

The exact procedures involved in implementing a lockout will depend on the circumstances of the individual workplace. Specific control measures at the source, along the path, and at the worker are often included in safe work procedures.

Job Planning

Perhaps the most important step in controlling electrical hazards is to plan each electricity-related job. This planning must involve the identification and assessment of electrical and other hazards. Once this process is complete, hazards must be controlled. Eliminating exposure to electrical and other hazards would be ideal. In some cases, however, controls along the path and at the worker may be the only realistic source of control.

Temporary Grounding

Grounding is the process of connecting a piece of electrical equipment to earth or some conducting body in place of earth. This process serves to complete the electric circuit and prevent electrical shocks. Portable temporary grounds must be applied before work begins on any electrical equipment that was energized over 750 volts before isolation. This control measure is along the path.

Bonding

Bonding is sometimes confused with grounding. Bonding is the connecting of two or more elements of an electrical system to keep them at the same potential. Bonding eliminates any potential difference in voltage between components and thereby eliminates electric shock hazards. It also provides a low resistance parallel path around a person's body should a fault occur. This control measure is also along the path.

Tools

Testing, inspecting, and repairing tools can prevent the occurrence of electrical hazards. An insulation-resistance test can be used to test the insulation of tools and allows the inspector to identify impending failure which may lead to a serious injury. Testing devices should only be used by workers trained to use specific equipment to perform these tasks.

Inspecting and maintaining power hand tools and using them only for their intended purpose will help reduce the risk of electrical shock. Where available, rechargeable battery-powered tools should be used. The elimination of extension cords will reduce the risk of electrical shock. Insulation-covered tools, such as insulated screwdrivers, pliers, and wrenches should be used where any work on live equipment is required. Their use may prevent a serious electrical flash in the case of an inadvertent move or mistake in identification.

Double-insulating tools is a manufacturing technique used in electrical components and tools. It provides protection for the user, without the use of a ground wire. The tool's case is made of an insulating material, like heavy plastic, a non-conductor. External metal parts, such as drill chucks and saw blades, are insulated from the live parts inside the tool. Under normal conditions, it is impossible for the user to contact any live part of the tool. A double-insulated tool must not be used if the case is cracked or broken. Double-insulated tools are clearly identified as such on the tool nameplate along with CSA certification, and serial and model numbers.

Ground Fault Circuit Interrupters (GFCI)

A ground fault circuit interrupter protects against shock. The device measures current going into the tool and coming out. Any discrepancy indicates that electricity is flowing where it should not. The GFCI is sensitive to low levels of current flow. Upon detection of this flow, it switches off the power before serious injury or damage can occur.

All electrical tools, including double-insulated tools, are hazardous when wet. Moisture along with possible metal or carbon dust could form a conductive path from inside the tool to the surface through cracks or ventilation holes. Since there is no ground wire to dispose of the stray current, the user might receive a shock. All electric tools should therefore be kept dry and a ground fault circuit interrupter used in wet or damp locations.

Barriers

Barriers can be defined as anything that effectively separates the person from the hazard. Most permanently-installed electrical equipment incorporates barriers into its design. This control measure helps to ensure that no worker can be exposed to a live conductor during normal operation of the equipment.

Portable barriers may be used by electrical maintenance crews. For example, rubber blankets are placed on the hazard while a worker is repairing or maintaining a specific part of the equipment.

These control measures are all along the path

Training
Some work involving electrical hazards can only be performed by qualified electricians certified under the *Trades Qualification and Apprenticeship Act*. Others with appropriate training can do some jobs that are associated with electrical hazards, such as setting up a ladder. Training is considered a control measure at the worker and must be accompanied by several other control measures in order to keep workers safe.

Personal Protective Equipment
All person protective equipment is considered a control at the worker. Those who work with electrical-powered tools and energized electrical equipment should wear footwear with soles resistant to electric shock. This footwear does not offer full protection should electrical contact occur. It can provide backup protection, but only if the footwear is relatively new, clean, and dry.

Properly-fitted industrial quality eye protection should be worn by persons when working on live electrical equipment. This takes the form of spectacles and side shields. Scratch-resistant clear polycarbonate lenses or plastic lenses with UV protection are recommended for all light conditions.

Ignition-resistant clothing should be worn when working on or around energized apparatus. Shirts should have full-length sleeves extending to the wrists. In some environments, special arc-flash rated clothing is required.

Workers who take voltage checks or perform work on energized electrical apparatus have special provisions for rubber gloves. Those gloves must be stored, maintained in good condition, be tested at regular intervals, and visually inspected before each use. Punctures, tears, or abrasions will impair the glove's ability to protect against electrical hazards.

Noise is unwanted sound. Sound is a form of mechanical energy caused by the vibration of the air. When sound vibrations reach the listener, they are detected by a delicate mechanism in the inner ear and perceived as sound by the brain. Sound has three principal characteristics: frequency, amplitude, and time pattern.

Frequency is perceived as pitch. It is the rate at which the sound waves are vibrating.

A high-pitched sound is one with a high frequency. Frequency is usually measured in cycles per second, or Hertz. Normal speech is in the 250 to 4,000 Hertz range.

Amplitude is perceived as loudness. It is the strength of the sound signal being received. The human ear is responsive to a very wide range of sounds. Amplitude is measured in decibels (dB). A decibel is one-tenth of a bel. The decibel scale is logarithmic rather than linear. This means that if there is an increase of one bel, the sound is ten times louder than before. The use of a logarithmic scale makes it possible to describe a very wide range of sound amplitudes.

Time pattern refers to the continuity and fluctuation of a sound. Continuous noise is that produced constantly. Impulse noise consists of separate pulses, which may or may not repeat a pattern and can have higher and lower sound levels.

Health Effects of Noise

Excessive noise has the potential to impair hearing, or even destroy it. Noise-induced hearing loss (NIHL) has a long latency period. The majority of workers who apply for NIHL benefits with the WSIB have an average age of 65. There is no cure for NIHL, but is completely preventable.

Noise may also put stress on other parts of the body causing the abnormal secretion of hormones, the tensing of muscles and other health effects. Sleeplessness and fatigue are among the symptoms. Noise also interferes with communication, which can affect normal functions including job performance and safety. The specific health effects depend on the type of noise involved and the duration of the exposure. To help understand these effects, it will be useful to briefly review the hearing mechanism.

Hearing begins when the outer ear collects and funnels sound waves to the eardrum through the pinna canal. The eardrum vibrates as it receives the sound waves. The vibrations are transmitted through three small bones: the hammer, the anvil and the stirrup in the middle ear.

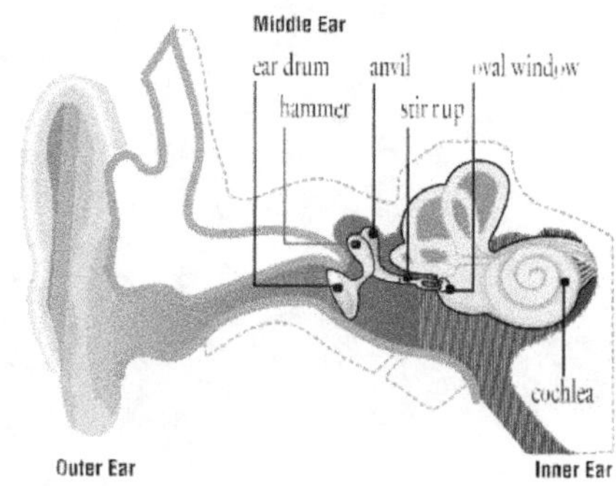

The middle ear acts as an amplifier. The stirrup sits on the end of a flexible membrane called the oval window. The oval window separates the middle ear from the inner ear which contains the hearing organs.

Attached to the other side of the oval window is a tiny, fluid-filled, snail-shaped structure called the cochlea. The fluid inside the cochlea is set in motion by vibrations intercepted at the oval window. The vibrations are then transferred to thousands of very small, very sensitive, hair-like cells resembling bristles. Each one connects with microscopic nerve endings that send messages to the brain, where the signals are interpreted as sound.

Hearing Loss

A hearing loss is any reduction in the normal ability to hear. A hearing loss can be temporary or permanent and it might be partial or total. Immediate and permanent damage to the ear can result from acoustic trauma when a person is exposed to a sudden and excessive noise, such as an explosion. This can cause damage to the delicate tissues of the middle ear. Prolonged exposure to continuous elevated noise can cause damage that is more gradual, but in the long run may be just as damaging. Noise-induced hearing loss, once established, is not reversible.

There is a natural hearing loss due to the normal aging process, which is called presbycusis.

Threshold Shift

A threshold shift is the loss of a person's ability to hear higher frequency sounds. It results from damage to the cochlea. The tiny hairs of this organ, or the nerves they are connected to, can be damaged by prolonged exposure to noise. The hair-like cells which are most receptive to the higher frequencies are often the first to go. This is true even if the noise that caused the damage was at a lower frequency. The most vulnerable hair-like cells are those responding to the 4,000 Hertz range.

The first symptom of a threshold shift is a loss of hearing at the higher frequency levels. In speech, the first sounds missed are the consonants s, f, t, p, and k, which have relatively high frequencies. Yet vowels may be heard normally. As the damage progresses, hearing loss extends into the lower frequencies, and poor understanding of speech becomes more apparent. A threshold shift can be permanent or temporary.

A temporary threshold shift can convince some people that they have become used to the noise. Intense noise, now perceived at a lower level, may continue to damage hearing and may result in permanent hearing loss. Tinnitus, or ringing in the ears, is one sign that exposure to noise has been excessive. It may be permanent or temporary.

With a temporary threshold shift, normal hearing will usually return after a period away from noise. The fluid in the inner ear may be changed by noise, but can revert to its original com-position. The time needed for recovery depends on the severity of the initial loss. An example of a temporary threshold shift might be a worker who has to turn up the volume on the car radio on the way home from work. The sound level that was adequate on the way to work in the morning is now difficult to hear.

Assessing Noise Exposure

A workplace inspection will usually reveal any areas with high noise levels. Inspections may have to be done at different times to ensure that all noise sources are identified. If it is difficult to carry on a conversation noise levels may exceed safe limits. The employer, JHSC member, or HSR should ask workers whether they have had any problems associated with noise. Common sources of noise include machinery, ventilation systems, and power tools.

Sources of noise could be specified on a floor plan, and the workers who may be exposed can be identified. Existing noise controls should also be identified. The next step is to assess the amount of exposure. Exposure assessments or sound level measurement should be conducted periodically in order to evaluate the effectiveness of controls.

Several different types of instrument are available for assessing noise levels. The sound level meter is the most useful. Others include noise dosimeters and frequency analyzers.

Sound Level Meters

A sound level meter consists of a microphone, an amplifier and an indicator gauge. Standard meters incorporate three different weighting systems, to approximate the varying response of the human ear to various frequencies. An "A" weighted sound level, or dBA, comes the closest to approximating human responses. The action of the meter can be adjusted to "fast" or "slow". A slow setting averages intermittent or variable sounds. The sound level meter needs to be calibrated regularly, preferably before and after each use. This ensures the accuracy of the sound measuring equipment.

Noise Dosimeters

In many work environments, workers move from location to location throughout their shift. Each location may have a different noise level. The noise exposure of the individual worker can be measured with a noise-exposure monitor, or dosimeter. It is worn by the worker and records the total noise energy that the worker is exposed to, preferably for a full work shift.

Frequency Analyzers

When designing noise control devices, it is important to know the frequency distribution of the noise. Different sound-absorbing materials work best in specific frequency ranges. An octave band or frequency analyzer is used to provide this information. It may also be used to determine a source of noise.

Survey Techniques

A noise exposure survey is a systematic approach to measuring noise level exposures in the workplace. CSA Standard Z107.56-18 Measurement of Noise Exposure provides information on methods of taking and interpreting sound measurements. Readings of sound level, duration and time pattern are required. They are taken at locations where workers may be exposed. Sound level readings are usually taken first to get an overall picture of where noise is generated. Then, if needed, dosimetry may also be carried out. It is essential that equipment be properly calibrated and operated by qualified persons. Professional consultants are usually brought in to conduct an assessment.

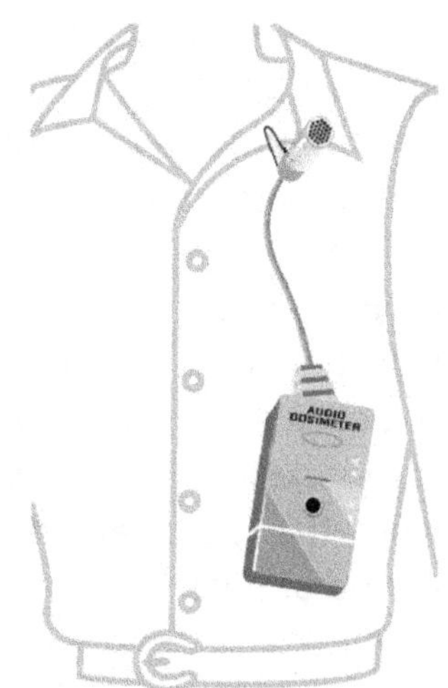

Controlling Noise

Noise can be controlled at the source, along the path, or at the worker. At the source, equipment may be replaced by quieter models, or less noisy work procedures can be adopted. In general, less friction and vibration mean less noise. Maintenance procedures such as lubrication may sometimes reduce noise by reducing friction. Equipment can sometimes be modified to reduce the amount of noise that is generated. Sound-absorbing material may be attached to the noise source. The frequency of the noise may be shifted to one that is less hazardous.

Noise can often be controlled along the path to the worker with the use of sound-absorbing paneling on walls or ceilings, and enclosures around noisy machinery.

Controls at the worker include both administrative controls and personal protective equipment.

Administrative controls modify how the work is carried out. The time employees spend in noisy areas may be reduced. Workers in noisy areas may be rotated to less noisy areas.

Noisy operations may be conducted outside normal working hours to reduce the number of people exposed.

Where noise exposures cannot be reduced by other methods, hearing protection is required. This includes ear plugs and earmuffs. Hearing protection devices must be properly fitted and must be appropriate for the level, frequency and duration of the noise involved. CSA Standard Z94.2-14 (R2019) Hearing Protection Devices – Performance, Selection, Care and Use, provides guidelines for selecting and using hearing protection. Everyone in the workplace should wear hearing protection when the sound level is greater than 85 dBA for any period of time.

Between 2006 and 2015, the WSIB supported approximately 30,000 people for noise induced hearing loss (WIHL). Ten percent of WSIB's annual heart care budget is spent on the WIHL program. In 2017, there were approximately 2,600 NIHL-related claims. Thirty-seven percent of claims came from the construction and manufacturing industries between 2016 and 2017. (www.toneitdown.ca)

On July 1, 2007 noise requirement in the Regulations for Industrial Establishments (Regulation 851, section 139) and the Regulation for Oil and Gas (Offshore (Regulation 855, section 41) were lowered from 90 dBA to 85 dBA. This brought the Province of Ontario into line with many other jurisdictions in the world.

Further changes took place on July 1, 2016 when Regulation 381/15 Noise was introduced and now applies to all workplaces covered under the *OHSA*.

Vibration

Vibration is a rapid alternating or reciprocating motion. It can affect all or part of the body. For example, driving a tractor over bumpy roads in a poorly designed seat vibrates the entire body. Prolonged use of a vibrating hand tool can affect the hands and arms.

Health Effects of Vibration
The energy from vibration is absorbed by the tissues and organs of the body. Whole-body vibration can lead to lower back pain. Hand-arm vibration causes damage to blood vessels, impairing circulation in the hand. This leads to a condition known as white finger, or Reynaud's phenomenon. When exposed to cold, the hands appear to be mildly frostbitten. The damage can progress to the point where it disables the victim. White finger disease is most common among operators of air hammers, air chisels, and chainsaws.

Vibration Monitoring
The evaluation of exposure to vibration is very technical. In general, the harm caused by vibration increases with its strength and with the duration of exposure. Exposure values have only recently been developed and are intended primarily for use by experts equipped with sophisticated equipment.

Certified members and health and safety representatives can make a preliminary assessment of vibration problems by talking with workers and observing the work. For example, the workplace floor may vibrate. Workers who use hand tools may report problems with their hands. A vibration specialist might be consulted to obtain a more accurate assessment of the problem.

Controlling Vibration
Vibration can be controlled at the source by redesigning the equipment to include vibration-absorbing mounts or shock absorbers. Older equipment can be replaced with newer vibration-free models. Control along the path involves the use of vibration-absorbing handles and vehicle seats, or remote control systems. Vibration-absorbing gloves are the most common form of control at the worker.

Temperature

The human body functions efficiently only within a very narrow range of internal temperatures. The normal *deep body temperature* is 37.6 degrees Celsius. The temperature taken under the tongue is a little lower, about 37 degrees. If the deep body temperature falls below 36.4 degrees or rises above 39.2 degrees, body functions are significantly impaired.

The body has automatic systems that maintain internal temperature within this narrow range under normal circumstances. If the body gets overheated, blood flow to the skin is increased to radiate heat. Sweat flows on the surface of the skin. When it evaporates, the body is cooled.

If the body is too cold, capillaries in the skin constrict, to reduce blood flow to the skin. Involuntary shivering causes muscles to burn stored energy and release heat. If the body is exposed to excessive temperatures for prolonged periods, these automatic heating and cooling systems get overloaded, and the body is placed under stress.

Exposure to Heat

High temperatures are encountered in many workplaces. Often the heat source is part of the work process, as in a steel mill or a laundry. In the summer, outdoor temperatures can reach 35 degrees, creating a possible hazard for some people working outside. If the body's cooling system is overloaded, the body is placed under heat stress.

Health Effects of Heat Stress

The health effects caused by heat stress include heat cramps, heat exhaustion, and heat stroke. Heat stress can also increase the risk from other health and safety hazards.

Heat cramps are caused by loss of fluid and body salts, sometimes in combination with heavy exertion. They can be very painful and affect several different muscle groups. Heat exhaustion results from the depletion of body fluid and salts. The symptoms include dizziness, nausea, and profuse sweating. Heat stroke is the failure of the body's temperature regulating system, leading to a rise in body temperature that can cause death.

Assessing Heat Exposure

Exposure to excessive heat can be recognized by a number of means. These include measuring temperature and humidity. Information about heat exposure can also be obtained by talking to workers and supervisors. If workplace heat is making them uncomfortable, further assessment may be necessary.

The assessment of heat exposure must take into account both temperature and humidity. High humidity hampers the body's ability to cool down by sweating, because sweat does not evaporate as quickly. The hazard from heat stress is also increased by radiant heat. Assessment should also take into account any acclimatization to heat a person may have acquired after a period of exposure.

The Wet Bulb Globe Temperature Index (WBGT) is a commonly used indicator for measuring the conditions that may cause heat stress. It is calculated with a formula that takes into account three different temperature measurements:

- The Dry Bulb temperature is measured by an ordinary thermometer.

- The Natural Wet Bulb temperature is measured by a thermometer which has the reservoir at the bottom encased in a wetted cloth. It measures the effect of humidity.

Wet Bulb Globe Temperature Index (WBGT)

The following formulas are used to calculate the Wet Bulb Globe Temperature Index:

Indoors, or outdoors with no sun:
WBGT = 0.7 WB + 0.3 GT
Outdoors, with sun:
WBGT = 0.7 WB + 0.2 GT + 0.1 DB
WB – natural wet bulb temperature GT
DB – dry bulb temperature.

- The Globe Thermometer temperature is measured by a thermometer encased in a black sphere or "globe". It measures the effect of radiant heat.

An electronic device is available that will measure all three indicators at the same time.

The *OHSA* does not include regulations setting exposure limits for heat. Many health and safety specialists use the Threshold Limit Values (TLVs) developed by the American Conference of Governmental Industrial Hygienists (ACGIH). The suggested TLVs for continuous work are a WBGT of 25 degrees for heavy work, and a WBGT of 30 degrees for light work.

Controlling Heat Exposure

Heat exposure can be controlled at the source by redesigning equipment and work processes. Examples include insulating and isolating heat sources. Control along the path includes ventilation or air conditioning to reduce air temperature and reflective barriers to reduce radiant heat.

There are several types of control at the worker. Work can be scheduled to provide work/rest cycles and worker rotation. Climate-controlled booths can protect equipment operators. Special clothing such as body-cooling vests and insulated or reflective clothing can also help to control heat stress. Provision should also be made for drinking water and rest periods.

Exposure to Cold

Workers are exposed to cold when they work outdoors or in refrigerated indoor environments. Workers in construction, forestry, utilities, and food processing and storage are most often affected. Working for prolonged periods in cold environments causes the body to decrease blood flow to the skin. The result can be cold stress.

Health Effects of Cold Stress

The immediate health effects of cold stress are restlessness, decreased alertness and lack of concentration. Performance of complex manual and mental tasks is impaired. Numbness and weakness may contribute to other health and safety hazards. In particular, a worker may become more vulnerable to injuries of the musculoskeletal system, such as muscle strain. If exposure is prolonged or extreme, frostbite or hypothermia may result.

What the Law Says
Exposure to Cold

- Section 129 of the Regulations for industrial establishments requires that inside air in a workplace must be heated to at least 18 degrees Celsius.

- There are a number of exceptions to this regulation. It does not apply where doors must be opened, where perishable goods are stored, where there is adequate radiant heating or in areas that are normally unheated or unoccupied. If the work process is a significant source of heat, the regulation does not apply for the first hour of the main operating shift.

Frostbite is the freezing of body tissues. The fingers, toes, ears, and nose are particularly vulnerable. Skin freezes at about -1 degree Celsius. If it is windy, this can happen quickly. Exposed flesh can freeze in about one minute at -10 degrees with a wind of 12 kilometres per hour. Frostbite can also be caused by contact with cold objects.

Hypothermia results when the body mechanisms can no longer maintain internal temperature above 35 degrees. Blood vessel constriction is no longer adequate to retain heat and shivering becomes the only mechanism available.

Assessing Cold Exposure

Moving air greatly increases heat loss from the body. For this reason, exposure to cold temperatures is usually evaluated according to the wind chill index. This is a combination of air temperature and wind speed. It can be calculated from a wind chill table.

The *OHSA* regulations do not include cold exposure values for workers who work outdoors, in areas that are not normally heated, or where perishable goods are stored. The ACGIH has suggested Threshold Limit Values (TLVs) for cold stress. The TLVs are organized by temperature and wind speed and provide work/warmup schedules for a four-hour period. For example, at -30 degrees Celsius, only one break would be needed for moderate-to-heavy work if there were no wind. But four breaks would be needed in a 15-mph wind and the maximum work period would be 40 minutes in a four-hour shift.

Controlling Exposure to Cold Stress

Control at the source is not generally possible outdoors. Indoors, it may be possible to reduce the number of workers exposed by modifying, enclosing, or isolating cold areas. In refrigerator rooms, cold can be controlled along the path by minimizing air velocity as much as possible. Insulated clothing is a form of control at the worker.

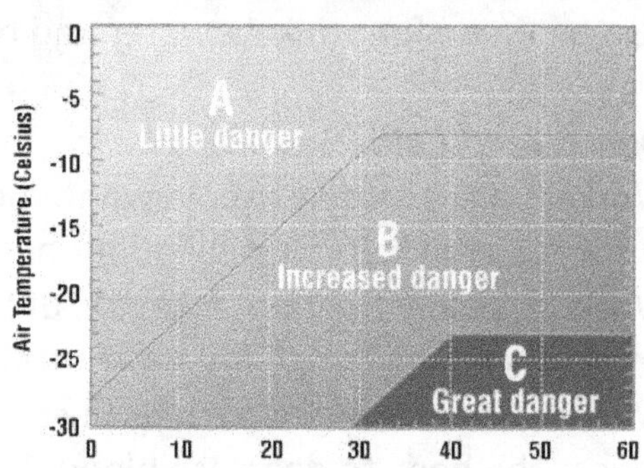

Outdoor controls are mainly at the worker. These include insulated wind-protective clothing, including mitts or gloves. Work practices should include a work/warmup cycle according to the ACGIH guidelines. Temporary shelters and other warmup areas may be provided.

Radiation

Radiation is the emission or transmission of energy as waves or moving particles. Although we are not often aware of it, radiation is absorbed by the body where it can affect the tissues and cells and lead to a variety of health effects.

Radiation can be divided into two main types: **ionizing** and **non-ionizing**.

Ionizing Radiation

Ionizing radiation is at the high frequency end of the electromagnetic spectrum, which means it has the shortest wavelengths. Ionizing radiation is considered the most harmful to humans. Ionizing radiation is produced by the natural decay of radioactive elements such as uranium. It has enough power to strip electrons from atoms and cause ionization. This can interfere with the body's cellular structure and cause genetic damage.

Ionizing radiation is produced by such devices as X-ray machines. There are several kinds of radiation and a complete description of them is beyond the scope of basic certification training. Different forms of radiation may have different routes of entry into the body.

A particular concern in many workplaces is Gamma rays, which for practical purposes can be considered the same as X-rays. Workers in radiology departments are potentially at risk to exposure to X-rays from the equipment they use.

The potential hazards are greater when radiation is used in areas where exposure is unexpected, and workers are unaware of the hazard. For example, portable X-ray equipment is used in industry to inspect welding, to measure the thickness of pipes, and for other diagnostic purposes.

Health Effects of Ionizing Radiation

The greatest effects of ionizing radiation are on cells that are rapidly dividing. The blood-forming system in the bone marrow is easily damaged. For the same reason, the embryo-fetus is also particularly vulnerable.

Ionizing radiation has the potential to cause cancer in many body organs. Cancer may appear after a latency period of as little as two to four years in the case of leukemia, and 5 to 30 years in the case of most other cancers. Ionizing radiation can damage the genetic material in the sperm or the egg cells, causing mutations. These mutations can be passed on to offspring.

Assessing Exposure to Ionizing Radiation

Radiation is measured by an international system of units (SI). The amount of radiation present at any one time can be detected with relatively simple equipment. The radiation dose to which a worker may be exposed is determined by the strength of the source, the type of radiation, the length of exposure, and the distance from the source.

The energy absorbed by the body from radiation is called the "absorbed dose" and is expressed in units of Gray (Gy). The "dose equivalent" measurement is called the Sievert (Sv). Different kinds of ionizing radiation are not equally harmful to the body. They take different routes into the body. For example, X-rays penetrate body tissues. Radon gas, in a uranium mine, is inhaled and absorbed through the lungs.

Most workers who are regularly exposed to radiation are covered by special legislation. Many of them are required by law to wear personal dosimeters to record the cumulative radiation to which they are exposed. Lifetime dose records for all radiation workers in Canada are maintained in the National Dose Registry and is administered by Health Canada's Radiation Protection Bureau.

Certified members who work in places where X-rays or Gamma rays are present should become thoroughly familiar with the regulations covering their workplace. Radiation safety officers are required by law in many of these workplaces.

Control of Ionizing Radiation
Exposure to ionizing radiation should be kept as low as possible. Radiation can be controlled at the source by shielding equipment which emits radiation. Control along the path is accomplished by increasing the distance from the radiation source to the worker, or through the use of radiation barriers. Control at the worker involves isolating the operator, limiting the time of exposure, avoiding unnecessary exposure, and wearing lead aprons, gloves, and goggles.

Non-Ionizing Radiation
Non-ionizing radiation is at the low end of the electromagnetic frequency spectrum. It lacks the energy required to cause ionization but can cause molecules to vibrate. The health effects depend on the particular wavelength of the radiation involved. The descriptions that follow are intended to familiarize certified members with the main types of non-ionizing radiation so that they can recognize these hazards if they are present in their workplaces.

Assessment and control of non-ionizing radiation are specialized issues, beyond the scope of this manual. Where non-ionizing radiation hazards are present in a workplace, JHSC members should learn about the specific assessment and control methods that apply.

Ultraviolet Radiation
Ultraviolet (UV) radiation is given off by the sun and also by artificial sources such as sun lamps and welding equipment. It can burn the skin as in sunburn. Long-term exposure can lead to aging of the skin and may cause skin cancer.

UV radiation can also damage the eye, forming lesions on the outer membrane. This is a particular hazard for welders, who must wear eye protection. Welding areas should be isolated so that other workers are not exposed to welding flashes.

Infrared Radiation
Infrared radiation is experienced primarily as radiated heat. Heating and warming equipment can cause an overexposure, leading to skin burns and eye damage. Shielding and enclosures may be required along with proper eye protection.

Lasers

A laser is an instrument or device that may be directed to produce a very intense beam of light. It produces specific electromagnetic radiation in the ultraviolet, infrared, and visible frequency ranges. Laser radiation can be used surgically to destroy tissue. Lasers are also used in some industrial applications. This type of radiation can potentially damage the eyes or skin.

Microwave and High Radio Frequency Radiation

Microwave and high radio frequency radiation is found in radar, communications, and cooking operations. Microwaves interact with the body by raising the temperature of body organs. It is suspected that the brain, the eyes, and the reproductive organs are vulnerable.

Low Frequency Radiation

The longer wavelengths including power line transmission frequencies, broadcast radio, and short-wave radio can produce a general heating of the body. The potential hazards are greatest for those working close to powerful radio transmitters.

Review

Physical agents are forms of energy. They can be hazardous if their energy is absorbed by the body. Physical agents hazardous to health include electricity, noise, vibration, temperature, and radiation.

Electrical injuries can range from shock to severe burns. A worker can, as a result of a shock, be thrown or fall if working at heights. As a result, workers can suffer broken bones or head injuries.

Noise has the potential to permanently impair hearing. Acoustic trauma is caused by a sudden and excessive noise such as an explosion. It can lead to deafness. A threshold shift is the result of damage to the cochlea, a tiny organ in the inner ear. The cochlea may be damaged by prolonged exposure to noise. The ear's sensitivity to the higher frequency ranges is the first to be impaired.

Vibration is a rapid alternating or reciprocating motion. Whole-body vibration is usually caused by moving vehicles. Hand-arm vibration results from contact with hand tools, such as jackhammers and chainsaws. It can lead to a condition known as white finger disease, which is potentially disabling.

Exposure to extreme temperatures can lead to heat stress or cold stress, as the body struggles to maintain its internal temperature. Heat stress can lead to cramps, exhaustion and eventually heat stroke when the body's temperature regulation system fails. Cold stress results in restlessness, decreased alertness and lack of concentration, any of which can contribute to other health and safety hazards. Prolonged exposure can result in frostbite or hypothermia.

Radiation is energy that travels in electromagnetic waves. This energy can enter the body and damage tissue and organs.

Ionizing radiation, such as X-rays, is the most harmful. It can damage the cells and cause genetic damage. Exposure to ionizing radiation can cause cancer, birth defects, and genetic damage to a worker's children.

Non-ionizing radiation is in the lower end of the frequency spectrum. It includes UV, infrared, microwave, and low frequency radiation. Non-ionizing radiation can cause burns to the skin or eyes and cause other health effects.

Chapter 11
Chemical Hazards

- States of Matter

- Health Effects

- Assessing Chemical Hazards

- WHMIS

- Exposure Monitoring

- Controlling Chemical Hazards

- Evaluating Chemical Hazard Controls

- Review

Chemical Hazards

Health hazards can arise from exposure to a large variety of chemical substances. Their toxic properties can harm the body. Chemical hazards take the form of solids, liquids, vapours, gases, dusts, fumes, or mists. They can be inhaled, ingested, absorbed, or injected into the body.

In order to prevent harm, we need to understand the toxic properties of chemicals. Toxic properties mean the ability of the chemical to produce adverse health effects. We also need to know the physical states chemical agents can take during the work process. This can help to determine how they might contact or enter the body and how exposure may be controlled. Chemicals serve many purposes in the workplace. Some are the raw materials used to make a product. Sometimes the product itself is a chemical. Other chemicals are fuels used to provide energy. Still others are byproducts of a process or are used for other purposes, such as lubrication and cleaning.

Chemicals that may cause an adverse health effect are called toxic. Some chemicals, such as corrosives, can harm the body without being toxic. Hazardous chemicals may also be referred to as hazardous substances or hazardous materials.

A very large number of chemicals are used in Ontario workplaces. There are many whose health effects are not entirely known. The problem is all the more difficult because the health effects of some chemicals can be subtle or may take years to develop. The best policy, therefore, is to regard chemicals as potentially hazardous until their effects are fully known.

The employer, as well as members of JHSCs, must know how to recognize, assess, control, and evaluate hazard controls of chemical hazards.

States of Matter

State of matter refers to the form of a substance. A substance can be in three states of matter: liquid, gas, or solid. Solids or liquids can also be suspended as particles or droplets in the air. Examples are dusts, fumes, and mists. Depending on the temperature and pressure conditions, a chemical can exist in more than one state. For example, water is a liquid above 0 degrees Celsius, but is a solid (ice) below this temperature. The physical state of a substance determines how it can enter the body. The state of a material may change as a result of the work process or other factors.

What the Law Says

OHSA

- Section 37 requires that all controlled products in the workplace be identified according to the WHMIS regulation and that safety data sheets for each of them be present in the workplace.

Chemicals exist in one of three states: solid, liquid or gas.

- A solid has shape and form, whether it's a dust particle or an ingot of steel.

- A liquid is a formless fluid. It takes the shape of its container but doesn't necessarily fill it. Solvents and oils are examples of chemicals in liquid form.

- A gas is a formless substance that expands to occupy all the space of its container. Oxygen and carbon monoxide are examples of chemicals in gaseous form. Gases are usually invisible, but they may be detected in some cases by their taste or smell.

A chemical is described as a solid, liquid, or gas according to its state under normal conditions of temperature and pressure. These normal conditions are called room temperature and atmospheric pressure.

Some chemicals move from one state to another with a change in temperature or pressure. Water is a chemical which is normally a liquid. At normal atmospheric pressure, it becomes a solid at temperatures below 0 degrees Celsius. Propane gas is a liquid while it is stored under pressure in a tank, but it becomes a gas when it is released at atmospheric pressure. The product known as dry ice is carbon dioxide. At atmospheric pressure, it becomes a solid at temperatures below 78.5 degrees Celsius. It changes directly into a gas at normal room temperature.

Knowledge of the physical states of hazardous chemicals is important to an understanding of their health effects. The physical state of a chemical determines which routes it may use to enter the body. For example, a gas may easily enter the body by inhalation. Some liquids are more likely to be absorbed through the skin. The fact that chemicals may change their state when subjected to work processes that involve temperature and pressure changes makes it all the more important that all of the possible states be taken into account.

Dust
Dust consists of very fine solid particles that can become airborne. Dust particles are created when a solid material is crushed, ground, or sanded. Dust also comes from the breakdown of materials like old plaster or insulation. Dust is created by many common workplace processes, such as crushing rock or transferring bulk materials into smaller containers. In addition, many raw materials and finished products are used in the form of powders which can readily become dusts. Some dust particles are made up of fibers from plants, minerals, or animals.

Examples are wood, asbestos and cotton.

Dust circulates in the air where it can be inhaled. The larger particles are trapped by the hairs in the nose or are captured by the mucous membranes in the breathing passages. Those that are small enough get past these natural defenses and enter the lungs. Those that are trapped in the mucous membranes may be swallowed with the mucous.

Dust eventually settles out of the air. It may land on clothing or skin or a work surface. It can also settle directly on a worker's food or be transferred to food from the worker's hands.

Fumes

Fumes are created when a solid substance melts. As it is heated, some of the solid vapourizes and enters the surrounding air. As this vapour cools, it produces solid particles which remain suspended in the air as fumes. Fume particles are usually very small, less than one micron in diameter. Fumes can therefore be inhaled. Welding is an example of a process that generates fumes.

Smoke

Smoke is produced when wood, coal, oil, or other substances are burned. All these materials contain carbon. Smoke is made up of carbon particles called soot, which is the result of incomplete combustion. Incomplete combustion means that some material is not consumed by the burning process. Smoke can also contain droplets of liquid tar as well as solid particles, and gases.

Airborne Liquids and Solids

Liquid and solid chemicals can become suspended in the air. When this happens, they are referred to as airborne.

The potential health hazards from liquid or solid chemicals normally result from absorption by skin contact or ingestion through the mouth. The conversion of liquids and solids into airborne forms may make them more hazardous. In addition, when airborne droplets or particles eventually settle, they may be spread more widely in the workplace. This means work processes, work practices, and housekeeping play a major role in workplace control.

Mists

The spraying or splashing of a liquid chemical can produce a mist. A mist is an airborne cloud of tiny liquid droplets. Some acids used in the workplace can produce airborne mists when they are sprayed, shaken, or stirred. Paint spraying is another workplace activity that produces mists.

Vapours

A liquid becomes a vapour when it combines with the air by the process of evaporation.

This process is affected by both temperature and pressure. Some liquids vapourize when heated. For example, water vapourizes into steam when it is boiled. Many workplace liquids vapourize without heating. The solvents used in paints, glues, and cleaners are examples of hazardous chemicals that may evaporate readily and rapidly at ordinary room temperature and pressure.

Liquids that evaporate rapidly are said to be volatile. Volatile chemicals that are left open to the workplace air may become airborne and may be inhaled. Xylene, toluene, and some chlorinated solvents are examples of hazardous chemicals that may become airborne as vapours.

When a toxic liquid chemical forms a mist or vapour it becomes more hazardous, and exposure may occur through absorption, inhalation, or ingestion.

Health Effects

This section describes potential health effects which have been linked to specific kinds of chemicals. Only a limited number of examples are used here, and they will not apply to every workplace. Many use different chemicals with different health effects, or the health effects may be unknown. The general approach to assessing and controlling the hazards will follow the description presented here.

Some Health Effects of Hazardous Materials

- Irritation
- Allergic reactions
- Depression of the central nervous system
- Asphyxia
- Pneumoconiosis
- Cancer
- Reproductive effects

Experience and research have established firm connections between many workplace chemicals and health effects among workers. Health effects can range from mild irritation at one extreme to death at the other.

Irritation

Chemicals that cause irritation are known as irritants. Irritants may affect the respiratory system, the eyes, or the skin.

Some Irritants of the Respiratory System

- Ozone
- Nitrogen dioxide
- Sulphur dioxide

Respiratory irritants cause irritation in the nose, lungs, and breathing passages. Bronchitis, or inflammation of the bronchial tubes, is an example. It can be caused by acid mists. Laryngitis, or inflammation of the larynx, is another example. Irritation can affect the lining of the nose and nasal passages.

Primary skin irritants are those that cause an immediate local reaction at the point of contact. The skin turns red and becomes itchy. This is known as irritant contact dermatitis. Primary irritants include some solvents that injure the outer layer of the skin. Others dissolve the skin's protective oils so that it can no longer retain moisture. As a result, the skin becomes dry and cracked. Some chemicals that are corrosive in strong concentrations are also irritants in weaker concentrations.

Allergic Reactions

Sensitizers are those substances that can produce allergic reactions. Skin sensitizers can cause allergic contact dermatitis. Other sensitizers can affect the respiratory system or the eyes.

Although it is possible to become sensitized to a substance after a single exposure, this usually happens only after repeated exposures. Later contact may cause an allergic reaction, when the immune system recognizes the foreign substance as something to be repelled. At this point the person is said to be sensitized to the material that triggers the allergic reaction. Continuing contact may make the person even more sensitive to the substance. Even a brief exposure, or contact with a very small amount of the substance, may cause a full-scale reaction. Most skin problems are caused by irritants rather than sensitizers.

Depression of the Nervous System

The body's nervous system is comprised of the central, peripheral and autonomic nervous systems. Chemicals can harm the nervous system by interfering with the body's own chemicals and slowing the transmission of nerve impulses. This can result in depression of the central nervous system producing such symptoms as headache, light-headedness, drowsiness, and unconsciousness. Chemical depressants can be ingested or inhaled, enter the bloodstream, and reach the central nervous system.

Substances Which May Cause Dermatitis

Primary Irritants – Corrosive Substances:

- Many chlorinated solvents
- Caustic substances
- Acids
- Many alkalis, including calcium hydroxide, ammonium hydroxide, sodium hydroxide and calcium chloride
- Organic solvents including toluene and xylene

Sensitizers:

- Epoxy glue materials, especially epoxy hardener
- Nickel
- Chromium
- Coal tar and creosote when combined with sunlight

Some Depressants - Central Nervous System

- Toluene
- Xylene
- Ether
- Acetone

Asphyxia

Asphyxia means suffocation. Any chemical that interferes with the supply of oxygen to the body is an asphyxiant. The person exposed to an asphyxiant begins to suffocate because there is no longer enough oxygen to sustain life. Oxygen normally makes up 21 percent of the air. If this level drops to 16 percent, health effects may appear. They include light-headedness, buzzing in the ears and an increased heartbeat.

Oxygen is required for life. If there is not enough oxygen in the air, asphyxiation occurs. Chemicals that are not themselves toxic but which displace the available oxygen in the air are called simple asphyxiants.

Chemical asphyxiants enter the body and may interfere with the transfer of oxygen to body tissues. For example, the carbon monoxide gas in engine exhausts displaces oxygen from the blood. Hydrogen cyanide blocks the use of oxygen by the cell. Hydrogen sulphide paralyses the breathing centre in the brain.

Pneumoconiosis

Pneumoconiosis is the medical term for a type of disease caused by dust in the lungs. It can arise from a number of dusts found in workplaces. For example, silicosis is a kind of pneumoconiosis caused by the presence of silica dust in the lungs. Silica is a mineral found in many underground mines and in some surface quarries.

Dust in the lungs can scar the lung tissues, a condition called fibrosis. The lungs lose their elasticity and become less efficient. The heart must work harder to maintain the oxygen supply. The exposed person suffers shortness of breath. Decreasing physical strength and death can follow in extreme cases of the illness.

Dusts that do not scar the lungs may nevertheless cause non-fibrotic pneumoconiosis and interfere with the proper functioning of the lung.

Cancer

Cancer is an abnormal, malignant growth of cells. Malignant means that the disease is growing or spreading. Malignant cancer cells invade nearby tissues and often spread to other locations in the body. According to Statistics Canada, cancer is now the leading cause of death (39%), followed by heart disease (26%), and stroke in third place (7%). While the exact process that causes cancer is still unknown, a few types of cancer can be linked to specific causal factors (for example, asbestos can lead to lung cancer, mesothelioma and other cancers). Chemicals that can cause cancer are known as **carcinogens**.

Effects on the Reproductive System

Some chemicals can harm the reproductive system of an exposed worker. Health effects can include loss of fertility, miscarriage, damage to the fetus, and inherited defects which are passed on to following generations.

Chemicals that can produce these effects have specific names depending on the effect:

- **Mutagens** may cause changes in human sperm or egg cells that may be passed on to successive generations. The result may be a birth defect. A child's cells may be altered so that they may develop some disease, such as cancer, in later life. These defects can be passed on through the female egg or through the male sperm. Mutagens which do not affect the reproductive system are called somatic cell mutagens.

- **Teratogens** are those chemicals which affect the developing embryo directly to cause birth defects. Fetal toxins are chemicals that can cause death of the embryo, impaired development or function, or behaviour problems after birth.

Assessing Chemical Hazards

This chapter has identified a number of workplace chemicals with particular health effects. There are tens of thousands of chemicals in use in Ontario, and those discussed here are only a few examples. They deal only with some of the best known linkages between chemicals and adverse health effects.

To recommend controls for chemical hazards, employers and members of joint health and safety committees and health and safety representatives must be able to assess chemical hazards, and link the products found in their workplaces with specific health effects.

An assessment of chemical hazards involves answering a series of questions about the work process:

- What is produced?

- What materials are used?

- What equipment is used?

- How does the production cycle work?

- What are the operating procedures and controls?

- How are workers exposed?

- Which workers are exposed?

- When are workers exposed?

- What is the degree of exposure?

- What is the health impact of exposure?

The workplace inspection can provide much of the information needed to answer these questions. A proper inspection includes talking to workers and supervisors and learning about any hazardous conditions or health effects they have observed.

A number of other tools and techniques are also used to gather information about hazards. They include the workplace inventory of hazardous chemicals, the workplace hazardous materials information system (WHMIS), and exposure monitoring.

WHMIS 2015

WHMIS first became law in October 1988. Canada is one of over 65 countries to adopt the globally harmonized system (GHS). WHMIS 2015 is aligned with the Globally Harmonized System of Classification and Labeling of Chemicals. GHS does not replace WHMIS but is an update to align with GHS elements. WHMIS 2015 is based on the 5th revised edition of the GHS.

WHMIS 2015 introduced new classification rules and hazard classes, new hazard pictograms, new supplier label requirements, and a new format for Safety Data Sheets (SDSs).

The following aspects of Canada's WHMIS program stayed the same:

- Worker education and training (Generic and Workplace Specific)
- Requirements for workplace labels
- Requirements for Safety Data Sheets (now 16 sections)
- Rules around confidential business information
- Workplace responsibilities for employers, supervisors, workers, and suppliers
- Inclusion of symbol for biohazardous infectious material from WHMIS 1988

Employers are required to educate and train workers about WHMIS 2015

Safety Data Sheets (SDSs)

The Safety Data Sheet (SDS) is produced by the supplier of the product and provides detailed information for the employer and workers. The GHS-formatted SDS will replace the old format of Material Safety Data Sheets (MSDS). The SDS has a standardized 16-section format and must appear in a specified order.

Section 1 – Identification

This section will identify the substance or mixture and provide the name of the supplier, recommended uses, and the contact information of the supplier including an emergency contact. Along with the recommended or intended use of the substance or mixture, restriction on use should also be stated.

Section 2 – Hazard Identification

This section describes the hazards associated with the substance or mixture as well as the pictogram or the name of the pictogram (e.g. "flame"), signal word, hazard statement, and precautionary statements. This section will also include information about other hazards that do not result in a classification but may contribute to the overall hazard of the material, for example, dust explosion hazard.

Section 3 – Composition/Information on Ingredients

The supplier will identify the ingredients of the product in this section. This includes impurities and stabilizers which may also be classified. If Confidential Business Information exemption has been granted, it will be noted in this section.

Section 4 – First Aid Measures

This section describes the initial care that can be given by someone who is trained in first aid. It describes the first-aid instructions by relevant routes of exposure: (inhalation, skin, eye, ingestion) as well as expected immediate and delayed symptoms. It also provides information on acute and delayed symptoms and where known, medical monitoring and antidotes.

Section 5 – Fire-Fighting Measures

This section provides information on the proper fire-extinguishing media and what measures to avoid. It also provides advice on specific hazards that may arise from the burning chemical (toxic fumes) and special protective actions for firefighters.

Section 6 – Accidental Release Measures

In the event of an accidental release, this section recommends the appropriate response in order to prevent or minimize the adverse effects on person, property, and the environment. Personal precautions, protective equipment and emergency procedures are detailed for non-emergency and emergency personnel. Methods and materials for containment and cleaning up are also provided.

Section 7 – Handling and Storage
This section provides guidance on safe handling in order to minimize hazards to people, property, and the environment. There are precautions on safe handling as well as advice on general hygiene (wash hands after use) and conditions for the safe storage including incompatibilities.

Section 8 – Exposure Controls / Personal Protection
This section provides occupation exposure limits or biological exposure limits when available. In keeping with the Hierarchy of Controls, it outlines appropriate engineering controls and individual protection measures, such as personal protective equipment.

Section 9 – Physical and Chemical Properties
This section identifies the appearance (physical state, colour), odour, odour threshold, pH, melting point/freezing point, boiling point/boiling range, flash point, evaporation rate, flammability, upper/lower flammable/explosive limit, vapour pressure, vapour density, relative density, solubility, partition coefficient-n-octanol/water, auto-ignition temperature, decomposition temperature, and viscosity. If specific characteristics do not apply or are not available, they still need to be listed on the SDS with the appropriate explanatory statement.

Section 10 – Stability and Reactivity
This section describes the reactivity hazards of the substance or mixture, as well as the chemical stability. If relevant, the SDS will describe possible hazardous reactions such as the release of excessive pressure or heat. Conditions to avoid as well as incompatible materials will also be detailed.

Section 11 – Toxicological Information
This section is intended for use by medical professionals, occupational health and safety professionals, and toxicologists. The hazards for which hazards should be provided include: acute toxicity; skin corrosion/irritation; serious eye damage/irritation; respiratory or skin sensitization; germ cell mutagenicity; carcinogenicity; reproductive toxicity; STOT-single exposure; STOT-repeated exposure; and aspiration hazard. If these hazards are not available, they should still be listed with a statement that data are not available.

Safety Data Sheet WHMIS 2015

1. Identification
2. Hazard Identification
3. Composition / Information on Ingredients
4. First-Aid Measures
5. Fire-Fighting Measures
6. Accidental Release Measures
7. Handling and Storage
8. Exposure Controls / Personal Protection
9. Physical and Chemical Properties
10. Stability and Reactivity
11. Toxicological Information
12. Ecological Information*
13. Disposal Considerations*
14. Transport Information*
15. Regulatory Information*
16. Other Information

* Sections 12 to 15 require the headings to be present. The supplier has the option to not provide information in these sections.

Information is required on the likely route of exposure, (inhalation, ingestion, skin, and eye contact) symptoms related to the physical, chemical and toxicological characteristics, delays and immediate effects, chronic effects from short-term and long-term exposure, and numerical measures of toxicity.

Section 12 – Ecological Information
The information in this section is to enable the evaluation of the environmental impact if the substance or mixture were to be released into the environment. Consideration is given to the impact on aquatic life, soil, and air.

Section 13 – Disposal Considerations
This section provides information for the proper disposal, recycling or reclamation of the substance or mixture, in order to determine the preferred waste management options.

Section 14 – Transport Information
This section provides classification information for the transportation/shipment of the hazardous substance or mixture by road, rail, sea, or air. Where the information is not available, or relevant the section still needs to be listed. The information required includes: UN number; UN proper shipping name; transport hazard class(es); packing group, if applicable; environmental hazards; special precautions for the user, and transport in bulk.

Section 15 – Regulatory Information
This section includes any safety, health, and environmental information specific to the product.

Section 16 – Other Information
This section includes the date of the last revision of the SDS as well as a key/legend to the abbreviations and acronyms used in the SDS.

Under Canadian Legislation Sections 12, 13, 14, and 15 require the headings to be present, but the supplier has the option to not provide information in these sections.

The most common routes of entry of hazardous chemicals into the body are inhalation or absorption through the skin. They may also be ingested. Airborne chemicals take the form of dust, gas, vapour, mist, fumes, or smoke. For this reason, monitoring the workplace air is the most common method of assessing exposure. These methods are appropriate for chemicals or other agents with known and proven sampling and analysis techniques.
Air sampling is a frequently used monitoring method.

Monitoring techniques, devices and strategies are introduced in Chapter 9 and described in greater detail in Chapter 19.

Safe Levels
The exposure limits in the regulations are based on an incomplete and sometimes controversial data. They cannot be used to determine precisely what is or is not a safe level for most hazardous chemicals.

For example, the Time Weighted Average Limit for ammonia is 25 parts per million (ppm). This does not mean that exposure to ammonia vapour in the air is necessarily safe at concentrations up to 25 ppm. And it does not mean that an average level of more than 25 ppm is necessarily unsafe for every individual.

Safe levels for chemical exposures are being disputed. At the 1992 United Nations Conference on Environment and Development, a declaration was passed on the 'precautionary principle' which states in part: "when an activity raises threats of harm to human health or the environment, precautionary measures should be taken even if some cause and effect relationships are not fully established scientifically."

This was reiterated after Severe Acute Respiratory Syndrome (SARS) resulted in 44 deaths and 330 serious lung disease cases in 2003 in Ontario. The severity of the outbreak may have been reduced if Ontario followed the precautionary principle, according to the 2007 SARS Commission. The Commission recommended adoption of the precautionary principle as "a guiding principle throughout Ontario's health, public health and worker safety systems…" Since 2006, the Ontario Health Care Health and Safety Committee under Section 21 of the *OHSA* has been reviewing occupational health and safety issues and supporting acceptance of the precautionary principle in health care settings and made this recommendation to the Ministry of Health.

ALARA
ALARA stands for As Low As Reasonably Achievable. This term expresses the principle that the exposure to any hazardous material should not only be lower than the stated exposure limit but as low as it reasonably can be.

Employers who use ALARA as a guideline believe it provides a more reliable standard of assessment. It guards against a "crisis" atmosphere where exposure levels may continually hover just below or above the regulated exposure limit. Maintaining exposure levels well below the maximum in the regulations also has the advantage of a wider margin of error whether the extent (or effect) of the hazard is known or not. If a control malfunctions, and exposure levels rise, the levels may still remain below the limit.

Occupational Exposure Limits
The regulations of the *Occupational Health and Safety Act* set maximum exposure levels for several hundred substances as well as noise and x-rays. The most important regulations are the following:

- Regulation 833 – for Control of Exposure to Biological or Chemical Agents which also covers 11 substances designated by the Ministry of Labour, Training and Skills Development;

- Regulation 490/09 Designated Substances – covers chemical agents considered designated substances listed in Section 1(2) and exposure limits are listed in Table 1

- The sector regulations for industrial establishments, construction projects, and mining and mining plants; and

- The regulation respecting x-ray safety.

Employers have a duty under the *OHSA* to ensure that no worker is exposed beyond these maximum levels. The regulations also require employers to "take all measures reasonably necessary in the circumstances" to protect workers from exposure to a hazardous agent.

The regulations are based on the American Conference of Governmental Industrial Hygienists (ACGIH) table adopted by Ontario. The regulations define three types of exposure values for airborne hazardous agents: time-weighted average, short term, and ceiling limits. The exposure values given in the regulation are stated as a concentration of the substance in the air. They are expressed either as parts per million (ppm) by volume or as milligrams per cubic metre of air.

Employers are required under section 4 of Regulation 833, Control of Exposure to Biological or Chemical Agents (the "Regulation"), to limit the exposure of workers to specified hazardous biological or chemical agents in accordance with the values set out in the "Ontario Table" (which is Table 1 in the Regulation) or, if the agent is not listed in the Ontario Table, the ACGIH Table that is incorporated by reference in the Regulation.

For ease of reference, the Ministry of Labour, Training and Skills Development has posted a table online containing **all** specific occupational exposure limits an employer must implement under s. 4 of the Regulation, i.e. it sets out information found in both the Ontario Table in Regulation 833 and the ACGIH Table.

In addition, the table includes listings (i.e. Petroleum ether, Rubber solvent and VM&P Naphtha) not included in either the Ontario Table or the ACGIH Table. The Ministry recommends that OELs for those substances be calculated using the recommended method referenced.

An employer has a duty and shall take all measures reasonably necessary in the circumstances to protect workers from exposure to a hazardous biological or chemical agent.
The table can be found at https://www.labour.gov.on.ca/english/hs/pubs/oel_table.php

Time-Weighted Average Limit (TWA)
The time-weighted average limit takes into account that the level of exposure may change throughout the working day or week. The regulations for many substances are based on the time-weighted average limit.

Carbon monoxide, which is found in vehicle exhausts, is an example. The time-weighted average limit (TWA) allowed for carbon monoxide is 25 parts per million (ppm). During one day, the actual levels in the loading bay of a shipping department might be:

16 ppm for 2 hours
30 ppm for 4 hours
20 ppm for 2 hours

According to the formula in the regulation, the cumulative exposure to carbon monoxide for the workers in this area during this 8-hour work day would be:

(16 ppm x 2 hrs) + (30 ppm x 4 hrs) + (20 ppm x 2 hrs)
$$32 + 120 + 40 = 192$$

To calculate the daily TWA, the cumulative daily exposure is divided by 8 hours, which is assumed for these purposes to be the normal working day:

192 ÷ 8 = 24

This is below the TWA of 25 ppm for carbon monoxide specified in the regulation, even though this level was exceeded for four hours during the day. The TWA is calculated by dividing the cumulative daily exposure by 8 and the cumulative weekly exposure by 40. The regulation does not specify the number of samples that are to be taken. The *OHSA* gives a worker member of a joint health and safety committee or the health and safety representative the right to be consulted about testing methods, and an opportunity to be present at the beginning of testing. The same concept of time-weighted averages is used for the designated substances.

Ceiling Limit (C)

Regulation 833/90 also includes ceiling limits (C) which are concentrations of the biological or chemical agent in the workplace air that must never be exceeded. Cs are used for fast-acting chemicals and are not listed for all substances in the regulation.

Short-Term Exposure Limit (STEL)

The regulation also includes short-term exposure limit (STEL) for many biological and chemical agents. The short-term values are higher than the daily or weekly averages. For example, the STEL for nitrogen dioxide is 5 ppm. A worker's exposure may not exceed this level for more than 15 minutes at a time. The STEL can be reached a maximum of four times in an eight- hour work shift and with at least one hour between exposures.

Section 4 3. of Regulation 833 states that where no C or STEL is specified, a worker may not be exposed to more than three times the TWA for more than 30 minutes or more than five times the TWA for any period. For example, the TWA for Carbon Monoxide (CO) is 25 ppm. A worker cannot be exposed to 75 ppm of CO for more than 30 minutes, or 125 ppm for any period.

Controlling Chemical Hazards

Chemical hazards may be controlled at the source, along the path, or at the worker.

Control at the Source

The best form of control is to eliminate or reduce the hazard. It may be found that a hazardous chemical is not an essential ingredient in the product, or that the process that creates exposure to a chemical is not necessary.

Four types of control can be used at the source. They are substitution, redesigning processes, enclosure/isolation, and local exhaust ventilation.

Substitution means finding a substance that can perform the same function and which may lessen the hazard or be more easily controlled. Care should be taken not to introduce any new hazards when selecting a substitute for a hazardous material.

Hazards can also be controlled at the source by redesigning the workplace or the work process. For example, where properly ventilated paint spray booths are not feasible, dipping a product in paint rather than spraying it can reduce hazards from mists.

Isolation is another method of control at the source. Isolation can be achieved by enclosing the process. For example, closed container systems can ensure that an entire chemical process takes place without the possibility of worker exposure.

Local Exhaust Ventilation

Local exhaust ventilation can be very effective in controlling chemical hazards. It is essential, however, that there is no possibility of the contaminated air being drawn back into the workplace. Consideration should be given to the environmental impact of hazardous materials being exhausted to the atmosphere.

Local exhaust ventilation removes the contaminant rather than diluting it. This type of ventilation is only effective if it is located close to the source of the hazard.

Local ventilation can be in a fixed position, perhaps at a chemical pouring station. It can also be movable, like the flexible hose systems for removing automobile exhaust in service centres. A local exhaust ventilation system has five key components:

Closed Container System

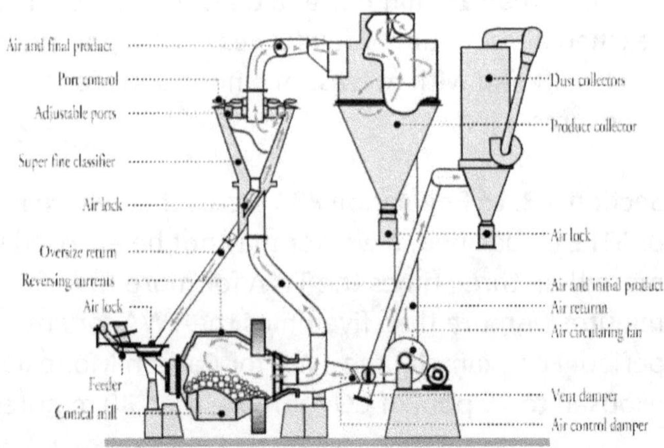

- a fan or a blower that draws in contaminated air;

- a hood that allows the effective capture of the contaminant;

- a system of ducts that transport the contaminated air away from the workplace;

- an air-cleaning device that removes the contaminants from the air;

- a source of make-up air that replaces the air removed from the workplace.

Fans

Fans are the driving force of a local exhaust ventilation system. They must provide enough negative air pressure to capture the contaminants, draw them into the hood, carry them through the duct work to the air cleaning device and exhaust the air outside. Special spark-proof motors may be needed if the contaminant is flammable.

Local Exhaust System

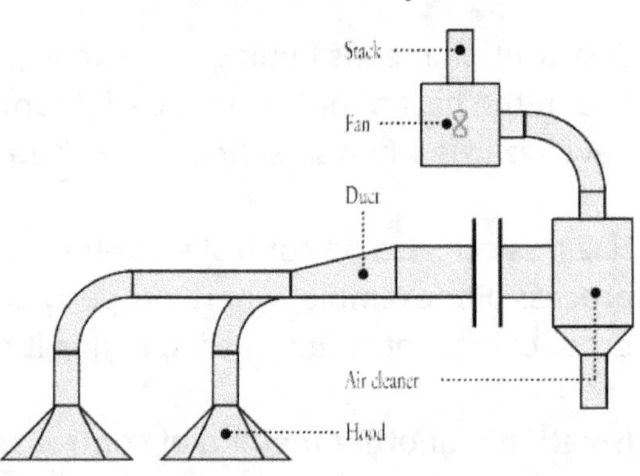

Hoods

Hoods should enclose the source of the contaminant as much as possible and be close to the source. They must provide enough air flow to ensure that the contaminant does not reach the worker's breathing area. A well-designed hood takes advantage of the natural movement of the contaminant.

Ducts

Ducts carry the contaminated air from the hood to the air-cleaning device. The speed of the air as it travels through the ducts is called the duct velocity. It must move fast enough that solid contaminants do not settle out in the ducts. As the air moves through the duct, it creates friction against the duct walls. Friction is greater at corners, bends, and obstructions of the duct. The overall duct length should be kept as short as possible with as few bends, as possible. Ventilation systems with more than one hood must be balanced to maintain proper air flow and velocities at each point of the system.

Air-Cleaning Devices

Air-cleaning devices capture and remove airborne contaminants from air that has been drawn from the workplace. Various types of devices are used, depending on whether the contaminant is a dust, fume, mist, gas, or vapour. The main types are fabric filters, charcoal filters, cyclones, electrostatic precipitators, and scrubbers.

Make-up Air System

All of the air drawn out of the workplace by a local exhaust ventilation system has to be replaced with fresh air. The local ventilation system itself should not be relied on to do this. Make-up air should move from cleaner areas towards the areas where contaminants may be present. Inlets for make-up air systems should be located so that no contaminated air from nearby exhaust stacks is drawn back into the building.

Recirculation

In some cases, cleaned exhaust air may be reintroduced into the workplace to conserve heat. This is discouraged for systems handling toxic contaminants. Recirculation may be acceptable provided that adequate precautions are taken. Precautions include multiple air-cleaning systems, and automatic sensing devices that warn of air-cleaner failure and divert contaminated air in the case of failure.

Control Along the Path

Ventilation is the principal method used for control of chemicals along the path. Maintenance, administrative controls, work practices, standard work procedures, housekeeping procedures, and safe practices are also controls which are implemented along the path.

General Dilution Ventilation

General dilution ventilation reduces airborne concentrations of chemicals by diluting the workplace air with cleaner air from outside. General ventilation can effectively remove large amounts of hot or humid air, or dilute low concentrations of low toxicity contaminants. General dilution ventilation does not eliminate exposure to airborne contaminants and is especially unsuitable for fumes or dusts.

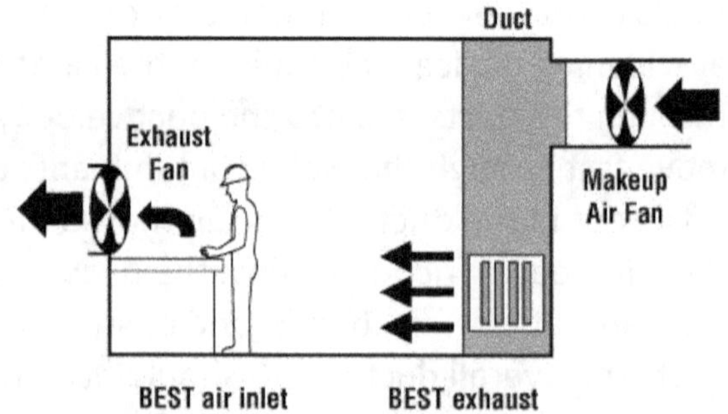

Maintenance

Like any other equipment, ventilation systems must be maintained. This work should normally be performed by the workplace maintenance staff. Maintenance involves systematic procedures for inspecting the equipment, monitoring system performance, and routine replacement or cleaning of components. Worn or damaged parts must be promptly replaced.

Inspection of ventilation systems involves regular checks of hoods, filters, belts, and air-cleaners. Periodic tests of system performance should include measurement of air velocities at key locations such as hoods and ducts. Smoke tubes or air current tubes may be used to visually check air flow. More sophisticated devices continuously measure the amount of air flow, velocity, and the negative air pressure in ducts.

Administrative Controls

Administrative controls involve changing the way people work with a hazard, rather than directly controlling the hazard itself. Some administrative controls rotate workers so that individual exposure is reduced.

For example, workers might be rotated between hot and cooler work areas.

Another type of administrative control is scheduling maintenance work during off-hours so unintended releases of toxic substances will affect the smallest possible number of workers.

Work Practices

Other controls should be supplemented by adherence to carefully designed work practices. Work practices should be spelled out in the control program. They might include standard work procedures, housekeeping procedures, and safe practices.

Standard Work Procedures

Standard work procedures help to ensure that each operation is performed in the safest possible way. They should be in writing. Written procedures can help in the training of workers and promote understanding among all workplace parties. They make sure that health considerations are part of every job. Written standard work procedures are also useful for purposes other than health and safety.

Housekeeping Procedures

Well-planned cleaning routines help to control exposure. They ensure that spills are promptly cleaned up and that hazardous dust does not accumulate and circulate in the workplace air. Some cleaning techniques may stir up dust and create an additional hazard. Planned housekeeping procedures will ensure that material is vacuumed rather than swept and that wet compounds and filters are used to prevent recirculation of contaminated dust. Once cleaned up, contaminants should be disposed of in a safe manner which avoids pollution of the environment.

Safe Practices

A control program should include safe practices to prevent the unintended release of a hazardous material. Safe practices may include:

- segregated storage for certain materials in well-ventilated areas;

- warning signs and labeling;

- prompt repair of damaged equipment;

- removal of obstacles from walkways and corridors;

- adequate lighting;

- safe transportation of materials;

- use of mechanical handling equipment; and

- minimizing the need for transport of the materials.

Control at the Worker

Control at the worker is generally less effective than control at the source or along the path. There are two types of control at the worker: personal hygiene practices, and personal protective equipment.

Personal Hygiene Practices

Personal hygiene practices and facilities can reduce the amount of a substance that is absorbed by the worker's body after he or she has been exposed to it. Some chemicals are released in a form that can accumulate on the worker's hands, hair, and clothes. For example, a control system may prevent lead from becoming airborne, but lead dust may be picked up on the hands.

Hygiene practices ensure that the worker does not swallow the substance. They also prevent hazardous toxic chemicals from being carried home on the body or on the clothes. This ensures that family members are not exposed to the hazard.

Hygiene practices at work include thoroughly washing hands and removing outer protective clothing before entering clean areas. Eating, drinking, and smoking must be done only in designated clean areas.

In some cases, the regulations under the *OHSA* require a system where workers remove soiled work clothing and place them in a locker in a "dirty" area. Workers may shower before entering the "clean" area where they have another locker containing their street clothes. Liquid shower and hand soap may also decrease the risk of contamination. Work clothes are laundered at the workplace or at a contract industrial laundry.

The sector regulations (Mining, Construction and Industrial Establishments) include a number of specific hygiene provisions and certified members and health and safety representatives should be familiar with those covering their sector.

Personal Protective Equipment
Personal protective equipment, like other controls at the worker, ensures protection when other controls at the source or along the path cannot eliminate the hazard either partially or totally. Circumstances in which personal protective equipment should be used include:

- while engineering controls are being installed or repaired;

- during an emergency;

- during occasional maintenance or repair, or work in confined spaces;

- when other controls are not possible or practicable;

- as a precautionary measure to back up other control systems; and

- where personal protective equipment is prescribed by regulations such as during asbestos removal or entry into confined spaces.

Personal protective equipment most commonly used for controlling chemical hazards includes barriers to skin or eye contact such as gloves, boots, protective clothing, face shields, and goggles. Respirators are used to protect against inhalation hazards.

Respirators must be the correct type for the hazard involved and must be carefully fitted and properly used. Respirators that remove contaminants from the air are called air-purifying respirators. They usually have replaceable filter cartridges. It is essential that the proper cartridge be used. Cartridges must be replaced at the recommended intervals to avoid clogging. There are several kinds of cartridges, identified by a colour coding system. The sector regulations include a number of more specific requirements for respirator use.

Special caution should be used whenever respirators are worn, because there are limitations in the protection they provide. They may interfere with communication or vision and can be uncomfortable. Workers must be trained in the proper maintenance and use of all personal protective equipment.

Guidelines for the selection, use and care of personal protective equipment are available through the Canadian Standards Association.

Assessment and Control Under the Designated Substance Regulations (DSR)

Some hazardous materials used in the workplace are subject to a special regulation under the *OHSA*. The *OHSA* give the Minister of Labour, Training and Skills Development the right to designate substances, assess, and control them. These regulations are made based on the recommendations of the American Congress of Governmental Industrial Hygienists (ACGIH). Ontario Occupational Exposure Limits (OELs) follow ACGIH standards closely.

Previous to July 1, 2010, each of the 11 designated substances had its own individual regulation. They are collectively known as the designated substance regulations (DSR). After July 1, 2010, the 11 designated substance regulations were repealed and moved into Regulation 490/09 (which amended the occupational exposure limits for 36 hazardous chemical substances). There continues to be a second separate regulation for Asbestos in Construction (Reg. 278/05).

Designated substances are treated much more strictly than other biological or chemical agents also regulated in the *OHSA*. If there is a designated substance in the workplace to which a worker may be exposed, the employer must do an assessment. If the assessment shows a possibility of exposure that could affect a worker's health, a control program must be implemented. The assessment and control program must be written and developed in consultation with the joint occupational health and safety committee or health and safety representative.

The DSR Control Program

A DSR control program generally conforms to the principles of control described in this chapter and in Chapter 9. It is much more than a general policy or procedure for reducing hazardous exposures. It is a specific written plan for a particular designated substance. Each part of the plan must follow conditions that are stated for the particular substance.

Exposure Control

The control program must contain both general practices and specific measures for the control of worker exposure at each step in the work process, emphasizing the importance of engineering controls to prevent exposure. The workplace must be reassessed whenever a change in the workplace could significantly affect the exposure of a worker.

Exposure evaluation is a mandatory part of any designated substance control program. Monitoring is required to provide a check on the effectiveness of controls. Exposure limits are described in detail in the regulation for each designated substance.

Monitoring codes apply separately to each airborne designated substance. The code sets the requirements for instruments, sampling techniques, methods of analysis, and record keeping. Monitoring results must be posted where they can be read by workers and be furnished to members of the JHSC or HSR.

Personal Exposure Records

The employer must provide a copy of a worker's exposure record to the doctor who examines or tests the worker.

Medical Examinations and Clinical Tests

Employers are required to provide medical examinations and clinical tests for workers. Worker participation is voluntary. Records of worker medical examinations must be retained by the examining physician in a secure place for a period of at least 40 years for the initial examination or 20 years for the most recent examination, whichever is longer.

The doctor must advise the worker and the employer whether the worker is fit, unfit, or fit with specified limitations for further work as a result of exposure to the designated substance. The doctor must not disclose any other particulars of the examination without the written consent of the worker. The DSR may also contain a code for taking and interpreting blood or urine tests.

Personal Protective Equipment

The DSR for a substance contains a code specifying the type, use and maintenance of any respiratory equipment used to protect a worker from exposure.

Timetable for Implementation

The control program should include a timetable for implementation. It should describe temporary measures to control exposure while permanent controls are being developed.

Copies of Control Program to JHSC or HSR
The employer must provide a copy of the current control program to the joint health and safety committee or health and safety representative.

Whereas previously there was a separate regulation for each designated substance, now Ontario Regulation 490/09 covers all the Designated Substances, with an additional regulation (Ont. Reg. 278/05) covering Asbestos in Construction. Committee members and health and safety representatives should become familiar with the DSR requirements for any designated substance in their workplace.

Evaluating Chemical Hazard Controls

As with all hazards, the work is not done, once control measures are put in place. The members of the joint health and safety committee and health and safety representatives must be diligent in evaluating whether the controls are effective. This is done during workplace inspections and in conversations with employees. There must be a system in place to determine that the required training is carried out and that regular maintenance is being completed, especially on ventilation systems. Any concerns from the workers must be taken seriously. Periodically, the employer should be undertaking exposure monitoring to determine that the control measures are effective.

Members of joint health and safety committees and health and safety representatives, where designated substances are present, have an opportunity to evaluate the control program and emergency plans, where applicable, put in place by the employer. If members of the joint health and safety committee or health and safety representatives receive information from the company physician that any of their members are fit with limitations, or unfit to work in relation to a designated substance, they must be prepared to make recommendations to the employer to improve the control measures. This is also program evaluation.

Review

Many health effects can be caused by chemicals. They include skin or lung irritation, asphyxia, pneumoconiosis, and cancer. Chemicals can also interfere with the central nervous system and the reproductive system. These effects can be complicated by the synergistic effects of exposure to multiple hazards. The physical properties of the chemical can make them more or less severe. Chemicals may affect different people in different ways.

Hazardous chemicals in the workplace can be assessed using a variety of tools and techniques. These include safety data sheets that are part of the WHMIS system. Members of the joint health and safety committee and health and safety representatives will be involved in decisions for ongoing training and implementation of WHIS programs.

Exposure monitoring for chemicals is most often accomplished by monitoring or testing workplace air. Exposure limits for more than 700 biological and chemical agents are included in Ontario Regulation 833/90, and Ontario Regulation 490/09.

Chemical hazards are controlled at the source, along the path, or at the worker. Elimination of the hazard or substitution of a less hazardous chemical are the most preferable methods.

Chemical hazards can also be controlled at the source by local ventilation, redesigning the work process, and by isolation of the hazard. Properly designed local ventilation systems can be very effective, because they can remove the hazard from the workplace before it reaches a worker's breathing area. Such systems must be carefully maintained and adjusted to operate effectively. General dilution ventilation is the principle means of controlling chemical hazards along the path. Maintenance, administrative controls, work practices, standard work procedures, housekeeping procedures, and safe work practices are also used along the path.

Control at the worker takes the form of personal hygiene practices and personal protective equipment. Good hygiene practices reduce the amount of a chemical that is absorbed by the worker's body after exposure. They also ensure that contaminants are not carried home. Personal protective equipment should not be a substitute for engineering controls, but it can be used during emergencies, while controls are being installed or maintained, or during maintenance and repair.

Eleven chemicals are designated under the authority of the *OHSA* and are subject to Regulation 490/09. Each designated substance requires special assessments and a written control program if present in the workplace. Asbestos is also covered in a second regulation due to its use in construction and building projects and abatement plans to remove it in a safe manner.

Once hazards are controlled, JHSCs and HSRs are involved in monitoring and evaluating the effectiveness of hazard controls.

Chapter 12
Biological Hazards

- Routes of Entry and Transmission

- Health Effects

- Assessing Biological Hazards

- Control of Biological Hazards

- Evaluating Biological Hazard Controls

- COVID-19

- Review

Biological Hazards

Biological agents are living things, or substances produced by living things, that can cause illness or disease in humans. Biological agents have many uses in the workplace, but some of them can be hazardous. They include bacteria, viruses, fungi as well as larger organisms such as parasites and plants.

Bacteria are microscopic single-celled organisms. They are found in the air, water and soil, and in living or dead animals and plants. Viruses are micro-organisms that can reproduce only by coming into contact with living cells. They are found only in living animal and plant matter.

Fungi are simple plants that feed on the living or dead tissues of animals or plants. Mold, yeast, and mushrooms are fungi. Yeasts are used in the manufacture of bread, beer, and wine.

Parasites live in the bodies of plants and animals, including, in some cases, the human digestive system. They reproduce by laying eggs.

Some plants produce substances that cause an allergic response in humans.

Routes of Entry and Transmission

Biological agents enter the body by inhalation, by ingestion, or by absorption through the skin. They can also enter by injection. The possible routes of entry are limited by the characteristics of the agent. For example, AIDS and hepatitis B are blood borne and are not transmitted through the air. In general, inhalation is the most common route of entry for biological hazards. Once inside the body, infectious agents can multiply and be passed from one person to another. Some can survive outside the body for a considerable length of time in an intermediate breeding ground such as water or food. Others die quickly without the protection of the body. The route they follow is referred to as the route of transmission.

Direct Transmission of Infectious Agents
The route of transmission may be direct or indirect. Direct transmission takes place when there is physical contact between an infected and a non-infected person. Direct transmission can also occur if there is a projection of droplets into the mucous membranes of the eye, nose, or mouth. This might happen during a cough or sneeze. Direct transmission might also occur if a person is injected or punctured with an infected needle or other sharp object which is infected.

Indirect Transmission of Infectious Agents
Indirect transmission may occur when infectious agents attach themselves to materials or objects such as food and water or cooking and eating utensils.

An infectious agent may also be transmitted by an insect. The insect may carry the infectious agent from the source to an uninfected person.

Some infectious agents may be transmitted through the air and are hazardous if inhaled.

Health Effects

Biological agents that are capable of causing disease are known as pathogens. Some of them are infectious and can multiply in the body. Persons who are most at risk from biological hazards include those who work with animals or plants or in health and child care. People who handle animals include those who work in zoos, animal breeding facilities, and veterinary services. Agriculture and food industry workers handle both animal and plant products. Others who may be affected include those who work with cutting oils or ventilation systems or work in municipal sanitation or sewage operations.

Diseases Caused by Infectious Agents
Bacterial diseases include tuberculosis, tetanus, and food poisoning. Infection through the skin can cause boils or blood poisoning.

Common fungal diseases are ringworm, which is a skin infection, and thrush, which infects the skin and mucous membranes.

Viral diseases include hepatitis, mumps, German measles and rabies.

Diseases Caused by Other Biological Agents
Parasitic worms enter the body when their eggs are ingested. They can also enter when their larvae in the soil penetrate the skin or through insect bites. The most common are roundworms and flatworms.

Biological hazards may be recognized by examining the materials used in the workplace or by a history of illness in workers. Some materials present in the workplace may not be biohazards themselves, but they may encourage the growth of bacteria or fungi.

In a workplace where biological hazards are present, unusual amounts of lost time due to illness might reveal that workers are being exposed to those hazards. The situation may be further assessed by discussions with workers and supervisors. These steps alone will not confirm exposure to a biological hazard. Medical assistance will be required to make a more accurate assessment.

Monitoring for biological hazards may be necessary in a workplace where workers may be exposed to plant or animal products, including those who work in health care or laboratory facilities.

Except for public health rules for bacteria in water and food, there are few standards for assessing exposure to micro-organisms.

The equipment used for monitoring biological hazards may be very specialized. Monitoring generally involves collecting samples from the workplace, placing them in a culture medium, and observing any "colonies" of micro-organisms that grow from them. Certified members who work where biological agents are present will need to familiarize themselves with the specific hazards involved and the means of monitoring them.

For workers who travel outside of North America, it is recommended that they consult the Public Health Agency of Canada's website to assess the need for travel immunization. http://www.travel.gc.ca

Control of Biological Hazards

Biological hazards may be controlled at the source of the hazard, along the path from the source to the worker, and at the worker.

Controls at the source involve eliminating or reducing exposure through elimination, isolation or containment of the hazard. This may be done through the proper design of equipment. Equipment – especially ventilation systems, which might harbour biohazards – must be regularly maintained, cleaned and sterilized. Where the hazard cannot be contained, steps can be taken to ensure that the hazard does not spread. Those inside the area must follow safe work practices and use protective equipment. Measures must be taken to ensure that contaminated protective equipment does not pose a threat.

Biological safety cabinets protect against exposure by forcing the surrounding air into a system that filters or captures the hazard.

Controls along the path include cleaning and disinfecting as well as the safe disposal of waste. It is important that all biohazardous materials, including waste, are labeled, handled and disposed of in a manner that avoids contamination of the handler or the environment. In health care facilities, all blood and other body fluids should be treated as potentially infectious.

Control at the worker may involve personal protective equipment such as gloves and masks. Immunization programs may be appropriate in some circumstances. For example, some health care institutions offer voluntary immunization against hepatitis B. Adequate hygiene facilities and good personal hygiene are very important components of a control program.

Safe Work Procedures and Training
Workplaces where biological hazards are present should have written safe work procedures and training to ensure that all workers know how to protect themselves.

- All contaminated equipment or material should be contained, labeled, and isolated.

- Spills should be cleaned up immediately.

- No one should eat, drink, or smoke in a potentially hazardous work area.

- Showers, lockers, and laundry facilities should be used to prevent hazards from leaving the workplace.

- Safe procedures should be designed to deal with the specific hazards of each workplace.

Biological Hazards

List of diseases due to viral, bacterial or other parasitic agents, which may be job-related.

Disease	Agent	Site of Infection	Occupation
Aids		Blood stream	Health, social and corrections workers
Amoebiasis	Protozoa	Bowel	Health and social workers
Anthrax	Bacteria	Skin and lungs	Animal handlers, wool sorters, tanners
Avian H5N1 Flu	Virus	Inhalation / Skin	Poultry workers
Brucellosis (undulant fever)	Bacteria	Blood stream	Livestock inspector, abattoir workers, veterinarians, farmers
Chicken Pox (and herpes zoster)	Virus	Skin	Teachers, health and social workers
Dermatophytosis	Fungus	Skin	Swimming pool attendants, dish washers
Dysentery (food poisoning)	Virus or Bacteria	Bowel	Claims allowed only if definite exposure associated with employment
Giardiasis	Protozoa	Bowel	Health and social workers
Hepatitis A and B	Virus	Liver	Health and social workers
Histoplasmosis	Fungus	Lungs	Any involving exposure to dust from bird droppings
Infected Blisters (septic infection)	Bacteria	Skin	Any
Insect Bites/Stings	Insects	Skin	Any
Mononucleosis (glandular fever)	Virus	Blood	Health and social workers
Ornithosis	Rickettsia	Lungs	Pet shop workers
Pertussis (whooping cough)	Bacteria	Respiratory system	Teachers, health and social workers
Rabies (hydrophobia)	Virus	Nervous system	Animal handlers, bush workers, farmers (claims allowed for prevention and treatment following exposure)
Rubella (German measles)	Virus	General	Teachers, health and social workers
Scabies	Mite	Skin	Teachers, health and social workers
Severe Acute Respiratory Syndrome (SARS)	Virus	Inhalation / Skin	Health and social workers, persons with weak immune systems
Sporotrichosis	Fungus	Skin	Teachers, health and social workers
Staphylococcal Infections	Bacteria	Nervous system	Health workers
Swine H1N1 Flu	Virus	Inhalation / Skin	Farm workers
Tetanus	Bacteria	Nervous system	Any
Tuberculosis	Bacteria	Lungs	Health and social workers, miners with silicosis
West Nile Virus	Blood	Skin	Outdoor workers

It is the job of the joint health and safety committee or health and safety representative to evaluate the biological hazard control measures in place at their workplace. In health care in particular, there are many measures and procedures that require the employer and committee to work together to evaluate the effectiveness of the program. Some of these include hygiene practices, control of infections, immunization, and soiled waste.

Joint committees and health and safety representatives may want to monitor handwashing, hygiene practices, and housekeeping as well as review absenteeism rates, and WSIB statistics for illnesses related to infectious diseases. In health care, at least once a year, the employer along with the joint health and safety committee or health and safety representative is required to review the programs and, if necessary, make recommendations for improvements. This is good practice and can be adopted in any sector.

COVID-19

Coronavirus Disease 2019 (COVID-19) is an infectious disease caused by a new coronavirus. The 2019 coronavirus causes a respiratory infection that originated in Wuhan, China. The first presumptive case of this infection in Ontario was identified on January 25, 2020. On March 17, 2020 Premier Doug Ford declared a state of emergency in the province of Ontario. The state of emergency originally prohibited organized public events of over 50 people. This later decreased to five. It closed restaurants and bars (except for take-out and delivery) indoor recreation centres, theatres, concert venues, private schools, daycares, and libraries. Grocery and convenience stores, pharmacies, public transit, manufacturing facilities, construction sites, and office buildings were allowed to remain open. The list of essential services decreased as time passed.

The pandemic mandated control measures in workplaces that were not familiar with managing biological hazards. As with any biological hazard, it is important to understand how it can be transmitted. COVID-19 is mostly spread by contact and droplet exposure. In rare cases, like during a procedure in a hospital setting, COVID-19 may become airborne.

Direct contact transmission occurs when the reservoir and the susceptible host touch each other. In other words, direct contact transmission occurs when transfer of microorganisms results from direct physical contact between an infected or colonized individual and a susceptible host (body surface to body surface). This happens when an infected person shakes hands with an uninfected person and the uninfected person touches their mouth, eyes, or nose before handwashing.

Indirect contact transmission involves the passive transfer of microorganisms to a susceptible host via an intermediate object, such as contaminated instruments or other inanimate objects in the immediate environment. Some other object carries the infectious organism from the reservoir to the host. Early research shows that the virus can last up to four hours on copper, 24 hours on cardboard, two to three days on plastic and stainless steel.

Droplet transmission is a form of contact transmission but requires special considerations. Droplet transmission refers to large droplets generated from the respiratory tract of the infected person during coughing or sneezing. These droplets are propelled a short distance, less than two metres, through the air and deposited on the nasal or oral mucosa of the new host. Large droplets do not remain suspended in the air.

Contact and droplet transmission enter the body by ingestion.

Using the hierarchy of controls, workplaces can manage this new virus. This pandemic is causing drastic changes to work environments and the economy and affecting the mental health of workers. Out of this this experience, will come innovation. Joint heath and safety committees and health and safety representatives will contribute to the advancements.

Elimination
- Setting up work-from-home arrangements for employees, where possible
- Conducting virtual meetings and training sessions
- Postponing in-person training and meetings
- Postponing all non-essential travel
- Temporarily closing down non-essential workplaces
- Requiring sick employees to stay at home and not spread the virus at work
- Eliminating non-essential visits by members of the public and contractors to workplaces and conducting appointments virtually, where possible

Engineering Controls
- Increasing ventilation rates in the workplace
- Installing physical barriers. These include locked doors with limited access to the public and contractors. Sneeze guards between shoppers and cashiers are in this category.
- Using drive-through windows

Administrative Controls
- Increasing sanitation and housekeeping in the workplace. This includes wiping down frequently-touched surfaces with cleaners known to kill viruses.
- Increasing medical monitoring for those workers who have high exposure to the virus
- Following pandemic plans and writing policies/procedures to manage several of the items that lead to the elimination of the virus spreading
- Instituting daily call-in meetings to keep workers up to date as the situation evolves
- Requiring workers to advise HR if they or a close contact has been diagnosed with COVID-19

- Requiring workers to self-isolate if they have been out of the country, or have come in contact with someone being tested for, or who has been diagnosed with COVID-19
- Providing current and factual access to current information on the pandemic
- Providing training for workers to implement any new measures, including donning and doffing personal protective equipment
- Creating social distancing opportunities in all aspects of work
- Adding shifts to the workday or week, so there is less contact among employees
- Staggering breaks and lunch periods
- Avoiding touching eyes, nose, and mouth
- Teaching employees to sneeze into their elbow or cover coughs or sneeze with a tissue, then throw the tissue in the trash, followed by 20 second hand washing
- Communicating with customers about the control measures in the workplace, and asking them to abide by the new rules
- Providing soap and water to employees and customers to wash hands
- Teaching workers how to properly wash hands for 20 seconds
- Providing hand sanitizer (at least 60% alcohol) when soap and water is not readily available
- Posting "Wash Your Hands" signs in all washrooms, "Stay Home if You are Sick" at all entranceways

Personal Protective Equipment
- Providing personal protective equipment as appropriate. This may include gloves, goggles, face shields, face masks, and respiratory protection, in front line health care jobs.

The joint health and safety committee and health and safety representative have an important role to play during a pandemic. Lessons learned will assist in planning for the next pandemic.

Review

Biological agents are living things, or products of living things. Biological agents include viruses, bacteria and fungi as well as parasitic worms and some plants.

Biological agents enter the body by inhalation, by ingestion or by absorption through the skin. Viruses, bacteria and fungi can be passed from one person to another. Infectious agents are transmitted by direct physical contact or by indirect transmission.

Indirect transmission can occur from injection. This could result from man-made sources such as a needle-stick from a used needle with a blood borne pathogen or an insect bite from a mosquito (West Nile Virus or malaria).

Biological hazards may be controlled at the source by eliminating or isolating the hazard. Biological safety cabinets are a common means of isolating and controlling biological hazards. Immunization programs prevent some illness and are therefore a control at the source.

Control along the path involves cleaning and waste disposal. Personal protective equipment along with safe work practices and training are means of control at the worker.

In the winter of 2020, COVID-19 gripped the world and affected every workplace. A thorough understanding of biological hazards is critical to keeping workers safe. As with all types of biological hazards, this virus can be controlled using hierarchy of controls.

Joint health and safety committees and health and safety representatives are integral to monitoring the effectiveness of the hazard controls for biological hazards.

Chapter 13

Musculoskeletal Hazards

- Health Effects

- Assessing Musculoskeletal Hazards

- Controlling Musculoskeletal Hazards

- Evaluating Musculoskeletal Hazard Control Measures

- Review

Musculoskeletal Hazards

Musculoskeletal disorders are a serious workplace hazard. They are the number one reason why workers file a claim and lose time from work.

The musculoskeletal system has two main parts. One part is the skeleton with its 206 bones. The other is the system of skeletal muscles attached to the bones. They give the body its ability to move. The musculoskeletal system also includes the tendons that connect the muscles to the bones, cartilage that covers the ends of the bones which form joints, and ligaments that bind the joints together and connect the bones. Tendons, cartilage, and ligaments are known as connective tissues.

Blood vessels and nerve systems provide the musculoskeletal system with oxygen and communication with the brain.

Work design hazards can create a situation that may cause injuries to parts of the musculoskeletal system. These injuries are known collectively by a number of titles. Some examples are musculoskeletal disorder (MSD), repetitive strain injury (RSI), and cumulative trauma disorder (CTD).

Injuries of the musculoskeletal system (MSD) make up an increasing proportion of workplace health problems. The explanation lies in the design of many jobs, both new and old, that require repetitive motions and strain on the part of the worker. One example is the supermarket cashier who must repeatedly perform lifting, pulling, twisting, and bending motions while at the same time operating a cash register and weigh scale.

Health Effects

Hazards caused by poor work design have received increasing attention as the incidence of reporting musculoskeletal injuries has increased. Many musculoskeletal conditions have been recognized for a long time. Bursitis of the knee is a painful, work-related condition that was once called housemaid's knee. Many other musculoskeletal injuries are identified by their occupations, rather than by their medical names. Thus we have postman's shoulder, carpet layer's knee, and telephone operator's elbow.

Musculoskeletal System

Connective Tissues

- Tendon: a fibrous tissue that connects muscle to bone. Tendons are inelastic and strong and vary in length and thickness.

- Cartilage: a tough, fibrous tissue that protects and connects bones. Cartilage has no nerves or blood supply.

- Ligament: a resilient and flexible fibrous tissue that binds joints together and connects bones and cartilage. The ligament allows joints to move while preventing their dislocation.

Musculoskeletal Disorders of the Arms and Legs

The most common musculoskeletal disorders of the arms and legs are described here using their medical names.

Bursitis

A bursa is a sac filled with fluid that lubricates joints like the knee, elbow and shoulder. It also protects other parts of the musculoskeletal system like the connections between tendons and bones and tendons and ligaments.

Bursitis is the condition that develops when the bursa swells and inflames. Carpet layers are susceptible to bursitis of the knee. Supermarket cashiers who work with stationary scanners are susceptible to bursitis of the elbow. Bursitis in the shoulder can be traced to tasks that involve exertion while the arms are lifted to shoulder height or above. The symptoms of bursitis are pain and limited mobility of the affected joint.

Epicondylitis

Epicondylitis is inflammation of the muscles and other connective tissues around the elbow joint. A cause of this condition is frequent rotation or twisting of the forearm, and exertion with a bent wrist. It is a problem common to workers who use hand tools, such as carpenters, electricians and pipefitters and is frequently called tennis elbow. Frequent picking up and carrying of heavy objects is another cause. The condition causes pain and swelling at the elbow.

Carpal Tunnel Syndrome

The carpal tunnel is a tunnel formed by the bones of the wrist covered by a fibrous sheath. It encloses the tendons that connect the arm muscles to the finger bones. It also surrounds the median nerve that controls most of the fingers. The term syndrome means a group of symptoms associated with an illness.

Carpal tunnel syndrome can occur when the tendons in the carpal tunnel become inflamed and swollen from overuse. They put pressure on the median nerve, causing carpal tunnel syndrome. The symptoms of this problem are tingling and numbness, most pronounced in the index and middle fingers and most often experienced at night. As the condition worsens, it causes burning and constant pain. The hand becomes clumsy and weak so that tools or other objects are hard to hold. Non-work-related conditions that may contribute to carpal tunnel syndrome are diabetes, hypothyroidism and pregnancy.

Carpal tunnel syndrome is most frequently seen in data entry workers, cashiers and meat cutters. All these jobs involve rapid and repeated motions of the fingers and hand. In many cases these motions are accompanied by exertion while the wrist is bent or by other types of body strain.

Ganglion Cyst

A ganglion cyst is a closed, fluid-filled sac which develops in a tendon sheath or the capsules around joints. This disorder is most often found in the wrist. Ganglion cysts are often not painful and may be caused by repetitive or forceful motion or a constrained position.

Tendinitis

Tendinitis is an inflammation of the tendon arising from small tears or wounds in the tissue. Because tendons have almost no blood supply they heal very slowly. When use of the tendon continues, it may become inflamed.

Tendinitis is most common in the tendons of the hand, wrist, shoulder, and forearm, but the foot and ankle may also be affected. The affected area becomes red and swollen and it is painful and tender. Hairdressers, sewing machine operators, and painters are among the workers frequently affected because they often work with their arms in unnatural postures for prolonged periods.

Tenosynovitis

Overactivity of the tendons from repeated motions and exertion, as well as awkward postures, causes inflammation of the protective sheath that surrounds them. The tendon sheath produces excess lubricating fluid which causes it to swell. A sudden increase in exertion may bring this condition on quickly, in which case it is described as acute tenosynovitis.

Tenosynovitis commonly occurs in the fingers and wrists. The hand becomes painful and swollen and difficult to use. It is most frequently seen in workers such as sheet metal workers who use cutting shears and data processors. It can also lead to carpal tunnel syndrome because it puts pressure on the median nerve.

Trigger Finger

Trigger finger is a non-medical name for chronic tenosynovitis. It results when the tenosynovitis is not treated and repeated movements and exertion of the fingers, thumb or wrist continue. The tendon sheath reacts by growing thicker, restricting the movement of the tendons or stopping it altogether. The index finger is the one most often affected, especially where a vibrating tool must be operated by finger pressure against a trigger or other control that is narrow or has sharp edges. The symptom is an inability to move the finger, sometimes accompanied by pain and swelling. Trigger finger is most frequently experienced by miners and assembly-line workers who use trigger-activated tools.

Common Musculoskeletal Disorders
Arms and Legs
• Bursitis
• Epicondylitis
• Carpal tunnel syndrome
• Ganglion cyst
• Tendinitis
• Tenosynovitis
• Trigger finger
• Sprains
• Strains
• White finger disease

Sprains and Strains

A sprain results from over-stretching of the ligament around a joint causing the ligament to tear. It causes pain, swelling and discoloration. Twisted ankles and wrists are examples. A strain is an injury to a muscle caused by overstretching. Some fibres of the muscle are torn by overuse, causing pain and swelling. Those in jobs that require bending, twisting, and lifting are at risk.

White Finger Disease

Known as vibration-induced white finger disease, this condition is caused by the impact of vibrating tools on the fingers. Continual use of such tools as jack-hammers, rock drills, and chain-saws causes the small blood vessels in the fingers to go into spasm. Given enough rest, they will recover their normal shape. Continuing exposure to vibration makes recovery difficult and may cause permanent damage to the blood vessels and nerves.

Victims of white finger disease experience tingling and numbness of the fingers. These signs are accompanied by swelling and stiffness of the knuckles and then whitening of the surrounding skin. Fingers become clumsy and difficult to use. The condition results from constriction of the blood vessels.

White finger develops more rapidly when vibrating tools are used in cold temperatures. Over years of this kind of work, the person's fingers become more and more sensitive to cold temperatures. Those most frequently affected include workers in forestry, mines, and construction.

Musculoskeletal Injuries of the Back

The spine encloses and protects the spinal cord. Its bones and their associated muscles allow the body to bend and twist. The spine and its muscles together are often referred to as the back. The back is susceptible to injury from work that involves harmful postures and practices.

Back injuries are a major cause of lost time from work. In some cases, this condition will prove to be chronic or continuing. It is often difficult to link back pain to a particular back injury or defect.

Degenerative Disc Disease

With increasing age, the discs which separate the vertebrae of the back gradually dry out and flatten. This brings the vertebrae closer together and reduces the space available for nerves and other tissues. Sometimes the space becomes so small that nerves are irritated, causing pain.

Degenerative disc disease is part of the aging process, but it can be accelerated by postures which put pressure on the discs. Jobs that involve long periods of sitting carry this risk. Examples are drivers and some office workers.

Herniated Disc

This condition arises from tiny rips or ruptures in the wall of the disc. These ruptures may allow some or all of the gel-like fluid in the disc to bulge. This reduces the ability of the disc to act as a cushion between the vertebrae and thus places pressure on the spinal nerves. The result may be pain in the back and legs.

Pinched Nerve

Pinched nerve can happen when a spinal nerve is caught between the vertebrae or when a bulging herniated disc puts pressure on the nerve. The symptoms of a pinched nerve may include pain, tingling, and numbness in the leg. Weakness of the leg may also be a sign of a pinched nerve. The pain felt in the leg is known as referred pain. The pain actually originates in the back but is referred or passed on to the leg.

The pinching of a spinal nerve can arise from degenerative disc disease or from a herniated disc.

Sprains and Strains

As with the ankles and wrists, sprains and strains of the back occur when the ligaments or muscles of the back are overstressed. Lifting and handling activities can lead to sprains or strains of the back, particularly when heavy exertion is required and awkward postures are assumed.

Common Causes of Musculoskeletal Disorder

Certain hazards or factors in work design increase the risk of musculoskeletal disorder. These include job demands; posture, exertion, repetition, and vibration. They also include workplace components; work station design, tools and equipment design, manual materials handling, work environment design, and work organization design.

Posture

The posture of a person's body at work can cause or contribute to a musculoskeletal disorder. Workers who must stoop, bend, crouch, or squat to do a job risk musculoskeletal disorder. Construction work often involves awkward postures.

Other occupations that involve awkward postures include nurses, ambulance attendants and child care workers. Even postures that are apparently comfortable can be risky if they are held too long. Sitting and standing tasks, like desk jobs in banks or offices or at checkout counters, can cause back, neck and shoulder problems and pooling

Musculoskeletal Disorders

The Back

- Degenerative disc disease
- Herniated disc
- Pinched nerve
- Strains and sprains

Back Injury Risk Factors

Connective Tissues

- Weight of the object being lifted or handled
- Distance of a lifted load from the spine
- Bending or twisting of the spine while lifting or handling
- Distance over which a load is carried
- Awkward shape or size of the load
- Frequency of lifting or other load handling activities
- Obstacles which interfere with a lifting or carrying activity
- Strength of the person
- Absence of convenient handholds on the load
- Deconditioned muscles

of the blood in legs if proper controls are missing. No one position is healthy for extended periods of time.

Exertion

Exertion, or force, is the amount of work a muscle must do to perform an action. Whether it's holding a heavy object or pushing against a lever to operate a tool, exertion is involved. Exertion is also needed to hold the body in a particular posture.

Muscles do static work even when the body is not moving. Holding a particular body posture like standing or sitting involves static work. Static work involves the risk of decreased blood flow and waste product build-up. The opposite of static work is dynamic work where the muscles alternately contract and relax to exert force and make the body move. Dynamic work is generally easier and healthier unless it requires abnormal exertion.

Common Causes of Musculoskeletal Injury

- Posture
- Exertion
- Repetition
- Vibration
- Workstation design
- Tools and equipment
- Manual material handling
- Work environment
- Work organization

Forceful exertion overloads the tendons and ligaments associated with muscle movement. Injuries to this connective tissue can occur regardless of the individual's muscle strength, or the weight involved. For example, a forceful grip may be needed to lift an article that is slippery or difficult to grasp because it has an awkward shape. Shippers and receivers in warehouses, garbage collectors, and health care workers may suffer back or other musculoskeletal injuries from manual lifting and from improper lifting.

Localized pressure and impact force are other factors in forceful exertion. The operator of a heavy staple gun exerts strong hand or finger pressure and may risk a trigger finger injury.

Repetition

Repeated movements affect the muscles, joints and connective tissues over time. When the same muscles are used again and again without rest, they begin to ache. This aching is the outward sign of muscle and/or connective tissue distress. Constant contraction or pull on the muscle decreases the flow of blood and with it the supply of nutrients. It also prevents waste products from being removed. Muscles begin to tire and cramp and other nearby muscles, not designed for the work, try to take over. This leads to further tiredness and cramping. The muscles are less able to stabilize the joints and the system becomes more prone to strain and sprain injuries.

In assessing the risk connected with repetitive work, four factors should be considered:

- frequency: how often the repetitive motion must be done;

- speed: how fast the motion is performed;

- duration: the period over which the repetitive work continues without rest; and

- position: the posture that the worker must assume.

Some kinds of jobs involve a lot of repetition. Data entry operators may have to do repetitive keying, sometimes with a bent wrist. Poultry processing and assembly line work are other examples. Without proper work design, persons in these and similar occupations may be at risk of an occupational injury.

Physical Condition
Muscles that are deconditioned due to illness, injury, inactivity, or aging are more vulnerable to musculoskeletal disorder.

Vibration
Vibration can affect the entire musculoskeletal system or certain parts of it. Vibration might be called externally-induced repetition.

The musculoskeletal disorder most often linked to vibration is white finger disease. Vibration from hand tools like chainsaws and jackhammers impacts on the blood vessels and sensory nerves that serve the fingers, hand and arm. This deprives the muscles of blood and affects the transmission of nerve impulses. It allows waste matter to accumulate in the muscle tissues.

Vibration can also affect the legs, because some workers do their jobs on vibrating surfaces and because vibration can be communicated from one part of the skeleton to another. Whole body vibration can be a special risk for drivers of vehicles.

WorkStation Design
The workstation is the specific place where a person works. Parts of the workstation design include work heights, reach distances, layout, sitting and standing durations, and displays and controls. If the workstation does not fit the physical dimensions of the worker, it will cause the worker to assume awkward postures and unnecessary force.

Much has changed in the design of the workstation. Health care professionals and workers on a shop floor are often keyboarding at computers while standing and sharing the space with multiple workers. Ergonomic design principles must be used to allow for the adjustability required and to minimize discomfort and workplace injuries.

Tools and Equipment

Workers need tools to do their jobs. These tools must be adequately designed for a natural grip that does not require a lot of force. Tools should not have pressure points on them, which can lead to contact stress, numbness, and a decrease in grip strength. Workers need to be able to work while holding their hands, and arm in neutral body positions. Tools must also minimize vibration.

Manual Material Handling

Manual material handling involves lifting, carrying, lowering, pushing, pulling, and shoveling. All of these activities can lead to muscle strains, tears, and pulls. About half of the injuries sustained while handling materials involve the lower back. Other vulnerable areas include the shoulders, arms, and abdomen. Good health practices, work procedures, and training can help to alleviate these effects.

Work Environment

A number of environmental factors in the workplace can also contribute to musculoskeletal disorder. These include temperature, vibration, and lighting. Working in extreme temperatures can put the body under heat or cold stress, as discussed in Chapter 9. And as discussed above, vibration may harm parts of the musculoskeletal system. Glare and the lack of direct lighting can force workers to adopt awkward postures in order to see their work. This can lead to eye, neck, and shoulder strain.

Work Organization

The organization of work includes such factors as how, when, and where a job is done, how quickly it is carried out, and the systems of compensation and supervision used. Poor work organization can contribute to a musculoskeletal disorder because workloads may be badly distributed, and individuals may be required to work under excessive pressure. Certain types of incentive systems are believed to contribute to the numbers or severity of incidents in some industries. For example, loggers are often paid based on the number of trees they cut, which encourages them to work long hours. The lack of adequate training is another work organization factor that can contribute to musculoskeletal injuries.

Interaction of Factors

Repetition, exertion, posture, and vibration can operate independently to cause musculoskeletal disorders. They may also operate in combination with each other or with other environmental factors.

The design and organization of work can potentially cause harm to the body by placing stresses and strains on the musculoskeletal system. The elements of work design include the design of the workstation, tools and equipment, the physical environment, and general work organization.

When these elements are not designed properly, they can overload and damage the muscles, tendons, ligaments, and associated nerves and blood vessels of the musculoskeletal system.

Work design affects those who work in a wide variety of occupations and workplaces. In addition to industrial workplaces, these include offices, health and other human care facilities, construction sites, warehouses, and service establishments.

Poorly designed work may involve frequent and prolonged repetitive movements combined with exertion from lifting, pressure on tools, or using improper lifting procedures. These factors may be further combined with awkward or uncomfortable postures and vibration. In addition, some or all of these combined factors may be at work in an environment of abnormal heat or cold or be aggravated by the effects of bad lighting. Some jobs in construction, forestry, and mining may combine all of these risk factors.

Assessing Musculoskeletal Hazards

Assessing work design hazards requires observation of individual job functions and work processes. When jobs are analyzed this way, factors like repetition, exertion, posture, and vibration can be measured. Environmental influences like temperature and lighting can also be taken into account.

To be effective, the assessment should be based on a thorough inspection which includes a careful job hazard analysis and interviews with workers and supervisors. Job hazard analysis is described in Chapter 9. Workplace inspections are covered in Chapter 17.

Controlling Musculoskeletal Hazards

The control of musculoskeletal hazards is based on a science called ergonomics. Ergonomics studies the relationship between work and the human body. The aim of ergonomics is to fit the work to the worker. Effective ergonomic design provides work stations, tools, and equipment which are comfortable and efficient for the worker to use. It also creates a work environment that is healthy, and it reorganizes the work process to control or eliminate hazards.

The Human Body
To fit the work to the worker, the capabilities and limitations of the human body have to be considered. Ergonomics borrows from a number of other fields of study for this purpose.

Anthropometry, a division of anatomy, provides data about body size and measurements like height, reach, and hand size. This information is used to help design work stations, tools, and equipment which are better suited to the human anatomy.

Physiology is the study of body functions. It helps in evaluating the physical demands of a job.

This data helps designers find ways to minimize muscle fatigue, blood pooling, and pressure on joints as well as friction on tendons and their protective sheaths.

Biomechanics studies the application of force or exertion in work activities like lifting, pushing, and pulling. Designers use this knowledge to find ways of getting the work done while minimizing the amount of exertion or stress on the musculoskeletal system. Psychology is the study of human behaviour. Knowledge of psychology can help ensure that equipment controls and displays are not misleading or confusing. It can also influence the design of the general work environment or surroundings.

The Design of Work

The design of work to fit the worker involves the application of engineering principles. The workers who do the jobs and the supervisors who organize and oversee the process know a lot about the design problems of a particular job. They should be consulted for ideas and information that can help in the redesign of work.

Work or job design examines the separate elements that make up the job. The objective is control or elimination of those work factors that cause or contribute to musculoskeletal injuries and other injurious health effects.

Work Design Elements

- Workstation
- Work Environment
- Tools and Equipment
- Work Organization
- Manual Material Handling

Workstation Design

Workstations are the particular places where people work. A workstation might be on an assembly line in an auto plant or at a desk in an office. Good design of a workstation will eliminate risk factors that might cause musculoskeletal injuries. It is also likely to increase efficiency and productivity.

Since workers come in different sizes and shapes, it's important that the workstation be able to accommodate these differences. A good guide to the principles of workstation design is the modern automobile. Auto makers must design the driver's seat and controls so that any driver can sit in comfort and conveniently operate the controls while maintaining a good view of the road ahead. The design of the driver's station thus allows the driver to react quickly and safely to changes in road or traffic conditions.

Workstation design requires application of the same principles. These can be summarized as designing for extremes and designing for adjustments within the extremes.

Designing for extremes, rather than averages, is a principle observed in many aspects of life. If the doorways in homes and workplaces were designed to fit the average person, those taller than average would regularly bump their heads. Workstations should be constructed to accommodate extremes of height, reach, leg length, and body shape.

Designing for adjustments allows individuals to adjust elements of the workstation across a range between the extremes so that their body features are accommodated comfortably. Ergonomically-designed computer work stations, for instance, have adjustable seats and armrests, tiltable keyboards, and movable monitor screens so that any user can adjust the work station for comfort and efficiency.

Reach and Arm Comfort

In general, workstations should be designed to permit workers to easily reach any object or control involved in the work, whether it is hand or foot operated. Hand controls are easiest to operate when they are placed between shoulder and waist level. It should not be necessary for the person to work with elbows or arms raised or to hold the arms away from the body or above shoulder height. Armrests may help those who must do delicate assembly work.

Ergonomists have devised guidelines for the placement and height of work surfaces which are most comfortable and efficient. For instance, for fine assembly work done by a standing worker, the worktable or work surface should be about 5 to 10 centimetres above the elbow height of the worker. Different distances apply to assembly of medium and heavy components. This means that the position of the worker or of the work surface, or both, should be adjustable to allow for the correct distance for the kind of job being done.

Chairs

Every workstation should be equipped with a chair or stool, where possible and practicable, even if most of the work is done in a standing position. Chairs give workers a chance to change body positions and reduce fatigue by getting their weight off their feet. In some jobs, like that of the supermarket cashier, the opportunity to sit and stand at intervals while continuing work can greatly ease strain on the legs, arms, and back. Adjustable sit/stand stools are best for this purpose.

Attached or separate footrests allow changes in posture and the easing of pressure on the feet. When the chair is not adjustable, footrests can provide support for people with short legs which might otherwise dangle above the floor.

Standing Surfaces

The floor or other surface on which the worker stands at the workstation can be equipped with a shock-absorbing pad to minimize pressure on the feet or to reduce the effects of machine vibration which is transmitted through the floor.

Instrument Displays

The instrument displays at workstations should be at or below the eye level of the worker. This means that seat height should be adjustable and that displays should be readable without the person having to bend or stretch.

Space

Work areas should not be cramped or crowded. People need sufficient room so that they can vary their body postures to relieve strain on particular muscles.

Work Environment Design

A properly designed workplace takes environmental factors into account. The environment includes temperature and humidity, lighting, air quality, and vibration.

Temperature and Humidity

The workplace atmosphere should be designed to maintain comfortable levels of temperature and humidity. For instance, cold is a well-known contributor to vibration-induced white finger disease. In addition, excessive dryness, dampness, cold, or heat produces discomfort. Discomfort tends to impair a person's concentration and accuracy, and this in turn can reduce attention to safe work practices. It also reduces the individual's work efficiency.

Some workplaces require abnormal conditions of temperature or humidity. For example, the molding of clay to make bathroom fixtures requires a humid atmosphere. Design features in such cases may include air-conditioned control rooms for operators.

Outdoor work can involve extremes of both temperature and humidity depending on the season. Protective clothing and indoor rest breaks may be necessary in such cases.

Ventilation

The circulation of fresh, clean air in the indoor workplace helps to ensure healthy working conditions. Stale air may cause discomfort. The placement of walls and room dividers should not restrict the flow of fresh air. Ventilation should circulate the air in the workplace without blowing it directly on those who work there.

Lighting

Lighting levels should be appropriate to the job. Every worker should have a clear view of the work. No one should be forced to bend and peer to make up for poor lighting. Intricate assembly requires more light than more general work. Special adjustable task lamps may be required to light some work, like technical drawing or woodworking.

Glare from computer screens can be adjusted by lighting and/or by the use of non-glare displays or by the installation of shields. In addition, proper positioning of computer workstations can reduce glare and reflection from windows and other reflecting surfaces.

Vibration

Vibration in the workplace environment can increase strain as muscles try to compensate. Where the vibration is caused by machinery, the source machines can be equipped with shock absorbing mounts. Shock absorbent floor coverings at workstations and shock absorbent footwear and gloves are less effective alternatives.

Tool and Equipment Design

Tools and equipment include such diverse items as screwdrivers, computers, and heavy machinery. Poor design of tools or equipment can cause musculoskeletal injury. Tools and equipment should be designed or adapted for ease and comfort in use. A job hazard analysis can help to ensure that the tools are properly suited to those who must use them. Some general rules apply to the design and selection of tools and other work equipment.

User-Friendly Tools

User-friendly tools are those that can be gripped without discomfort or slippage. Their use should not require an unnatural or uncomfortable hand position. Examples can be seen in the ergonomic design of knives for poultry processing. Traditional straight-handled knives have been replaced with angled handles. These permit the user to perform the cutting task while maintaining the wrist in a neutral, unbent position. Greater force can be exerted with hand tools that allow the worker's wrist to stay in the neutral position.

Hand tools should also be designed to accommodate both left-handed and right-handed users, and to incorporate non-slip handles. A tool that can be used in either hand helps workers to relieve strain by periodically switching hands. Thermoplastic grips gradually mold themselves to the shape of the user's hand.

Shock Absorption

Both powered and non-powered hand tools can transmit harmful vibration to the body of the user. Some tools use vibration-dampening materials to reduce the amount of vibration transmitted in this way. This design feature is particularly important in the case of vibrating power tools like chainsaws, jackhammers, and rock drills which cause musculoskeletal disorders such as white finger disease. Some vibrating tools or equipment can be mounted in special cradles so that the user can control them without absorbing vibration.

Balance and Torque Absorption

A well-designed tool is correctly balanced. Its centre of gravity is located close to the operator's body, close to the handles and in line with the centre of the operator's hand. Unbalanced power tools generally produce excess noise and vibration and require a tighter grip by the operator's hand.

Some hand-held power tools, like heavy twist drills, exert considerable torque. Torque is a twisting force in the direction opposite to the drill motion. A badly designed tool can injure the wrist by suddenly pulling on the user's arm. Proper tool design will involve double handles or other features to prevent injury from torque.

Convenient Location of Adjustment Mechanisms and Other Controls

Some equipment requires operators or maintainers to assume uncomfortable postures to carry out maintenance or make adjustments. Some have badly placed controls that require abnormal wrist positions or exertion to operate. When such equipment is being replaced or renovated, care should be taken to relocate controls, where possible, so that they can be used without discomfort or risk of musculoskeletal disorders.

Regular Maintenance of Tools and Equipment

A regular preventive maintenance program keeps tools and equipment in safe working order. Maintenance includes the sharpening of knives, chisels, and other hand tools. Poorly maintained equipment may generate excess noise and vibration. It may also increase the exertion required of the worker.

Work Organization Design

When and where people work, and at what pace, are important factors in the control of musculoskeletal injury. Muscle and tendon strain from repetitive work is the cause of injuries like carpal tunnel syndrome and tendinitis. Where repetitive work cannot be avoided by control at the source, the reorganization of work can provide the necessary relief.

Workers and supervisors can provide valuable advice in the design and redesign of work organization.

Machine and Incentive-Paced Work

Some improperly engineered machine-paced and incentive jobs can lead to musculoskeletal disorders. Where possible, employees should be involved in the establishment of work standards so as to give the individual the ability to perform the work appropriately and meet production targets by the application of skill and good work organization.

Where workers operate under incentive rate systems, workloads and quotas should not push them beyond their physical capacities.

Relief from Repetitive Work

Continual repetitive work motions have been identified as the direct cause of a number of musculoskeletal disorders. Where changes in equipment or processes cannot be used to eliminate repetitive tasks, the reorganization of work can provide relief.

Relief from repetitive tasks can take the form of regular rest breaks or the rotation of tasks. Alternate tasks allow workers to rest some muscles while they are exercising others. Task rotation may also involve a greater variety of body postures during a work shift. These kinds of work organization help prevent musculoskeletal injuries from developing.

In some jobs, it may be possible to assign a number of related tasks to a group of two or more individuals. They can then decide for themselves how to divide the work.

Material Handling

The manual movement of materials in the workplace is a major cause of injury to the back. The avoidance of injury through the reorganization of work is an important preventive control. The elimination of manual lifting is a major step in this direction. It requires the substitution of mechanical lifting devices. For example, many hospitals use a mechanical lifting device to transfer patients in and out of beds. Where some manual lifting is still required, it can be made less risky by the installation of convenient handholds on containers and by smaller loads.

Manual lifting can also be made easier by devices such as spring-loaded pallets which keep the lifting surface at a constant level. Mechanical conveyors, forklift trucks, and other specialized material-handling equipment are the best substitute for the manual carrying of loads over distances.

Containers which display their weight on a label can help workers to recognize lifting hazards and get the necessary assistance from other workers or mechanical devices. Written work practices for safe material handling should be developed and workers trained in how to follow safe operating procedures.

The control of work design hazards requires the application of ergonomic principles so that work is fitted to the worker. These principles can be applied to the design of the work station, the work environment, tools and equipment, and to the organization of the work.

Evaluating Musculoskeletal Hazard Control Measures

As with all hazards, one must evaluate the success of the controls that have been implemented. This can be done through observations and when completing workplace inspections. Are workers using the controls and are they using them correctly? Evaluate whether new hazards have been introduced. It is appropriate to ask workers if they feel the control measures are working. This can be done one-on-one or more formally, with a survey. If workplace injuries continue to show up, do not be discouraged; those injuries may be a result of exposure to hazards far before the control measures were implemented. Focus on worker comments, body mechanics, and feedback from supervisors.

Review

Musculoskeletal Disorders (MSD) can result from hazards created by faulty work design. MSD is a rapidly growing cause of lost time and production in Ontario.

The human musculoskeletal system consists of the skeleton, made up of 206 bones, together with the skeletal muscles and connective tissues. It also includes the network of blood vessels and nerves which serve the system.

Poor work design can cause musculoskeletal disorders of the arms and legs and their joints, and injuries of the back. MSD may be caused by repetitive motions of the arms and legs, by exertion of the muscles, by abnormal working postures, and by vibration from hand-held power tools and equipment.

The control of work design hazards involves the application of ergonomics to the workplace. Ergonomics is known as the science which fits the work to the worker. The use of ergonomics in the design of workstations, the work environment, tools and equipment, and of work organization can reduce or eliminate the risk of musculoskeletal disorders to workers.

Once control measures are implemented, it is important to evaluate the effectiveness of the controls.

Chapter 14

Psychosocial Hazards

- Stress

- Violence

- Harassment

- Organizational Stressors

- Health Effects

- Assessing Psychosocial Hazards

- Controlling Psychosocial Hazards

- Evaluating Psychosocial Hazard Controls

- Review

Psychosocial Hazard

A psychosocial hazard is any hazard that affects the mental well-being or mental health of a worker. Psychosocial hazards include, but are not limited to stress, violence, and harassment.

Stress

Stress is a normal component of the body's response to demands that are placed on it. When we are frightened or angry, the body responds to this stress with a number of physical reactions that prepare it for action. Factors that trigger this stress response are known as stressors.

Stressors are encountered in almost every aspect of our lives. Excess stress, or distress, has been identified as an important factor in many types of illnesses. Heart disease is one of the health effects that has been linked to excessive stress. Workplace stressors can lead to distress because they are, in many cases, beyond the individual's control. The individual may be exposed to the same stressors day after day. Occupational stress is often the combined effect of several stressors. The health effects of different stressors cannot be easily separated. Nonetheless, an understanding of the different types of stressors is essential to recognizing, assessing and controlling these potential hazards. Workplace stressors include physical and organizational factors.

Physical Stressors
The body has automatic mechanisms that attempt to protect it from physical agents such as noise and extreme temperature. Physical stressors can be harmful because they force body systems to continuously compensate for conditions that are outside the normal range.

Exposure to excessive heat and excessive cold may be workplace stressors. Other physical agents that cause excessive stress are high levels of noise and vibration.

Workstation design may cause excessive stress. Heavy manual labour may have similar effects. Work on rotating shifts may place the body under physical stress, because the body's natural cycles, known as the circadian rhythm, are forced to readjust. Several days may be needed for this adjustment to take place, when workers change from one shift to another. In the meantime, their appetite, sleep, body temperature and blood pressure may be affected.

Violence happens in our communities, and therefore, also at work. In Ontario, in 2007 the Workplace Safety and Insurance Board (WSIB) registered 2,150 allowed lost-time claims that were attributed to assaults and violent acts. By 2018, that number increased to 4,179. This may be in part, to an increased recognition, and therefore reporting of violence in the workplace.

In Ontario, on December 15, 2009, Bill 168 received royal assent. Bill 168, the *Occupational Health and Safety Amendment Act* (Violence and Harassment in the Workplace) 2009 amended the *Occupational Health and Safety Act* (*OHSA*) to impose new obligations on employers with respect to workplace violence and harassment. It came into force and became law on June 15, 2010.

"Workplace violence" means:

a) the exercise of physical force by a person against a worker, in a workplace, that causes or could cause physical injury to the worker;

b) an attempt to exercise physical force against a worker, in a workplace, that could cause physical injury to the worker; or

c) a statement or behaviour that it is reasonable for a worker to interpret as a threat to exercise physical force against the worker, in a workplace, that could cause physical injury to the worker.

Domestic violence is also part of the legislation and therefore employers "who are aware or ought to be aware" must protect workers from incidents of domestic violence that may occur in their workplaces.

Harassment

In Ontario, workplace harassment is defined as "engaging in a course of vexatious comment or conduct against a worker in a workplace that is known or ought reasonably to be known to be unwelcome, or workplace sexual harassment." Employers also have to be aware of the Human Rights definition of discrimination as discrimination is a type of harassment.

Harassment occurs when someone:

- makes unwelcome remarks or jokes about someone else's race, religion, sex, age, national or ethnic origin, colour, sexual orientation, marital status, family status, or a conviction for which a pardon has been granted or a record suspended;

- threatens or intimidates; or

- makes unwelcome physical contact with you, such as touching, patting, pinching or punching, which can also be considered assault.

Workplace harassment may escalate to threats or acts of physical violence or a targeted worker may react violently to prolonged harassment in the workplace. It is important for employers to recognize these behaviours and to deal with them promptly because they could lead to workplace violence.

Sexual Harassment

In July 2016, the *Occupational Health and Safety Act* was amended to include workplace sexual harassment.

Workplace sexual harassment means "engaging in a course of vexatious comment or conduct against a worker in a workplace because of sex, sexual orientation, gender identity or gender expression, where the course of comment or conduct is known or ought reasonably to be known to be unwelcome, or making a sexual solicitation or advance where the person making the solicitation or advance is in a position to confer, grant or deny a benefit or advancement to the worker and the person knows or ought reasonably to know that the solicitation or advance is unwelcome."

Organizational Stressors

Organizational stressors result when people face anxiety or frustration from aspects of their work that they cannot control. Examples include situations where people are not able to exercise their full skills and knowledge potential or may not understand what they produce, and how. They may face conflicting demands. They may not receive the respect or recognition they expect for their accomplishments. Organizational stressors may cause specific reactions in the body that can lead to potential health effects. One European study correlates the degree of stress with the amount of responsibility and control a person has over the job.

Work Overload or Underload
A person may become frustrated at work due to a number of circumstances, such as repetitive tasks without the opportunity for variation or for undertaking greater responsibility and learning, and not receiving adequate recognition.

Excessive work demands may be stressful and potentially lead to emotional stress when they exceed the person's capabilities. Excessive work without appropriate breaks may also be stressful. Work overload may weaken a person's confidence in their own abilities and adequacy to do the job.

Role Uncertainty and Role Conflict

The responsibilities placed on individuals are often positive aspects of their work. Meeting responsibility and "doing a good job" are important factors in self-esteem. Where job responsibilities conflict or are unclear, work can be confusing and frustrating and may lead to excessive stress.

Responsibility for Others

Jobs which involve accepting responsibility for the care and welfare of other people can be emotionally draining. The distress that results can eventually lead to a condition known as burnout, which means that the person is emotionally and physically exhausted. People in this situation may begin to blame themselves when things go wrong or become indifferent towards the people in their care. This can happen without the affected person even being aware of it. Health care, custodial, and social workers are particularly vulnerable.

Isolation

When a person feels, or is in fact, isolated for long periods of time, they may become stressed. Some work processes separate people and can create feelings of isolation, which may cause stress.

Job Satisfaction

Lack of job satisfaction may contribute to excessive stress. The lack of promotional opportunities or restrictive job functions and uncertainty about job performance may be contributing factors.

Job Security

A concern for job security may contribute to stress. A feeling of insecurity can come from several sources. The potential for layoffs due to lack of work, job loss due to discriminatory dismissal, and sexual or racial discrimination or harassment are examples of stressful situations.

Health Effects

Individuals respond differently to psychosocial hazards. Personality, general health, and the support of friends and colleagues all affect this response. A group of people exposed to the same type of stressors may experience different health effects. Nonetheless, the body's physical response to stress is generally the same for everyone. It is commonly known as the generalized stress response.

Excessive stress has been associated with heart disease, high blood pressure, digestive ailments, skin rashes, insomnia, nervous or emotional disorders, substance abuse, and interpersonal and family dysfunction.

As long as stressful experiences are brief and infrequent, the body quickly returns to normal. In nature, this phenomenon is known as the fight or flight reaction. A person who is in a continuous state of stress throughout every working day may experience a wide variety of potential health effects.

Assessing Psychosocial Hazards

In accordance with the *OHSA*, employers with more than five employees are required to assess the risk of violence in their workplace. The assessment must consider the nature of the workplace, the type of workplace, conditions of work, and circumstances specific to the workplace. The results of the assessment must be shared with the joint health and safety committee or health and safety representative, if the assessment is in writing. It is recommended that this assessment be written.

The standard CSA Z-1003/BNQ 9700-803 *Psychological Health and safety in the Workplace – Prevention, promotion, and guidance to staged implementation,* was developed by the Bureau de normalization du Québec (BNQ) and the CSA group, in 2013. It addresses psychological health and safety aspects which are within the control responsibility, or influence of employers. These aspects may have an impact within, or on, the workplace.

The model identifies thirteen workplace factors to assess. They include:

1. Psychological support;
2. Organizational culture;
3. Clear leadership and expectations;
4. Civility and respect;
5. Psychological job demands;
6. Growth and development;
7. Recognition and reward;
8. Involvement and influence;
9. Workload management;
10. Engagement;
11. Work/life balance;
12. Psychological protection from violence, bullying, and harassment; and
13. Protections of physical safety.

As well as assessing the 13 identified risks, the model recommends that the employer identify and assess opportunities to promote psychological health.

Another assessment tool which is available to workplaces is Guarding Minds @ Work (GM@W). It is a set of resources designed to promote psychological health and safety in the workplace. GM@W's free resources address the 13 psychosocial factors. GM@W was developed by researchers from the Centre for Applied Research in Mental Health and Addiction (CARMHA) within the Faculty of Health Sciences at Simon Fraser University.

An employer that is interested in assessing their risk to psychosocial hazards in the workplace has a number of excellent resources available. The members of the joint health and safety committee have an opportunity to be involved in choosing a method and tool that best fits the workplace.

Controlling Psychosocial Hazards

Excessive stress may be controlled or reduced by eliminating the source of the excessive stress, or by helping people to cope. Control at the source is preferable where it is possible and practicable.

Control at the source may involve changes to the physical environment or to the organization or conditions of work. Physical stressors, such as excessive temperatures, or noise and poor air quality, may possibly be reduced or eliminated. Workstations may be designed to reduce repetitive and strenuous movements.

Excessive stress caused by shift work may also be reduced. Eliminating shift work is usually impossible, but schedules can be designed on a forward rotating basis to minimize the disruption of body rhythms. Ideally, the persons on shift should be involved in developing their schedules.

Organizational stressors may be eliminated or controlled through changes in working conditions, such as job rotation. Increased job responsibilities and opportunities allow people to learn and apply new skills. Employee involvement in the decision-making process, clear work assignments to avoid work uncertainty, and policies that eliminate harassment and discrimination in the workplace can help to reduce excessive stress.

Controls along the path such as administrative controls are required. The *OHSA* obligates employers with more than five employees to implement violence and harassment programs, based on the hazards identified in the workplace.

Administrative controls include understanding the relationship between health and productivity. Some programs which may help in workplaces include:

- support of work/family/life issues,

- flextime,

- part-time schedules,

- child-care benefits,

- personal leave,

- wellness-health programs,

- family counselling,

- intranet pages so that employees can obtain accurate information on stress/mental health,

- courses for employees on how to cope with stress,

- free counselling for all employees available during the working day,

- Mental Health First Aid courses for employees,

- social events to promote healthy lifestyles such as showing a film (at lunchtime or after work) about a health-related topic and providing an opportunity to discuss issues arising with experts,

- individual assessment of employee lifestyle (perhaps as a work benefit) and helping them plan for a healthier future,

- genuine concern for employee welfare, and

- nurturing relationships with colleagues.

Controls at the worker are also important. Programs to help employees cope with excessive stress include employee assistance programs (EAP). Some companies conduct seminars for this purpose. Workplace meetings that allow people to share their views about work procedures and design and organizational issues may also help.

It is also essential that workers maintain regular eating patterns, which include a balance of fruits, vegetables, proteins, and dairy products. Workers need to sleep as normally and routinely as possible. They should eat family meals together regularly and remember that exercise and social activities are important.

Generalized Stress Response

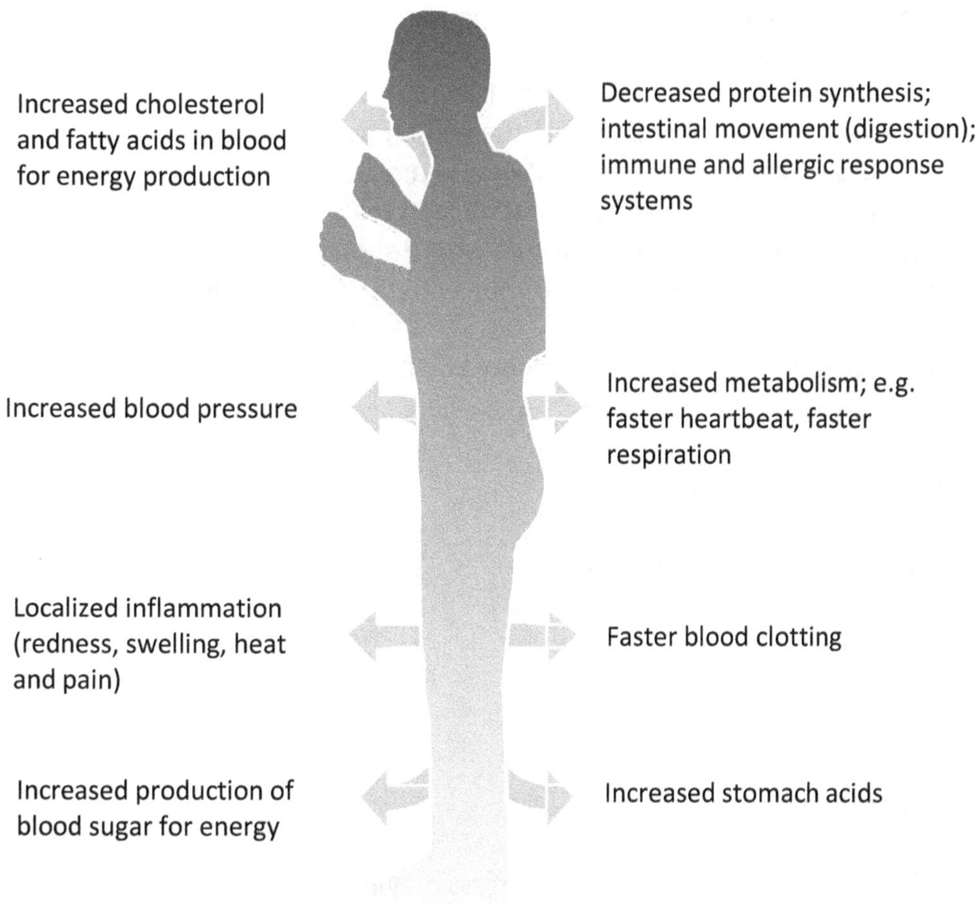

Source: Occupational Health and Safety: A Training Manual, 1982

Evaluating Psychosocial Hazard Controls

As with all other control measures, the programs implemented to manage psychosocial hazards, must be evaluated. The evaluation may include a review of audit findings. Were corrective actions identified? Was the joint health and safety committee or health and safety representative involved in implementing new programs?

It is important to include staff and to find out what their perceptions are. Do they feel the psychological hazards have been reduced in the workplace? What do your statistics tell you? An employer may also choose to survey its employees to get anonymous feedback on the value of control measures implemented in the workplace. This feedback should be shared with the joint health and safety committee or health and safety representative.

Psychosocial hazards include stress, violence, and harassment.

Stress is a normal component of our everyday lives. Excessive stress is the effect of prolonged excessive physical or emotional pressure on the human body. Factors that may cause excessive stress, such as physical agents and organizational characteristics, are called stressors. Some physical agents such as excessive noise, vibration, and temperatures are stressors. Other physical factors that may lead to stress include workstation design, ventilation, and lighting. Shift work may cause excess stress by interfering with the worker's body rhythms.

Organizational factors which can lead to anxiety and frustration are also stressors and may include:

- Work overload or underload;

- Role uncertainty and role conflict;

- Responsibility for others;

- Isolation; and

- Job dissatisfaction;

The health effects of excessive occupational stress may be more severe where the causes are likely to be persistent and continual, and when the person may not have control over them.

The body reacts to excessive stress in different ways. The general pattern of physical reactions is known as the generalized stress response. Heart disease and high blood pressure and other health effects have been associated with excessive stress.

By law, employers are required to assess the risk of violence in their workplaces. There are also voluntary tools such as the CSA/BNQ standard and Guarding Minds @ Work to assist employers to assess and implement psychosocial/psychological programs in their workplaces. Employers can implement any number of programs to assist employees to balance work and life stressors.

Psychosocial hazards may be controlled by eliminating the source of the hazard or by helping people to cope. Where possible and practicable, the former approach is preferable. All control measures need to be evaluated, once implemented.

Chapter 15
Safety Hazards

- Machine Hazards

- Confined Space Hazards

- Material Handling Hazards

- Hand Tool Hazards

- Ladder Hazards

- Review

Safety Hazards

Safety hazards include machine hazards, confined space hazards, hand tool hazards, and ladder hazards. The specific hazards found in Ontario workplaces are too numerous to be covered in detail here. A number of hazards are common to many workplaces. These issues are the subject of this chapter. They are discussed in general terms, so that they are relevant to as many workplaces as possible.

Machine Hazards

Machines increase the efficiency of the workers who use them by substituting external energy for their own muscle power. Machines can be dangerous. The biggest hazard comes from moving machine parts which may come into contact with a worker's body causing injury or death.

Workers may be crushed when a part of their body or clothing gets caught in rotating shafts, belts, or pulleys. Body parts may be severely injured or even severed by presses, blades, and saws. Flying projectiles from materials or machine parts can puncture the body.

Burns from hot surfaces or exhausts and shock from contact with electrical wiring are also consequences of machine hazards. The consequences can be severe. In seconds, a worker can be crippled for life.

Ideally, machines should be designed so that moving parts, as well as heat and electrical sources, are enclosed or otherwise protected so they can never come into contact with a worker. If a machine has not been designed this way, external guards will be needed. The term guard refers to any device, barrier or equipment used to protect workers from contact with the moving parts of a machine.

Even where appropriate guards have been provided, a worker may still be injured by a machine if it malfunctions, if procedures are not followed, or if it breaks. Mechanical equipment deteriorates as it is used. Friction wears away moving parts. Material fatigue can lead to sudden fractures or other breakdowns. Machine components can be damaged or become misaligned because of vibration. Pumps, valves, filters, and mechanical mechanisms can become clogged with residue from work processes.

The unexpected failure of a machine can injure the operator or cause hazardous exposures to chemical, biological, or physical agents. Maintenance refers to a systematic procedure for inspecting and repairing machinery before it wears out or suddenly breaks down. Along with guarding and safe work procedures, maintenance is an essential ingredient of machine safety.

Machine Guarding

There are many different kinds of guards. They range from covers over pulleys and belts to barriers preventing workers' hands from coming near cutting or punching tools. There are several principles involved in their design and operation:

- A guard prevents human access to hazard points during normal operation of the machine.

- A guard should not create another hazard.

- Workers must be trained to use guards properly. They must understand the hazard being guarded, and they must know how the guard operates.

- Temporary protection must be provided when a guard is removed for any reason.

- When a guard is removed, it must be completely replaced and checked by trained personnel before work is resumed.

- The materials used for guards must be strong enough to withstand impact from internal and external forces.

A proper guard design takes into account all the possible exposures of workers to the point of operation or other machine parts under normal operating conditions. The design must also provide for safe maintenance procedures. When a machine is shut down for service, it may be necessary to test it with the guards temporarily removed or other safety measures bypassed. This should be done only under very carefully controlled circumstances.

Start-up Controls

There are a number of other safety devices used to protect workers from exposure to machine hazards. Strictly speaking, they are not guards because they are not a barrier to a hazardous part of the machine. Instead, they work by preventing the machine from starting until the operator is in a safe position.

There are many different types of start-up control. The following are the most common:

- Control covers prevent inadvertent operation of the control.

- Emergency stop controls, such as panic buttons, bars or pull cords, stop the machine in an emergency.

- Two-hand controls require the operator to have both hands on the controls, and therefore out of the machine, before it can be started.

- Presence-sensing devices stop the machine if a worker gets too close.

Another method of preventing worker contact with the point of operation is a pull back or hold back. Pull backs are devices that pull the worker's hands away from the machine when it is activated. Hold backs restrain the operator's hands from entering the danger zone.

Safe Work Practices for Guarded Machines

Guards are a widely used way of preventing incidents. To be effective, they must be used properly. This means following safe work procedures. There are several safe work practices that should be incorporated into any procedure for operating a guarded machine:

- Missing or defective guards should be reported to a supervisor promptly.

- Machinery should never be started unless all guards are securely in place and operating properly.

- No worker should remove, adjust or bypass any guard.

- Before guards are removed for adjustment or maintenance, the power to the machine must be turned off and a lock-out procedure put into effect. Lock-out procedures are discussed in Chapter 10.

- Workers using machines should not wear loose clothing or jewelry or leave long hair unconfined. Loose items can get past a guard and be caught in moving parts.

In addition to these general practices, a safe work procedure includes specific practices that account for the individual circumstances of the workplace.

Machine Maintenance

Preventative maintenance is an organized program for preventing the gradual breakdown or sudden failure of machines and equipment. A typical preventive maintenance program involves planned maintenance of critical parts according to a prearranged schedule. It includes periodic cleaning and lubrication as well as regular inspections of machine functions to detect faults. When defects are found, the parts are repaired or replaced. A preventive maintenance program includes maintenance schedules, procedures for keeping records of maintenance work, and procedures for ensuring the availability of spare parts.

Equipment Repairs

Repairs to equipment are sometimes needed between scheduled maintenance operations. Repairs are required any time the machine fails to operate within the manufacturer's specifications. Sometimes the needed repairs will be beyond the ability of maintenance workers, and factory-trained service personnel will be called in.

Repair work can be potentially hazardous because it often involves less predictable conditions. It is sometimes performed with guards and safety devices temporarily removed. Careful adherence to documented safe work procedures is the best protection.

What the Law Says

Preventive Maintenance

- The *Occupational Health and Safety Act* places a duty on employers to maintain equipment, materials and protective devices in "good condition".

- Some of the sector regulations include other requirements. For example, Section 93 of the Construction Regulation requires that equipment shall be maintained in a condition that does not endanger a worker.

A confined space is a fully or partially enclosed space:

- That is **not** both designed and constructed for continuous human occupancy, **and**

- In which atmospheric hazards may occur because of its construction, location or contents, or because of work that is done in it.

Confined spaces are found in a wide variety of workplaces. Examples include storage tanks, vats, vaults, trenches, pipes, ducts, and tunnels.

There are many hazards associated with confined spaces. Rescue operations in confined spaces also involve a number of specific hazards.

Atmospheric Hazards in Confined Spaces

The atmosphere in confined spaces can become hazardous due to limited air circulation. In addition, there may also be a build-up of toxic gases. The air may be contaminated by a material stored or retained there or by one that enters from outside. Confined space atmospheres are particularly hazardous because they can change very quickly and without warning.

Air testing by a trained and competent person must be carried out before entry into confined spaces where a hazardous atmosphere is likely to be present. Records of all test results must be kept. Even though the air is tested and found to be safe before a worker enters, contaminants can enter while the worker is inside or can be created by the work itself. These contaminants may be poisonous. They may form an explosive or combustible mixture when they combine with the air. They may irritate the skin or respiratory system, or they may displace oxygen and asphyxiate the worker.

The means of monitoring and controlling atmospheric hazards are specific to each situation. These controls include procedures for purging contaminated air from the confined space by pumping in cleaner air. Maintaining air circulation while workers are in the confined space is essential. The correct selection and use of personal protective equipment, especially respirators and self-contained breathing apparatus where it is required, is also an important control.

Other Hazards in Confined Spaces

Confined spaces, by their very nature, pose difficulties of getting in and getting out. Hazards may be associated with the work environment. They may be part of the work being done. Hazards may be inadvertently brought in from outside the space.

Getting workers and equipment in and out of confined spaces can be difficult. Openings may be small and in awkward locations. The openings may be large but may require the use of ladders and hoists which can hinder quick escape. Entry and exit routes must be carefully planned and kept clear or guarded.

In addition to the general hazard associated with entry and exit, confined spaces may involve a number of more specific hazards:

- Electricity is a special hazard in confined spaces because the enclosures themselves are often made of metal or have metal components or contain materials that can conduct electricity. All potential electrical hazards should be identified and locked out. Tools should be grounded, double-insulated and in good repair.

- Supply lines and pipes into confined spaces may contain substances that can spill into the confined space and endanger the people working there. They must be disconnected and blocked off.

- Working surfaces inside confined spaces may be constricted, irregularly shaped, sloped or elevated. This can increase the risk of slipping and falling. Work under these conditions must be carefully planned.

- Poor visibility from inadequate lighting, smoke, fumes, or mists creates additional hazards, which must be foreseen and controlled.

- Noise and vibration are intensified in confined spaces. The walls cause sound to reverberate, raising the noise level. Appropriate personal protective equipment may be needed.

- Extreme temperature and humidity are often encountered in confined spaces. Temperature and humidity must be taken into account when planning the work.

The key to controlling the hazards of work in confined spaces is to carefully evaluate the hazards and prepare detailed safe work procedures to avoid them.

Rescue Operations in Confined Spaces

A large percentage of fatalities associated with confined spaces occur during attempted rescues by coworkers. In Ontario, when work is done in a confined space, an onsite rescue plan is required. It is essential that there be an attendant outside the space, as well as people trained and equipped for rescue operations.

A worker entering a confined space often wears a safety harness with a lifeline attached. The free end of the lifeline should be secured outside the space under the control of an observer who is trained in first aid and cardiopulmonary resuscitation (CPR).

Self-contained breathing apparatus and reviving apparatus should be conveniently available outside, along with a safety harness and rope. The attendant requires a means to summon help from the rescue team.

Many other hazards may be associated with confined spaces. This brief overview is intended only as an introduction to the subject. Certified members and health and safety representatives should become familiar with confined spaces in their workplaces. They should also read the Confined Spaces Regulation 632/05.

Material Handling Hazards

Almost every workplace depends on the physical movement of material. Factories receive raw materials and ship finished products. Stores receive merchandise in bulk and break it down into smaller packages. Construction projects require large amounts of raw material. In fact, virtually every workplace depends on a regular flow of supplies.

Material handling is a major cause of injury. Injuries can result from manually lifting, moving, and carrying objects. They also result from incidents involving mechanized material handling equipment, such as fork-lifts and conveyors.

Preventing injuries during material handling requires an understanding of how the injuries happen. Quite often there is an engineering solution. Handling procedures may also need to be reviewed and revised. Walking and working surfaces may require improvement. Load sizes may be adjusted. Where this is not feasible, a number of workers may have to share the load. Sometimes material movements can be assisted by mechanical means. But mechanized material handling has its own particular hazards. These hazards must also be controlled.

Health care workers face particular problems in handling heavy loads. They are often called upon to move people with mobility issues. Most of the hazards associated with material handling also apply to these situations. Mechanical lifting devices and sufficient assistance from other workers to ensure the safety of both the patient and the worker are important controls. Manual material handling and the associated musculoskeletal hazards are discussed in Chapter 13.

Mechanical Material Handling

Mechanical material handling devices can help prevent damage caused by manual lifting. These devices include forklift trucks, conveyors, and cranes used in industry as well as the special lifting devices used to move patients in health care facilities. Mechanical devices may introduce new hazards. The hazards are specific to each type of device. Important categories of mechanical material handling equipment and the hazards that are associated with them are listed below.

- Fork-lift trucks are finely balanced and can easily overturn. These hazards can be effectively controlled by training fork-lift operators and others who work around them, by choosing the right equipment for the job, and by using the correct operating procedures.

- Cranes are hazardous because they move heavy material over spaces where people may be working, and they may come in contact with electrical cables. Each crane must have a safe working procedure that takes account of the specifics of the equipment and the locations in which it is used. Above all, crane operators need special training. For many types of cranes, a special Ontario operator's qualification is needed. The sector regulations contain detailed requirements for material handling and the use of cranes.

- Conveyors can be hazardous because of their many moving parts. There are many pinch points between pulleys, belts, and rollers. Injuries can happen when workers attempt to clear jammed mechanisms while the equipment is energized. These hazards can be controlled with enclosures and guards on moving parts, and by lockout procedures.

- Hand carts and trucks can be hazardous. Fingers and hands can be caught between the cart and walls or other stationary objects. A worker using a cart can experience arm, shoulder, or back strain. Safe working procedures are important to control the hazards from these vehicles.

- Patient-lifting devices can be hazardous. These hazards can be effectively controlled with proper training and assistance from other workers.

Hand Tool Hazards

Hand tools have many uses in our workplaces. It is important that workers use the correct tool for the job, that tools are maintained, and that workers receive appropriate training prior to using any tool.

Tools can lead to injuries. Tools which are designed to cut material, can also cut people. Workers can suffer puncture wounds, tissue tear, and abrasion injuries from hand tools.

There are many hazards associated with hand tools. Workers can be struck by tools. This may include being struck by a hammer while learning to drive a nail. A repeated motion from using tools can lead to a musculoskeletal disorder.

There are several safe practices which are associated with the use of hand tools. First and foremost, employers must ensure that workers have the proper tools to do the job, and workers must select the correct tool for the job. Opening a paint can with a screwdriver can lead to hand injuries. A wrench should not be used as a hammer. Every hand tool has a purpose and is designed accordingly.

Tools need to be inspected, maintained, and stored in a safe manner. Sharp tools should have a protective sheath around them when not in use. Workers must wear the proper personal protective equipment such as safety goggles and well-fitted gloves. Using tools as intended, maintaining them properly, receiving appropriate training, and wearing personal protective equipment will minimize the risk of worker injury.

Ladder Hazards

There are many types of ladders used in our workplaces. Ladders may be fixed or portable. They may be straight, extension, or stepladders and may be manufactured from wood, metal, plastic, or fiberglass. They can be light, medium, heavy, or extra heavy duty. They can be as short as two feet (stepstools), up to 18 feet for extra heavy-duty step ladders, and 40 feet or longer for extension-type ladders. Most ladders are manufactured, while others can be built for job sites, as long as stringent standards are met.

Even a good ladder can be a serious safety hazard when used by workers in a dangerous way. It is important therefore to use them correctly and take proper precautions to prevent a fall. Some simple rules to follow when using a ladder:

- Choose a ladder which is suitable for your use;

- Always inspect a ladder before use;

- Metal ladders conduct electricity and should never be used around electrical equipment;

- Tie-off ladders at the top and secure the base to prevent ladder from slipping;

- Face the ladder when climbing up or down;

- Always maintain three-point contact on a ladder;

- Place the ladder feet not less than ¼ and not more than ⅓ of the ladder's working length away from the base of the structure; and

- When using a straight ladder or extension ladder on a higher work surface, be sure to extend the ladder one metre (three feet) above the landing.

Workers need to be taught how to select and use ladders correctly. Ladders are not used for transporting materials. If someone is carrying material, he or she cannot maintain three-point contact. The worker needs to find another way to carry material or choose another tool for the job; perhaps a scaffold or elevated work platform.

Members of joint health and safety committees and health and safety representatives may observe and/or discuss these issues while completing monthly workplace inspections. This is one way to evaluate whether workers have and are using the proper tools for the job.

Review

Every workplace has its own unique set of hazards. Many of them are specific to the industry involved or the occupation of the worker. This chapter reviews several categories of hazards that are found in a broad variety of workplaces.

Machine hazards include the danger of workers being struck, cut or pinched by moving machine parts. Workers may also be injured from flying projectiles. There are two important methods for controlling these hazards. Machine guards prevent human access to hazard points during the normal operation of a machine. Preventive maintenance prevents the gradual breakdown or sudden failure of machines and equipment.

Generally, confined space hazards are enclosed areas in a workplace where there may be a hazardous atmosphere. Other hazards in confined spaces include difficulty of entry and exit, poor working surfaces, poor visibility, and extremes of temperature and humidity.

Material handling hazards result from mechanized movements of material. Mechanical material handling equipment can cause injury. Forklift trucks can tip over or run into workers. Cranes can strike fixed objects or drop heavy materials on people working below. Conveyors have many moving parts, including numerous pinch points.

Hand tools are powered by hand, or manual labour. Some hand tools found in our workplaces include hammers, pliers, wrenches, screwdrivers, and chisels. Choosing the proper tool for the job, as well as using it as it was intended will minimize the risk of injury. Hand tools need to be regularly maintained and stored safely.

There are many different types of ladders. Ladders can be fixed or portable. Portable ladders include step, platform, straight, and extension. Each ladder has its own use. Workers need to follow some simple rules when setting up and using ladders safely.

These are only the most common safety hazards found in the workplace. Certified members should be familiar with the specific hazards found in their workplaces, and the means of recognizing, assessing, controlling, and evaluating their hazard controls.

Chapter 16

Hazard Management Tools

- Completing a Hazard Management Tool

- Step One – Recognizing Hazards

- Step Two – Assessing Hazards

- Step Three – Controlling Hazards

- Step Four – Evaluating Hazard Controls

- Review

A Hazard Management Tool is an instrument that allows a step-by-step approach to hazard recognition, assessment, control, and evaluation of controls. There are many different tools available. It is important to choose one that fits the type of work that you do, and the sector within which you work. This manual adapts a tool which was developed by the Workplace Safety and Insurance board. The assessment portion uses a task-based qualitative risk estimation matrix found in the CSA-Z1002-12 (R17) Standard "Occupational Health and Safety – Hazard Identification and Elimination and Risk Assessment and Control".

Completing a hazard management tool brings together many concepts. On paper, one can see how a hazard is recognized, assessed, controlled, and how hazard controls are evaluated. It allows workers, managers, and members of the joint health and safety committee to have a conversation about hazards in the workplace.

Step One – Recognizing Hazards

Column A – What activity can cause an injury or illness?

Identify what job titles, work activities, and work areas to assess. Remember to think about tasks that may be performed in normal and abnormal or emergency situations.

Column B – What hazard groups (categories) can cause injury or illness?

An occupational health or safety hazard is anything in the workplace that has the potential to cause harm to the human body.

Hazards can be group as:

- Physical
- Chemical
- Biological
- Musculoskeletal
- Psychosocial
- Safety

Recognize

A	B	C
What activity can cause an injury or illness?	What hazard categories can cause injury or illness?	What potential hazards can cause the worker injury and illness?
• Job titles • Work activities	• Physical • Chemical • Biological • MSD • Psychosocial • safety	

The following factors contribute to creating hazards:

- **P**eople (training, supervision, coaching, education, communication)
- **E**quipment (protective equipment, repair and maintenance, adequate clearance)
- **M**aterials (correct use, size and shape, proper storage)
- **E**nvironment (noise, temperature, air quality, lighting, layout, housekeeping)
- **P**rocess (work design, workflow, reporting requirement, work practices, policies and procedures)

Review the following workplace information to help identify hazards in your workplace:

- Worker comments, feedback and reports of concerns
- Workplace inspection records
- Incident investigation reports, first aid reports
- Supervisor's inspection reports and shift notes
- Safety data sheets (SDSs)
- Hazard alerts or bulletins
- Regulations, technical standards and codes (e.g. building code, fire code)
- Industry best practices
- Manufacturer's instructions and specifications
- Established occupational exposure limits
- Human resources related data such as absentee records and turnover rates.

You may need to consult with a health and safety expert where specialized expertise is needed. It may be necessary to take measurements or samples to determine if a hazard is within recommended limits.

Column C – What potential hazards can cause the worker injury or illness?

Identify what potential hazards can cause injury or illness to the workers if exposed to each hazard.

For example:

- Exposure to chemicals
- Fall from heights or ladders
- Coming into contact with moving parts of machinery
- Exposure to noise
- Exposure to heat/cold extremes
- Exposure to situations where harassment and violence may occur.

Assessment of hazards should be carried out without taking into account any existing controls. This way, if controls fail, the risk is properly understood.

Assess			
D	E	F	G
How severe can the injury be? • Minor • Major • Permanent injury or death	What is the exposure to the hazard? • Infrequent • Frequent	What is the probability of occurrence? • Unlikely • Likely (use the answers from D,E, and F and plot on the risk estimation matrix)	What is the risk evaluation for this hazard? • Low • Medium • High • Very high

Column D – Severity: How severe can the injury be?

When determining severity, the worst credible severity of harm needs to be selected.

Severity	Level	Description
S0	Minor	Injuries that could require first aid treatment
S1	Major	Injuries that could require medical treatment (more than first aid)
S2	Permanent injury or death	Injuries that could result in permanent injury or death

Column E – Exposure to the Hazard: How often are workers exposed?

Estimating exposure to a hazard should take into account the reasons for assessing the hazard, the proximity to the hazard, duration of the work in the danger zone, the number of workers exposed to the hazard, and the number of tasks to be carried out.

Exposure	Frequency	Routine Non-Routine	Description
F1	Infrequent	Non-routine activities	Non-routine maintenance activity changeover (set-up), teaching
F2	Frequent	Routine activities	Activities performed multiple times as a part of production cycle or over successive production cycle activities conducted on a regular basis

Column F – What is the probability of occurrence?

Probability of occurrence refers to how likely it is that the person will come into contact with the hazard. It is necessary to consider each person's activities and how they relate to the identified hazard. All activities with a classification of "could happen" or "it's possible" are combined into the "likely" category. This is using a conservative approach.

Probability	Unlikely or Likely	Description
P1	Unlikely	It is unlikely that the person can come into contact with the hazard or get hurt
P2	Likely	It is possible or likely that the person can come into contact with the hazard or get hurt

Column G – What is the risk evaluation for this hazard?

Severity + Frequency + Probability = Risk

The purpose of risk evaluation is to assist in making decisions about whether work should be done, which risks need to be controlled and in what order or priority, and future actions.

Plot, using the risk Estimation matrix, the Severity from Column D, the Frequency of Exposure from Column E, and the Probability of Occurrence from Column F. This helps determine the level of risk for each hazard. It also helps to prioritize hazards so that the hazards with the highest risk are controlled first.

Severity	Frequency of Exposure to Hazard	Probability of Occurrence	Risk
S0 Minor	F1 Infrequent	P1 Unlikely P2 Likely	Low Low
	F2 Frequent	P1 Unlikely P2 Likely	Low Low/Medium
S1 Major	F1 Infrequent	P1 Unlikely P2 Likely	Medium Medium
	F2 Frequent	P1 Unlikely P2 Likely	Medium Medium/High
S2 Permanent Injury or Death	F1 Infrequent	P1 Unlikely P2 Likely	High Very High
	F2 Frequent	P1 Unlikely P2 Likely	Very High Very High

When the risk is identified as low, no action is required. Improvements should be made when feasible. For medium, high, and very high-risk work, work may require a redesign to remove hazards. In addition, using the hierarchy of controls, other safeguards will need to be implemented.

Column H – What legal requirements and/or standards apply to the identified hazards, work processes, work activities?

Identify the legal requirements and standards as they apply to the identified hazards, work processes, and activities.

Ensure that all legislative authorities and standards / guidelines are consulted. This will ensure that what should be in place is known to the managers, supervisors, and workers. If the standards are not being met, then the changes can be put into the Hazard Assessment Tool under Column J for future consideration.

Legislation/Regulations/Standards are subject to change from time to time and should always be consulted during this review process.

Control		
H	I	J
What legal requirement or standards apply to the identified hazards, work processes, work activities?	What is currently being done to eliminate or control the hazard?	What future actions are needed to eliminate or control hazards? Apply hierarchy of controls.

Column I – What is currently being done to eliminate or control the hazard?

Identify which control measures are currently in place.

Column J – What future actions are needed to eliminate or control hazards?

Ideally, controls should be designed to eliminate a worker's exposure to the hazards. Make sure the hazard controls do not create new hazards. You should work through the hierarchy of controls:

- Eliminate the hazard or substitute with less hazardous materials;

- Use engineering controls to prevent access, limit exposure, or reduce energy available that may harm workers;

- Use administrative controls such as training, procedures, job rotation, housekeeping; and

- Use personal protective equipment, and ensure appropriate selection, use and maintenance of it.

Remember controls like personal protective equipment only control the exposure to the hazard not the hazard itself.

Column K – Severity: How severe can the injury be now?

After implementing controls, you should reassess the hazard with the control measures in place to determine if the hazard has bene eliminated or adequately controlled. The goal is to reduce the risk to an acceptable level. The workplace will need to decide how to proceed when risk levels cannot be reduced to acceptable levels.

Using the same method as in Column G, plot the answers from Columns K, L & M on the Risk Evaluation Chart to determine the risk level in column N.

Communication and Ongoing Monitoring of Hazards and Controls

Implementing controls for hazards is not the end of the journey. Communication is important for keeping everyone involved, informed and up to date. Ensure workers know the hazards that were identified, the risks associated with the hazards, and the measures to be used to eliminate or control the hazards.

Monitor for continuing effectiveness of controls and reduce the risk further as better control measures become available. Look for changes in the workplace that may require adjustments in the methods of controlling hazards. At the very least review all your hazards annually.

Evaluate

K	L	M	N
How severe can the injury be now?	What is the exposure to the hazard now?	What is the probability of occurrence now?	What is the risk evaluation for this hazard now?
• Minor • Major • Permanent injury or death	• Infrequent • Frequent	• Unlikely • Likely (use the answers from K, L, and M and plot on the risk estimation matrix)	• Low • Medium • High • Very high

HAZARD MANAGEMENT TOOL

Name of Firm:	Assessment Date:	
Person Completing:	JHSC/Representative Review Date:	
Work Area/Department:	Sr. Management Review Date:	Signature:

RECOGNIZE			ASSESS				CONTROL			EVALUATE			
A	B	C	D	E	F	G	H	I	J	K	L	M	N
What activity can cause an injury or illness? • Job titles • Work activities	What hazard categories can cause injury or illness? • Physical • Chemical • Biological • MSD • Psycho-social • Safety	What potential hazards can cause the worker injury and illness?	How severe can the injury be? • Minor • Major • Permanent injury or death	What is the exposure to the hazard? • Infrequent • Frequent	What is the probability of occurrence? • Unlikely • Likely (use the answers from D, E, and F and plot on the risk estimation matrix)	What is the risk evaluation for this hazard? • Low • Medium • High • Very high	What legal requirement or standards apply to the identified hazards, work processes, work activities?	What is currently being done to eliminate or control the hazard?	What future actions are needed to eliminate or control hazards? Apply hierarchy of controls	How severe can the injury be now? • Minor • Major • Permanent injury or death	What is the exposure to the hazard now? • Infrequent • Frequent	What is the probability of occurrence now? • Unlikely • Likely (Use the answers from K, L, and M, and plot on the risk estimation matrix)	What is the risk evaluation for this hazard now? • Low • Medium • High • Very high

Severity	Frequency of Exposure to Hazard	Probability of Occurrence	Risk
S0 Minor	F1 Infrequent	P1 Unlikely P2 Likely	Low Low
	F2 Frequent	P1 Unlikely P2 Likely	Low Low/Medium
S1 Major	F1 Infrequent	P1 Unlikely P2 Likely	Medium Medium
	F2 Frequent	P1 Unlikely P2 Likely	Medium Medium/High
S2 Permanent Injury or Death	F1 Infrequent	P1 Unlikely P2 Likely	High Very High
	F2 Frequent	P1 Unlikely P2 Likely	Very High Very High

This tool brings together many concepts discussed in Section Two of this manual, including the hazard categories; physical, chemical, biological, musculoskeletal, psychosocial, and safety. The five factors which contribute to a hazard are also included: people, equipment, materials, environment, and process (PEMEP). Assessment of hazards includes the severity, exposure to the hazard, and the probability of occurrence, to determine the risk evaluation of the hazard.

Next, hazard controls are applied, considering what is done presently, and what can be done in the future. Control measures are applied using the Hierarchy of Controls.

Finally, hazards are evaluated with the control measures in place.

Hazard management is ongoing. New equipment and chemicals may become available, workers will have new ideas, and legislation will change. A workplace that is committed to the health and safety of its employees will review hazards, jobs, and processes on an ongoing and regular basis. Members of joint health and safety committees and health and safety representatives have a vital role to play in the overall management of hazards

3 TOOLS

Chapter 17

Workplace Inspections

- Preparing for an Inspection

- Conducting an Inspection

- Review and Reporting

- Follow-Up

- Review

Workplace Inspections

The purpose of a workplace inspection is to identify hazards that could endanger the health or safety of anyone in the workplace. It can also determine whether established procedures are being followed.
An inspection achieves its purpose by seeking answers to four questions:

- Is a hazard or potential hazard present in the workplace?

- Is any worker or other person exposed or likely to be exposed to the hazard?

- Has anyone suffered injury or a health effect as a result of this exposure, or is anyone likely to do so?

- Are established procedures being followed?

Action can then be taken to control or remove the hazard in order to prevent work-related incidents, disease or injury.

Planned inspections are carried out at regular intervals both by the employer and by designated worker members of the joint health and safety committee in a workplace. In workplaces with 6-19 workers, a health and safety representative completes monthly inspections. Those completing the workplace inspections may cover the entire workplace or cover different work areas on separate occasions.

Inspections are not only for industrial workplaces, mines, and construction sites. Any kind of workplace can be involved. Laboratories, offices, warehouses, and stores may all contain hazards to health or safety. These hazards can be identified by inspection. The workplace might be a bus moving along city streets, or it might be a number of power line sites visited by a crew of hydro line maintainers.

- Section 8 of the *Occupational Health and Safety Act* requires a health and safety representative to inspect the physical condition of the workplace at least once a month.

- Section 9 of the *Occupational Health and Safety Act* requires the members of a joint health and safety committee who represent workers to designate one of their number, preferably a certified member, to inspect the physical condition of the workplace at least once a month.

- Different worker members of the JHSC may be appointed to perform separate inspections.

- If it is not practical to inspect the workplace at least once a month, the designated member or a health and safety representative is required to inspect the whole workplace at least once each year and some part of it at least once a month. In this case, a schedule of inspections will be established.

- The constructor or employer and the workers shall provide the designated member or health and safety representative with any information and assistance needed to carry out the inspection.

- The designated member must inform the JHSC of any situation discovered by the inspection that may be a source of danger or hazard to workers. The JHSC must consider this information within a reasonable amount of time.

An effective inspection is a procedure made of four stages:

- Preparation;
- Inspection;
- Review and reporting; and
- Follow-up.

To be effective, inspections should be planned and laid out in advance. Effective planning for an inspection will include reviewing available information, and assembling inspection tools, as well as other preparations.

Pre-Inspection Information

Pre-inspection information is specific information about work processes, hazards and controls that are present in the place to be inspected. This information will help the joint health and safety committee member and a health and safety representative to concentrate on the things most likely to need attention. Four types of data are important:

Pre-Inspection Information

Workplace Layout Data
- Building Pan
- Interior Layout, Showing Equipment and Machinery
- Process and Work Flow Patterns
- Hazardous Materials Used, SDSs, Labels, and Available Inventories
- Non-Work Access and Exit Routes and Emergency Exit Locations
- Access and Exit Routes and Emergency Exit Locations.

- Workplace Layout: What goes on where and when, and what materials are used?

- Standards: What legal regulations, industry standards and employer rules apply to the processes and equipment used in the work area?

- Controls: What controls, emergency procedures, and protective equipment are used there?

- Problem Indicators: What concerns have been reported about this area that may indicate potential hazards?

Workplace Layout

The data on workplace layout allows the persons conducting an inspection to visualize the layout of the area and the flow of the process or processes carried out there.

Standards and Controls

Standards indicate what legal regulations, industry standards or employer rules should be applied in the work area. These standards indicate what controls, if any, are in effect to establish control over known health or safety hazards. These are benchmarks against which the person conducting the inspection can measure what is actually happening in the work area. Where there are differences or deviations, they may indicate the presence of an actual or potential hazard.

Problem Indicators

Problem indicators may be identified from various reports regarding the area to be inspected. They include outstanding issues from previous inspections, first aid reports, incident reports, and the reports of complaint investigations. The person doing the inspection should read this information and look for trends or patterns that might indicate a potential hazard to be investigated.

In addition, the employer may provide other information which has a bearing on the area. It could be a recent scientific or medical report on a chemical used in the workplace. It might be an example of a safe work procedure adopted at another workplace in the same industry. These specifics may help the persons conducting the inspection to select items to be given more attention during the inspection.

Inspection Tools

Inspection tools help the person doing the inspection to ensure that all relevant items are examined during the inspection and that observations of these items are properly recorded.

The four most commonly used inspection tools are:

- block diagrams;

- process or operations flow charts;

- materials records; and

- machinery and equipment records.

In less complex workplaces, some of these tools may be unnecessary.

Block Diagram

A block diagram is a floor plan of a work area, showing the location of machines and equipment and other physical features of the area such as stairwells, ventilation ducts and so on. It will also show the dimensions of the area. Care should be taken to get the most recent versions so that renovations, or changes in the location of equipment, are incorporated. Differences between the plan and what is observed during the inspection can be noted on the diagram.

Process or Operations Flow Chart

The flow chart is a supplement to the block diagram or floor plan. It contains notes and diagrams that explain how the various elements of a process or operation interact with each other.

Flow charts are useful for any workplace, whether goods or services are produced. It is particularly suited to the study of material handling operations where lifting and moving takes place. It can also be used to analyze and separate job components in workplaces like hospitals and retail stores where workers move between different groups of clients, customers, or patients.

The flow chart will note where work is sequential, passing from one work station to another. It will also show where several operations are carried out separately but at the same time.

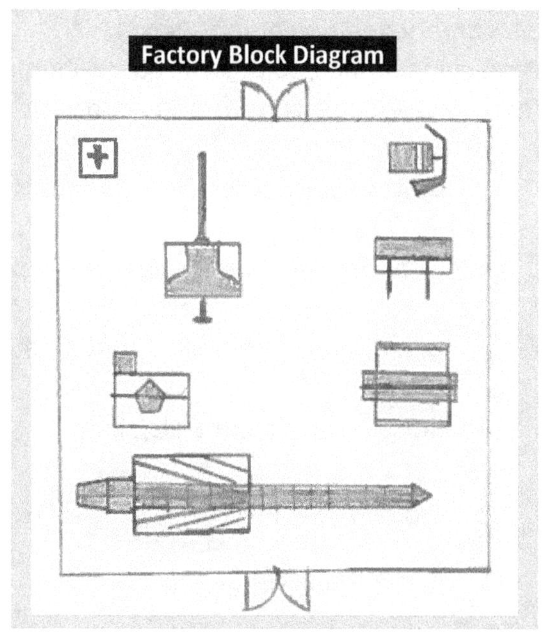

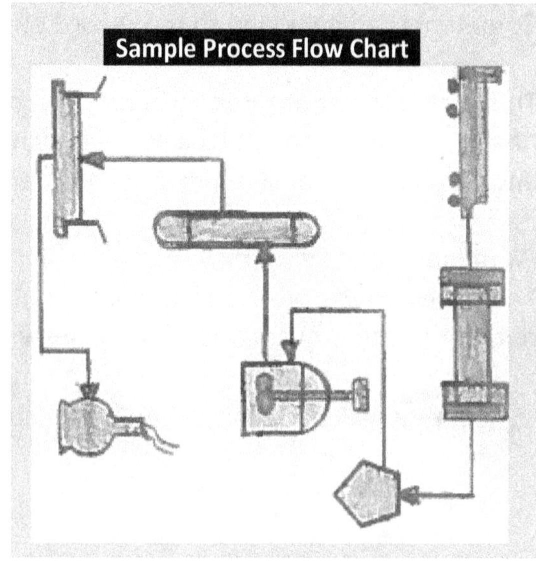

Materials Record

The materials record is a reminder of which materials are present in the work area and how they are used and stored there.

A materials record should include a brief description of known or suspected health effects and any air sampling results for the substance. Hazardous materials inventories, where available, safety data sheets, and other health and safety reports are good sources for the creation of a materials record.

Machinery and Equipment Record

A machinery and equipment record should describe each device used in the work area to be inspected. The description should include such details as:

- power source (electrical, hydraulic, etc.);

- location of exhaust outlets, air supply and methods of ventilation;

- guarding (on what parts of the device);

- noise level and controls, if any;

- ergonomic factors; and

- maintenance intervals.

Comments can be added to the record during the inspection.

These tools may not all apply in some workplaces. Where they are used, they will help the joint health and safety committee members and a health and safety representatives to save time and focus on the most important considerations.

Planning

The review of the pre-inspection information provides the basis for planning the inspection. A number of other questions must be answered:

- Who will participate in the inspection?

- How long will it take?

- Have the necessary arrangements been made to ensure entry to the work area?

- How will the inspection be organized? Where will it begin, what parts of the work area will be visited, and in what order?

This stage of inspection planning is also the time to make sure all required tools have been prepared and assembled and are ready for use.

The object of the inspection is to conduct a systematic examination of anything or any procedure that might pose a hazard to the health or safety of any person in the workplace. Examples include follow-up inspections of recently-installed controls to see if they are working, as well as verification of compliance with an inspector's order.

During workplace inspections, safety hazards are generally easier to detect than health hazards because they are usually more obvious and visible. The health hazards posed by inadequate ergonomic design, inadequate work practices, airborne dust, fumes or mists may be more difficult to recognize. They are not as readily observable. In addition, the health effects of these potential hazards are seldom immediately obvious.

Although inspections are meant to focus on the workers regularly employed in the work area, it is also important to be aware of others who move in and out of the area to conduct maintenance, make deliveries, or perform some other task.

As the physical inspection of the work area proceeds, the JHSC member or HSR should take advantage of two reliable inspection techniques:

- talk with workers and supervisors and consider expressed concerns and points of view; and
- use human senses, supported by adequate knowledge and training.

Talk with Workers and Supervisors
Sufficient time should always be allowed by JHSC members and HSRs to talk with those who work in the area. They may provide many insights into the way things work and alert the member to hazards they might otherwise overlook.

Changes in health, illness symptoms, or equipment problems may be revealed by workers or supervisors who are familiar with a work area. Workers and supervisors can also report whether the conditions at the time of the inspection are more or less typical or normal. JHSC members and HSRs conducting an inspection should ask if any changes have occurred since the previous inspection.

Information about the quality and suitability of training may also emerge from talks with workers and supervisors. Because of their knowledge and experience, they are often the source of useful suggestions or concrete proposals for health and safety improvements. Personal attitudes and human relations sometimes contribute to the existence or continuation of a hazard, and knowledge of these factors can only be learned from those in the work area.

Workers newly hired or transferred into the area should not be ignored. Often, they are able to pick up on potential hazards to which their more experienced colleagues have become accustomed or have not identified.

Using the Senses
The ability to see and identify potentially hazardous conditions is the most obvious use of the senses during an inspection.

The ear can detect noise and the nose and taste buds can sometimes discover the presence of gases, fumes, or vapour in the air. In either case, those who work every day in the area may have become so accustomed to these indicators that they ignore, or accept, the possible presence of a potential health hazard.

Adequate knowledge and training reminds the members that there may be potentially hazardous substances present which are colourless, odourless, and tasteless. The presence of potentially hazardous circumstances may be identified from conversations with workers and supervisors. This evidence may then be confirmed through further investigation.

Recording
Everything of significance and everything that prompts a question in the mind of the members should be recorded. Inspection tools such as floor plans, flow charts, and checklists are good places to record observations or questions. Observations that don't fit on one of these forms should be recorded separately, if necessary. Careful recording makes the later preparation of the inspection report relatively easy. It also helps to ensure that the report contains a thorough and useful account of the inspection. Consider a data management system in your workplace that can assign action items and track ongoing completion.

Review and Reporting

An inspection should begin with preparation and it should end with a report. The *OHSA* requires that the joint health and safety committee members report inspection findings to the joint health and safety committee. Before the report can be written, the information from both the preparation and inspection stages must be reviewed and organized.

A health and safety representative provides the inspection report directly to the employer.

Review
As soon as possible after the inspection, the member reviews the notes taken during the inspection together with observations jotted on the floor plan and flow chart.

Any potential hazards determined should be classified according to their potential for injury to health or safety. Obviously, hazards which threaten death, serious injury or illness should be given the highest priority for action. They must be reported to the employer or supervisor immediately.

Health effects and environmental monitoring results associated with these potential hazards should be listed for each potential hazard. The need for specific potential hazard assessments and exposure controls should be assigned in a similar fashion. Assessment and control measures for recognized hazards can then be given the right priority.

The members may conclude that further information is needed to help in the analysis. For example, it may be necessary to study monitoring results for a particular part of the inspection area in order to check out problems reported by workers or supervisors. Some of the information gathered in the preparation stage of the inspection may also help in the analysis. Careful organization and analysis of the facts can confirm a conclusion about needed controls.

Writing the Report

The report should be prepared as soon as possible following the inspection so that prompt action can be taken on any potential hazard which has been identified.

Basic Information

An inspection report must provide basic information about the inspection site, the date and time of the inspection and the name of the members who conducted the inspection.

Categorizing Hazards

Some workplaces assign a hazard category to hazards. A common practice is an "A", "B", and "C" system.

A Class "A" hazard is a major condition or practice that is likely to cause serious injury, permanent disability, death, or an extensive loss of building assets, equipment or materials within the workplace. This class must be dealt with immediately.

A Class "B" hazard is a serious condition or hazard that is likely to cause moderate harm resulting in a temporary disability, some property damage, but is not disruptive to operations. This class can be dealt with in a week's time.

Inspection Report Contents

Basic Information

- Work area inspected
- Date and time of inspection
- Name of person who performed the inspection

Findings

- Description of potential hazards identified
- Whether or not hazard was identified by previous inspection
- Other supporting information
- Conclusions about potential hazard cause

Recommendations

- Description of any corrective action taken during inspection
- Recommended control action

A Class "C" is a minor condition or practice that results in a first aid and non-disruptive property damage. This class can be assigned a longer time frame, for resolution.

Findings

The findings of the inspection consist of descriptions of any identified potential hazards, plus supporting information from the preparation stage or from further investigations carried out following the inspection.

A copy of the floor plan, flow chart or other inspection document should be attached to the report if it can help to pinpoint the location of a hazard.

Conclusions made by the members or the HSR should be noted last in the findings.

Recommendations

Recommendations should begin by noting any corrective action taken at the time of the inspection. Then recommendations for further investigation, control of the hazard, or for the collection of additional information should be described.

Report Forms

Special report forms are sometimes established to make the reporting process easier and faster. Forms also ensure that each inspection report follows a consistent order which makes it easy to understand. Increasingly popular data management systems capture the report immediately.

Prompt Action

The report should be handed over as quickly as possible to the joint health and safety committee for review. The committee will discuss the report, and may use it to help prepare recommendations for action that will be forwarded to the employer. Serious concerns should be immediately reported to the employer or supervisor. In workplace where a health and safety representative is required, he or she will make recommendations directly to the employer.

The inspection report becomes part of the permanent records of the JHSC or HSR and is available for study by a Ministry of Labour, Training and Skills Development inspector upon request.

The report should also be posted in the workplace for the information of workers and supervisors.

The member conducting the inspection must report any identified potential hazard to the JHSC, and the committee must review the report within a reasonable period of time. The HSR reports findings directly to the employer. All employees have an obligation to report any hazards to the employer.

The *OHSA* requires the employer to reply to a JHSC or HSR recommendation in writing within 21 days. The employer is not required to agree with a JHSC recommendation or to act upon it. The employer's duty is to comply with the *OHSA* and regulations.

The *OHSA* requires that, where the employer agrees with a joint health and safety committee or health and safety representative recommendation, a timetable for acting on the recommendation must be provided. Where the employer disagrees with a JHSC or HSR recommendation, the reasons for that disagreement must be provided.

Where the same hazard is repeated, or where agreed control action has not been taken, the JHSC or HSR may decide to hold a special discussion with the employer on this item. Further action may include a complaint to a Ministry inspector where a violation of the *OHSA* is claimed and the employer has failed to take corrective action on the recommendations.

The inspection report may result in a JHSC or HSR recommendation for further follow-up evaluation. This might take the form of a hazard-specific assessment, additional air sampling, a health survey to assess health effects, or a job hazard analysis to study a potential work design hazard. A follow-up report should include a list of proposed action required, the person responsible, and a target date for completion. Follow-up reports should also become part of the pre-inspection information reviewed in advance of further inspections in the same work area.

Thorough follow up of inspection reports and JHSC or HSR recommendations helps to ensure the prompt and effective control of potential health and safety hazards. Data management systems are a powerful tool to manage inspection follow up.

The purpose of a workplace inspection is to identify potential hazards that could endanger the health or safety of anyone in the workplace so that corrective action can be taken.

An inspection achieves its purpose by seeking answers to four questions:

- Is a potential hazard present in the workplace?
- Is any worker or other person exposed or likely to be exposed to a potential hazard?
- Has anyone suffered injury or a health effect as a result of exposure to a potential hazard or is anyone likely to do so?
- Are established procedures being followed?

Action can then be taken to control potential hazards and prevent work-related disease and injury.

The *OHSA* requires that a worker member of the joint health and safety committee be designated to conduct a physical inspection of all or part of the workplace at least once a month. The member so designated must prepare an inspection report to be given to the JHSC. In smaller workplaces and on some construction projects, a health and safety representative shall complete and prepare the report. The *OHSA* requires the employer to help the member or HSR with information and to provide other assistance.

In most workplaces, employer and worker member or health and safety representative conduct the inspection together. The frequency of inspections can be varied by agreement of the employer and worker representatives or by the inspector.

There are four stages to an inspection.

The **first stage** includes information gathering, the assembly of inspection tools, and other preparations. This process ensures that the members conducting the inspection are well informed about the area to be visited and better able to identify hazards. Inspection tools include floor plans of the area, flow charts of the work process, checklists, and other records.

The **second stage** involves the physical inspection of the workplace or work area. It should involve talks with workers and supervisors, and the use of the inspecting member's senses, knowledge and training to help detect hazards to identify hazardous situations that could develop under certain conditions.

Where hazards are discovered during the inspection that immediately endanger the health or safety of a worker, the member should take the steps required by law, and by the employer's health and safety program, to have the danger removed immediately. This includes immediately reporting the situation to the employer.

One purpose of the inspection is to verify that controls installed as a result of a previous inspection are in place and are working properly.

Immediately following the inspection, the member should carry out the **third stage**, which is review and writing of the report. The written report should state the place, date and time of the inspection, and name the person(s) who conducted it. The findings of the report should describe the potential hazards identified, classify them by priority categories and provide any other relevant information. Classification identifies those potential hazards that need immediate attention. The report may draw conclusions about the potential hazards that have been identified, and recommend controls to reduce or eliminate worker exposure to the potential hazard.

The report should be delivered to the JHSC as soon as possible so that it can be discussed at the committee's next meeting. It is the role of the JHSC to decide on recommendations to be made to the employer for action on the hazards. The HSR delivers the report directly to the employer and makes any necessary recommendations.

The inspection report becomes a permanent record and should be posted in the workplace for the information of workers and supervisors. It also becomes part of the pre-inspection information for the next inspection of that work area.

The **fourth and final stage** of the inspection is follow-up. Follow-up is intended to make sure that the information provided in the inspection report is acted upon in a timely manner. The *OHSA* requires an employer to respond in writing within 21 days to any written recommendation received from the JHSC or HSR.

Chapter 18
Incident Investigations

- Investigation Procedures

- Investigation Techniques

- Assessing Incident Trends

- Coroner's Inquests

- Review

Incident Investigations

Investigations and reporting are important tools for assessing and controlling potential health and safety hazards. The purpose of these activities is not to find fault or lay blame, but rather to identify causes of incidents so that controls can be put in place to prevent further occurrences.

Much has been written about the difference between "accidents" and "incidents". The social movement began in the early 90s.

The Collins English Dictionary defines an accident as "an unforeseen event or one without an apparent cause; anything that occurs unintentionally or by chance". It is difficult in occupational health and safety to consider a worker who falls to his/her death with no training, fall protection systems, or supervision, as a situation with no apparent cause.

The CSA Z1005-17 Incident Investigation Standard no longer uses the term "accident". It uses the following definition:

> **Incident** – An occurrence, condition, or situation arising in the course of work that resulted in, or could have resulted, in injuries, illnesses, damage to health, or fatalities.

This is the definition we will use in this reference guide. We will no longer use the term "accident", unless it is stated in legislation.

If an incident results in a fatality or a critical injury, the worker members of the joint health and safety committee will designate one or more of its members to investigate the incident. Only one of those designated members has the right to inspect the actual site, subject to the limitations set out in section 51 of the *OHSA*. In smaller workplaces, the health and safety representative has this right.

An important consideration in an incident investigation is that an incident rarely has a single "cause". Most often, an incident is the result of a number of contributing factors.

The purpose of an incident investigation is to prevent the reoccurrence of the incident. The focus should be on the incident, not the injury. It is essential to look beyond the immediate cause of an incident and look for the contributing factors and several causes. The biggest mistake that incident investigators can make is jumping to conclusions on the basis of immediate appearances. A proper investigation has to look deeper.

It is important to look beyond the immediate and superficial explanations to find the true causes of the incident. This doesn't mean that temporary action should not be taken to remove the immediate hazard. The investigation should continue until all the contributing factors have been identified.

There are a number of steps that can be taken to ensure that the investigation considers all of the possible causes. A systematic approach also ensures that no one else is endangered and that all reporting requirements are met.

Investigation procedures vary, but there are at least four major steps:

- secure and manage the scene;
- fulfil government reporting requirements;
- investigate causes; and
- prepare report.

The report may contain recommendations for corrective action. The investigator should follow up later to make sure that the recommended controls have been put in place.

Secure and Manage the Scene

The first priority is to provide first aid or medical response for anyone who was injured in the incident. A call to emergency services will send fire, ambulance and police to the scene. The job of the police is to determine whether criminal activity has taken place. The employer or supervisor is responsible for ensuring that the scene is secured so that there is no risk of further injury. Securing the scene also preserves evidence that may be important in the investigation.

If a workplace incident results in a death or critical injury, the *OHSA* states that an inspector's permission is required before the scene can be disturbed. Until

---

What the Law Says

Critical Injuries

Ontario Regulation 834/92 defines "critical injury" as an injury of a serious nature that:

- Places life in jeopardy;
- Produces unconsciousness;
- Results in substantial loss of blood;
- Involves the facture of a leg or arm;
- Involves the amputation of a leg, arm, hand or foot;
- Consists of burns to a major portion of the body; or
- Causes the loss of sight of an eye.

What the Law Says

Right to Investigate Incidents

- Section 8 of the *Occupational Health and Safety Act* specifies that a health and safety representatives shall investigate cases where a person is killed or critically injured.
- The HSR findings are reported in writing to a Director.
- Section 9 of the *Occupational Health and Safety Act* specifies that the worker members of a JHSC shall designate one or more of their members to investigate cases where a worker is killed or critically injured.
- The JHSC designated worker member's findings are reported to the JHSC and a Director.
- One of the worker committee members or health and safety representatives may inspect the place where the incident occurred.
- Time spent completing investigations is paid at regular or premium rate as may be proper.

such permission is received, no person may interfere with, disturb, destroy, alter or carry away anything at the scene of, or connected with the occurrence. There are exceptions for the purpose of saving life, relieving human suffering, maintaining an essential service or utility, or preventing unnecessary damage to equipment or property.

If the incident is serious, senior management must be informed immediately. They are responsible for contacting the families of injured workers and initiating investigation procedures. Management is also responsible for reporting the incident.

Fulfil Reporting Requirements

Management has a duty to report incidents and illnesses under a variety of circumstances. While not strictly speaking part of the investigation process, it is normally at this stage that the appropriate reports are filed. If the incident involved a fatality or a critical injury (as defined by the *OHSA*) it must be reported to an inspector, the joint health and safety committee or health and safety representative and the union, if any, immediately by direct means. In addition, the employer must send a written report to the Ministry of Labour, Training and Skills Development within 48 hours. If the workplace is covered by the Workplace Safety and Insurance Board, additional reporting requirements are involved. The employer must give written notice of serious incidents to the Ministry of Labour, Training and Skills Development the joint health and safety committee or health and safety representative and the union, if any, within four days.

Investigate Incident Causes

Regardless of any specific system that might be used in a workplace, there are a number of key steps to an incident investigation.

Survey the Scene

The first step is to survey the incident scene. The investigator should itemize the things that need to be explained and make a list of people who were present at the site of the incident who should be interviewed. This is the time to take photographs and measurements and write down the immediate facts. If the incident resulted in critical injuries or fatalities, the incident scene must be preserved in accordance with the provisions of Section 51 of the *OHSA*.

Interview Witnesses

Everyone who has information relevant to the investigation should be interviewed. This includes eyewitnesses, workers on other shifts, technical experts and, sometimes, equipment designers or suppliers. Eyewitnesses should be interviewed first, while the details are still fresh in their minds. Detailed notes should be kept for later analysis.

Physical Investigation

Physical evidence includes details of equipment damage, breaks, rips, burned materials, skid marks, and signs of impact. Photographs and diagrams or measurements are often important. Details of the work environment, such as visibility, noise level, temperature, and exposure to hazardous materials should be noted. At this stage, documents such as equipment specifications, maintenance schedules, and work procedures may also be taken into account.

Organize the Facts

All information should be organized and subjected to a thorough analysis. Where possible, separate facts from opinions. Identify gaps in the information and re-interview witnesses and confirm facts. Ask the questions: Who? What? When? Where? Why? and How?

Prepare Report

The investigation report should explain the circumstances of the incident, identify the causes, and recommend controls to prevent a recurrence. The report should be submitted to senior management and the joint health and safety committee. The Ministry of Labour, Training and Skills Development must also receive a report on the findings of the investigation.

Investigation Techniques

There are a number of techniques that can contribute to an effective investigation. They include proven methods for interviewing, analyzing, report writing, and using information sources.

Conducting Interviews

The purpose of conducting interviews is to find out what the person knows about an incident or about possible causes. The interview may also identify additional people to be interviewed.

Interviews should be conducted as soon as possible after the incident. Interviewers should be courteous and try to put the person at ease. They should explain that the purpose of the interview is to prevent a recurrence and avoid any suggestion that blame is being assigned. Interviews should be conducted separately and privately, so that people are not influenced or intimidated by the presence of others.

Interview questions should be simple and to the point. Ask the person to explain what happened, or what they know about the possible causes of the incident or illness. Don't ask questions that suggest the answer. Don't tell the person what the answer should be or what may be expected. Don't interrupt. Instead, ask clarifying questions later. Try to avoid questions that invite a "yes" or a "no" answer.

Make careful notes during the interview and, if necessary, ask the person to repeat their answer to ensure accuracy. At the end of the interview, review the key points and confirm that they are accurate. If the interview is conducted at the worksite, the person may be able to point out relevant objects. Otherwise diagrams or photographs may be used.
At the end of the interview, arrange to stay in contact in case the person remembers additional details later. Thank them for their help, and let them know that they have helped to prevent a recurrence.

Using Photographs and Drawings

Photographs of incident scenes are a useful way of recording information. They make a permanent record of the location of equipment, tools and other objects in the workplace. They can be used later to check details during an analysis, and to illustrate the investigation report.

Sketches are another way to record information from an incident scene. They do not have to be elaborate. They have the advantage that they focus only on the elements relevant to the incident. They can be helpful when interviewing witnesses and performing an analysis.

Sometimes, more detailed drawings are required. It may be necessary to record the exact distances involved. In this case, the drawing can be made to a precise scale and drawn on graph paper. Each object should be measured from at least two reference points to verify the accuracy of the drawing.

Analyzing the Facts

Analysis is an organized method of solving a problem by breaking it down into its constituent parts. The immediate "cause" of the incident may already be apparent. The purpose of an analysis is to find all of the contributing factors.

An analysis systematically reviews all of the factors that could contribute to an incident. There are a number of ways of classifying the factors that can contribute to an incident. For example:

- People factors;
- Equipment factors;
- Material factors;
- Environmental factors; and
- Process factors.

These factors are often associated with the acronym PEMEP. These are the same factors that were discussed in Chapter 16 in relation to Hazard Management Tools.

Each factor must be carefully checked against the facts to see if it could have played a role in the incident. This is easier to do if the facts are first grouped into categories. For example, an investigation might have assembled the statements of witnesses, photographs, physical evidence, and written evidence such as work procedures.

When all of the factors that might have contributed to the incident have been identified, the sequence of events can be reconstructed. At each step, the suspected cause can be checked against the facts.

Report Writing

If a comprehensive report is prepared, it should be clear, concise and logical. Its purpose is to identify the causes of the incident or illness and make recommendations for remedial action. A typical report might be organized as follows:

- A description of the incident;
- A sequence of events;
- The consequences;
- The contributing factors;
- The corrective action taken; and
- Recommendations for further action.

A report may be illustrated with photographs or diagrams, or supporting documents.

The report should not contain the personal opinion of the writer or anyone else if it is not substantiated. If some points are unexplained, there should not be any attempt to answer them hypothetically.

Follow Up

The incident report usually includes recommendations to management for controls to prevent a recurrence. If the report is submitted by the JHSC or health and safety representative, the employer has a duty to respond in writing to any recommendations in the report. If the employer agrees to implement the recommended controls, the committee or health and safety representative should follow up to ensure that all of the corrective actions are actually implemented.

Many employers record regular statistics of incidents. These reports can be classified according to a number of factors. It is then possible to detect patterns or trends in the data. It may also be possible to detect these patterns from claims data provided by the Workplace Safety and Insurance Board.

The usefulness of this type of data depends on how well it is classified. For example, one classification for incidents might be "falls". A pattern of falls in the workplace could trigger further investigations. If the data allowed a segregation of "falls from ladders", for example, the nature of the underlying problem would be more apparent.

Coroner's Inquests

Under the Coroner's Act, notice of death from an industrial incident must be provided to a coroner immediately. The coroner, who is a medical doctor, may decide to hold an inquest into the death. Inquests are mandatory for deaths in the construction and mining industries. In other sectors, coroners use their discretion and may or may not hold an inquest. The decision of a coroner may be appealed.

Inquests involve formal procedures resembling those in courts of law. Their purpose is to determine the cause of the death and make recommendations to prevent future deaths. There is no legal requirement that their recommendations be implemented. Following receipt of recommendations from a coroner's inquest, the Ministry of Labour, Training and Skills Development prepares a detailed response to the chief coroner concerning implementation.

If a coroner calls an inquest, the members of the joint health and safety committee or health and safety representatives can apply to the coroner in writing and request standing. A person granted standing has the right to participate in the inquest, to call witnesses, and present evidence. Families of the deceased and employers get automatic standing. Persons with standing can be represented by a lawyer or agent.

The testimony of witnesses at coroner's inquests cannot be used against them in any legal action, except for perjury. If charges are laid, the inquest will be suspended until the charges are dealt with by the courts.

The type of evidence presented at coroner's inquests is the same as might be used in any incident investigation. In effect, an inquest is a formal and very detailed incident investigation.

Further information about inquests can be found on the Ministry of the Solicitor General website www.mcscs.jus.gov.on.ca. Here, you can find verdicts and recommendations posted by the Office of the Chief Coroner.

Investigations are often carried out to find the causes of incidents, and to find ways of preventing recurrences. Investigations are normally the responsibility of the employer. If an incident resulted in a fatality or a critical injury, the worker members of the joint health and safety committee and health and safety representatives have the right to conduct their own investigation.

Incident investigations seek to identify the underlying causes that led up to the incident, not just the apparent cause. Incident investigation procedures are designed to systematically evaluate the role of every conceivable causation factor.

Incidents may also be investigated using statistical data. Reports of incidents may be retained and classified. Patterns or trends in the frequency of certain types of incidents may indicate the need for additional controls.

All types of investigation require clear, concise reporting. The object of a report is to describe the incident or illness, identify its causes and consequences, and recommend corrective action.

Finally, the effort of an investigation may be wasted if no action is taken on its recommendations. The investigator should follow up to see that effective controls have been implemented to prevent a recurrence.

Coroner's requests which are public hearings, are held to learn about and provide information to the public about circumstances surrounding a death. They are mandatory if a death occurs on a construction site, mine, pit, or quarry.

Chapter 19
Monitoring Strategies

- Monitoring Objectives

- Developing a Monitoring Strategy

- Monitoring Techniques and Tools

- Analysis and Reporting

- Review

Monitoring Strategies

Monitoring in the workplace is often called exposure monitoring or air monitoring. These terms refer to the detection and assessment of agents to which workers may be exposed in the workplace environment. The purpose of monitoring is to determine actual exposure levels of the agents and, where necessary, to determine where controls may be required.

Persons in the workplace may be exposed to agents without being immediately aware of the exposure, because the hazardous substance in question cannot be readily detected by the human senses. Even when it can be seen or smelled, the senses provide no reliable indication of the level of concentration.

This chapter concerns itself with measuring exposure to airborne solids, liquids, and gases. They are monitored using a variety of air sampling techniques and devices.

Monitoring Objectives

A strategy is an overall plan for achieving an objective. A monitoring strategy, as it applies to workplace health and safety, is a plan for determining the methods necessary to properly measure the level of a substance in the air.

Ensuring that proper controls are identified and, where necessary, established to protect the health of people in the workplace is the main objective of any monitoring strategy. This goal can be supported by a number of more immediate objectives. There are at least four separate reasons for conducting workplace air sampling.

Compliance with Regulations

The air is sampled to make sure that concentrations of a particular substance are below the exposure limits stated in the designated substance regulations of the *OHSA*, or the limits stated in other regulations or guidelines.

Concerns or Requests

The JHSC or HSR may request air sampling in a work area because of an inspection finding. A concern raised by an individual may also lead to air sampling. The concern may be based on symptoms of illness experienced by persons who work in certain parts of the workplace.

Monitoring may be used in such cases to identify a substance that has been tentatively identified as a possible cause of the symptoms. Monitoring can also measure the concentration of one or more known substances in the air.

Control
Sampling may also be conducted by the employer to locate the source of a known substance so that effective engineering controls, if appropriate, can be applied at the source to contain it.

Where controls are already in place for a known hazardous substance, air sampling can be used to evaluate the effectiveness of those controls. Continuous monitoring is a method of control sometimes used where especially hazardous materials are involved. The continuous monitoring device should be linked to an alarm mechanism or a continuous readout so that any failure of the control will produce a warning.

Monitoring is sometimes performed on a continuous basis for a specific period of time at the work station of a particular person who regularly works with a hazardous material.

The Role of the JHSC and HSR in Monitoring
The employer is responsible for having the monitoring conducted in the workplace.

The JHSC or HSR are entitled to information from the employer or constructor about monitoring tests. A designated member of the committee who represents workers or the health and safety representative are entitled to be present at the beginning of any hygiene testing to ensure the validity of test procedures and results.

The JHSC or HSR may make recommendations to the employer on health and safety matters. A recommendation might include provisions for monitoring the effectiveness of any health and safety program or control. It is important for members of JHSCs and HSRs to be knowledgeable about monitoring strategies and sampling techniques in general. They should also be familiar with the sampling techniques used in the various areas of their own workplace.

The previous section dealt with why sampling should be undertaken. Developing a monitoring strategy involves answering seven additional questions:

- What should be sampled?
- How to sample?
- Where to sample?
- Who should be sampled?
- When to sample?
- How long to sample?
- How many samples?

What Should Be Sampled?

An efficient monitoring strategy should deal with the most serious potential hazards first. An assessment should be conducted to identify all the hazardous substances in the workplace.

Next, the situations that are considered serious enough to warrant monitoring should be selected. A situation might be considered serious either because there is a high risk of overexposure or because the substance is particularly hazardous.

Any of the designated substances identified in regulation 490/09 of the *OHSA* may require an assessment that includes exposure monitoring.

How to Sample?

Air monitoring must involve a validated and known air sampling procedure. That means the sampling equipment, the volume of air sampled, the durations (time) of sampling, calibration methods, and analysis methods are all known and understood by the person conducting the sampling. There are many different methods and types of equipment available to do air monitoring. In some cases, the concentration of the substance can be read directly from a monitoring device. The choice of monitoring method is influenced by several factors.

What the Law Says

Regulation 490/09 Designated Substances

- If there is a designated substance in the workplace, the employer is required to perform an assessment and to implement a control program, if the assessment shows that there is a possibility of exposure that could affect a worker's health.

- Hygiene monitoring is a regulated part of any control program. Section 20(2) 1 and 2 of Regulation 490/09 stipulates that all control programs provide engineering controls, work practices, hygiene facilities and practices to control worker exposure to designated substances; and have methods and procedures to monitor airborne concentration in the workplace and worker exposure to a designated substance.

Information Needed

The sampling is most often conducted for a specific substance so that the exact concentration of that substance in workplace air can be determined. The monitoring method must be selective and accurate. If the air was being monitored for an unknown or suspected contaminant, a method capable of capturing a broad range of substances would be the best choice.

Urgency
Where sampling involves potential high-risk substances, methods that provide fast, accurate results will be favoured. Some substances may require direct-reading instruments. Particularly hazardous substances may be the subject of continuous monitoring.

Availability of Equipment
The choice of sampling method also determines which equipment is required. Specialized sampling may be contracted by the employer to a consulting firm that specializes in hygiene monitoring. These companies have access to a wide range of equipment, and people who know how to operate it. Alternatively, the employer may lease equipment and have in-house staff who are qualified to operate it.

Where to Sample?
The sampling location will vary depending on what is being sampled, the type of device being used, and the type of information sought. There are three ways to sample: area, personal, and source sampling.

Area Samples
When area samples are taken, the air collection device is placed so that the sample will reflect the general concentration of the substance in that part of the workplace. They have the advantage in that they can give an estimation of exposure for an entire process.
Area samples are also useful for evaluating ventilation.

Personal Samples
Personal samples are collected by a device attached to a worker. They are designed to measure the specific exposure of that worker. Placement should be as close as possible to the worker's breathing zone so that the sample will accurately reflect the worker's exposure. Many of these devices operate on battery power, and collect a continuous sample throughout the shift.
Passive dosimeters do not have pumps and do not require batteries.

Source Samples
Source samples are intended to identify the source of an airborne substance. Samples are collected in a variety of suspect areas until the source is identified.

Who Should Be Sampled?
Workers who are suspected of being exposed to the greatest hazard should be given priority in a monitoring strategy. This is sometimes called a worst-case strategy. If the worst-case worker is exposed at a safe level, then the other workers are also likely to be. A number of workers may be chosen randomly for sampling. Several factors influence the choice of a worker for monitoring:

- proximity of the worker to the source of contamination;

- mobility of workers that determines whether they are constantly exposed or only occasionally exposed;

- air movement that may affect the airborne concentration and concentrate contamination in an unexpected site; and

- work practices that may increase or decrease the airborne concentration to which a worker may be exposed.

When to Sample?

The airborne concentration of a substance may fluctuate significantly over time. Operations or the work process may change or the raw materials being handled may differ. A proper sampling procedure determines the overall or average concentration of a particular substance and may also determine peak or short-term levels of concentration. This can indicate whether overexposure has occurred or if the controls are working. There are several factors to consider in deciding when to sample. Unless a worst-case sample is desired, sampling should reflect the entire work cycle. This means that samples should be representative. They should be taken on every shift, at different times of the day or week and, where necessary, in every season. Sampling should be done when machines or processes are in operation. Anything that might cause significant changes in the airborne concentrations of hazardous substances should be taken into account in the design of a monitoring strategy.

How Long to Sample?

The duration of the sampling period is also part of a monitoring strategy. Technical and practical factors will guide this decision. The minimum and maximum sampling periods are determined by the equipment used. Some equipment is very sensitive and can quickly detect even small concentrations of a contaminant. Other equipment may take longer to draw a sufficient sample of air. Some devices can become overloaded with contaminants if the sample period is too long.

The type of measurement needed also affects the decision about how long to sample. For example, an exposure limit under Regulation 833/90 might require a 15-minute sample for a short-term exposure level. A time-weighted measurement might be based on eight-hour, full shift samples. For some purposes, a brief grab sample might be needed.

The length of the work activity being sampled is also a consideration. If the activity takes less than a full shift, the sample might last only for the duration of the work activity.

How Many Samples?

The number of samples needed depends on the reasons for sampling, the nature of the job, and the level of concentration of the contaminant. A small number of samples may be sufficient to evaluate the effectiveness of a control. The number of samples needed to measure the time-weighted average exposure level for a 40-hour week may be greater. A routine job with little variation will require fewer samples than a complex one. Many samples will be needed if the level of concentration of a hazardous material varies through the work cycle.

A wide range of monitoring instruments is available. The instruments used to monitor hazardous physical agents are discussed in Chapter 10. This section deals with methods for monitoring airborne contaminants.

Some monitoring instruments are based on sophisticated technology. The certified member and health and safety representative should not be concerned about their apparent complexity. In most cases, using them requires a knowledge of some fairly simple principles. It is not necessary to understand their inner workings. Nonetheless, there are certain instruments which must be calibrated or operated by specially-trained personnel.

There are two main methods of sampling: direct-reading methods and indirect-reading methods.

Direct-Reading Methods

Direct-reading methods provide virtually instantaneous results. They do not require that samples be sent to a laboratory. Direct-reading instruments include colorimetric tubes and specific gas analyzers as well as a variety of other devices.

Colorimetric Tubes

When a colorimetric tube is used, a pump draws a fixed volume of air through a transparent tube containing a reagent. A reagent is a chemical that reacts with the substance being monitored. The reagent changes colour and the stain length is in proportion to the concentration of the monitored substance. The stain length is compared to a concentration scale marked on the outside of the tube to estimate the concentration of the substance in the air.

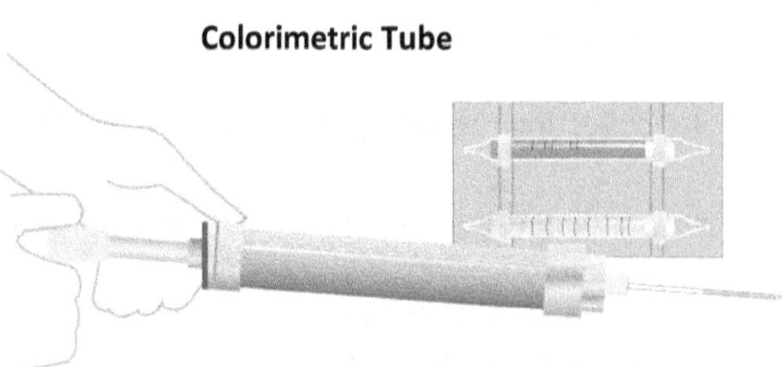

Colorimetric Tube

Colorimetric tubes are available for more than 600 different contaminants. They are convenient, but they are subject to a number of limitations.

One problem is interference from substances other than the one being monitored. The manufacturer's instructions list substances that may react with the reagent in the tube.

Another problem is that the reagent in the tubes may deteriorate over time, especially if they are not stored properly. They are usually good for at least two years. Storage instructions and expiry dates are provided on the package.

Colorimetric tubes have varying error rates, sometimes changing from one batch to another. The accuracy of some tubes is as low as plus or minus 25 percent. However, this can still be a good indicator of whether a substance is present. Moreover, they can be used only for grab samples. Passive colorimetric indicator tubes can be used for determining average concentration over extended periods, and they do not require pumps.

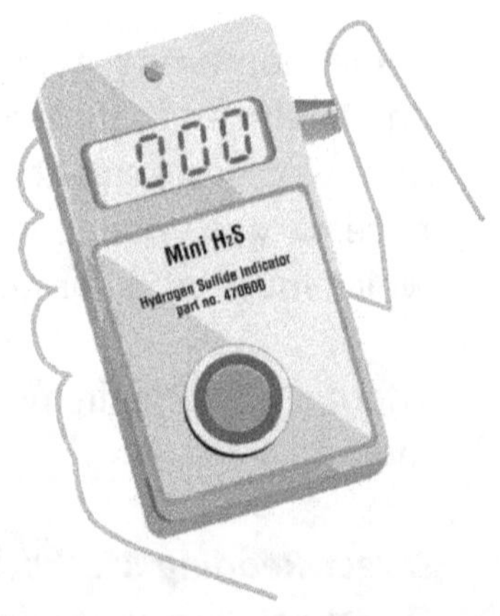

Specific Gas Analyzer

Gas Analyzers

A variety of specific gas analyzers is available. Most of them are hand-held electronic detectors that can provide a convenient and accurate method of evaluating atmospheres.

They are useful wherever a grab sample is appropriate. For example, they may be used to check inside a confined space or after cleaning up a spill. They can also be adapted for continuous monitoring and be connected to an alarm device.

Portable spectrophotometers and gas chromatographs are sophisticated devices that can measure a variety of gases and vapours in the air. These devices require careful calibration and must be operated by trained personnel.

Indirect-Reading Methods

Indirect-reading methods involve a three-stage process:

- sampling an exact volume of air;

- collecting the workplace air with a filter or other device; and

- sending the sample to a laboratory for analysis.

A variety of devices is available to do this, but the most convenient and commonly used device is a sampling train. This is a series of devices that use a pump to draw air from the workplace. A device such as a critical orifice or needle valve may be used to maintain a constant flow rate. They are usually battery operated so they can be used for personal monitoring.

If the sampling concerns a respirable dust, a known volume of air is passed through a size-selection device, which admits only the small particles that are capable of being inhaled into the respiratory system. The next stage is a collection medium or device that traps the contaminants from the air as it passes through. This is most often a filter of some kind.

Sampling Train

The sampling train is operated for a fixed period of time and then the filter or other collection device is sent to a laboratory for analysis. The amount of dust, fumes, or fibres can be measured and, using the volume of air sampled, the average concentration of the contaminant over the duration of the sample, can be calculated.

To maintain accuracy, the sampling train must be calibrated. It is essential that the air flow rate be set at specified levels. If the sampling train does not have an automatic flow-regulating device, the flow rate must be manually adjusted.

Analysis and Reporting

When sampling has been completed, the material collected on the filter or other sample medium will be analyzed in a laboratory. The laboratory report will normally be a statement of the facts:

- Identification: What substance was found. There may be more than one substance.

- Concentration: The concentration of that substance in the sampled air. This figure will be a calculation based on the quality of the substance found and the volume of air that has passed through the sampling device over the measured time period of the sampling.

Concentration are sometimes stated in terms of parts (of the substance) per million (parts of air), or ppm. They may also be stated in weight per volume terms such as milligrams (of the substance) per cubic metre (of air), or mg/m3.

Interpreting Sample Results

Those interpreting the sampling results should review the original sampling strategy, the techniques employed to carry out the strategy and the instruments used to validate the analysis. This review should reveal whether the results are representative and accurate. Both these terms have specific meanings related to monitoring tests. They can be stated in the form of questions to be answered by the interpreter.

- Representative: Did the sampling strategy ensure that the air samples collected truly reflect the actual exposure levels experienced by those in the workplace?

- Accurate: Was the right equipment used to identify, collect, and measure the contaminants? Was the sampling equipment calibrated properly and checked regularly during the sampling period? In other words, did it perform properly, and did it accurately measure the concentration of the substance in the air?

If a consultant has been hired to complete the exposure monitoring, the report should be written in a manner that is easily understood by the JHSC or HSR. If there are any questions, it is reasonable to ask the consultant for clarification at a JHSC meeting, or one on one. If the representation or accuracy of the sampling results are placed in doubt, the employer should consider having the sampling repeated.

Conclusions

With the assumption that the samples are both representative and accurate, there are usually special conclusions that can be drawn from the monitoring results:

- no exposure (within detection limits of analysis);

- acceptable exposure (below recognized exposure levels); or

- overexposure (above recognized exposure levels).

These results need to be interpreted, based on the duration and type of sampling carried out, to determine the degree of exposure which may have occurred or may likely occur.

The results of a good sampling strategy will provide information about employee exposure in the workplace and show whether existing controls are functioning properly. They may also indicate the need for additional controls, such as ventilation, materials movement, improved work practices, or personal protective equipment. The results may suggest that immediate action is necessary to implement temporary controls until permanent remedial action can be taken. The results will provide meaningful insight into the workplace atmosphere.

Regulations, standards, and guidelines provide the acceptable average exposure levels that are legally permissible. These are not "limits", unless specifically stated.

Monitoring needs and practices will vary from one workplace to another: from no monitoring required in some cases to continuous readouts in others. The complexity and size of the operation as well as the number and toxicity of hazardous substances used are contributing factors in the sampling strategy.

Air quality can be a concern in office buildings as well as in factories, but it is approached very differently in terms of a monitoring strategy. The sampling in office environments is usually focused toward evaluating ventilation rather than specific chemical hazards.

Certified members and health and safety representatives should be familiar with the hazardous substances, if any, that are present in their workplace, and the means by which these substances may enter the workplace air. They should have a basic understanding of the principles of air sampling and a thorough understanding of the specific air sampling strategies, techniques and instruments used in their workplace, if any.

The most common form of workplace monitoring is air sampling. Air sampling may be used to detect hazardous substances in the workplace air and to measure their concentration.

Strategy is a term for the plan used to reach an objective. Monitoring strategies are used to ensure that the devices used, the method of sampling, the time of sampling, and the process are representative of normal activity. This then ensures that the results of the tests indicating the concentration of hazardous substances in the workplace air can be compared with the exposure limit standards stated in the regulations and guidelines of the OHSA.

Monitoring is performed for several reasons. They include compliance with legal standards, confirmation of hazards, and ensuring that overexposure of workers does not occur. They are also used to check the efficiency of existing controls and contribute to occupational health research.

Under the OHSA, the joint health and safety committee and health and safety representative have the right to obtain information from the employer about monitoring tests and have the right to be consulted about these tests. The committee may designate a member representing workers to be present at the beginning of testing if they so choose. A health and safety representative may also be present when testing takes place.

One of the most common forms of workplace monitoring is air sampling. It is used to detect a number of hazardous substances in the workplace air and determine their airborne concentration. A monitoring strategy must be both representative and accurate to be useful. The monitoring or sampling strategy must consider seven factors:

- What should be sampled?
- How to sample?
- Where to sample?
- Who should be sampled?
- When to sample?
- How long to sample?
- How many samples?

These factors determine which techniques and instruments should be used to obtain air samples that are truly representative and accurate.

A wide range of monitoring methods and instruments may be used. Monitoring instruments use sophisticated technology. The JHSC member or HSR are not involved in the actual sampling process nor required to have detailed knowledge of the instruments used.

The JHSC members and the HSR should, however, be aware of the different methods of sampling, such as direct and indirect, colorimetric tubes and specific gas analyzers, and how the equipment and methods used affect the analysis which may be required for a specific agent.

Direct-reading methods provide instant results. Indirect sampling methods involve the collection of samples from the air and their analysis in a laboratory. Indirect sampling methods use a sampling train. The train is a series of devices that use a pump to draw air, a critical orifice or needle valve to maintain a constant flow rate, and a collecting medium that traps the air. The device is designed to admit only those particles that would normally be able to enter the human respiratory system.

Air samples are analyzed in a laboratory. The lab results normally state which substance was found and its concentration. This information can be compared with the standards stated in the regulations or guidelines included in the *OHSA* for compliance purposes.

Chapter 20
Health and Safety Research

- Researching Health and Safety Issues

- The Research Plan

- Gathering Information

- Evaluating and Analyzing Health and Safety Information

- Conclusions and Recommendations

- Review

Health and Safety Research

Knowledge is a powerful tool for improving health and safety. The more everyone in the workplace knows about occupational health and safety, the better equipped they are to play effective roles in the creation of a safe and healthy work environment.

There is an enormous amount of information available about occupational health and safety. To make the most of this resource, it is essential to know where to find it and how to use it. This "finding and using" information search process is known as research. Good research skills are important to the information-gathering phase of a workplace inspection or an investigation. This chapter provides an outline of the basic research methods used to gather and evaluate information.

The type of information search referred to in this chapter is not the same as the pure research, normally involving scientific skills, which is performed in a laboratory or think tank. Therefore, where the term research is used in this reference guide, it should not be confused with the pure scientific research. For our purposes, the required qualifications for research are familiarity with the workplace, organizational ability, time, and effort.

Research is the systematic collection and evaluation of information. It starts with a series of questions. Then, information is found relating to those questions. Based on those data, objective conclusions can be reached and recommendations made. For most people, it is a part of daily life. Deciding which car to buy by testing several models and comparing food prices at several supermarkets are both forms of research.

Researching Health and Safety Issues

Health and safety research is usually conducted to identify potential safety hazards in the workplace or to assist in determining the cause of a health concern that crops up too often to be explained by "normal" circumstances. In both cases, instinct may convince the joint health and safety committee or health and safety representative people that a problem exists. Its members may even be fairly certain of the cause of the concern. Research helps support that opinion with enough facts to determine whether or not there is a case for preventive action. Other reasons to conduct research could include:

- employee safety concerns;

- introduction of a new substance or technology;

- reports of problems in similar workplaces;

- a sudden increase in the number of workers' compensation claims or first aid treatments;

- a high incidence of disease or early death;

- an investigation report of a critical injury or death;

- an appeal of an inspector's ruling;

- a request for assessment or reassessment;

- a stop-work situation, or a worker refusing unsafe work;

- a request or need for educational materials;

- a need for information about the health effects of a particular chemical; or

- preparation of JHSC or HSR recommendation to the employer.

Conducting research isn't difficult, but it can be very detailed and time-consuming. A research plan provides a useful framework which JHSC members and HSRs can use to guide them through the process.

Since the heart of research is information, learning how to find and interpret that information is vital. There are many different sources of data and all are useful.

Data is information gathered by the researcher and may consist of information collected within the workplace. These data may include such items as first aid treatment statistics, inspection reports, employee surveys, health surveys, and other information that originates in the workplace.

Studies, articles, or books written by someone else are another source. The safety data sheet is an example. Most other sources of data may be found outside the workplace. Many employers also maintain good collections of reference material on health and safety subjects.

An Example of Research

A workplace employs a number of welders, many of whom are concerned about severe, frequent headaches. Since the number of concerns raised is so high, the JHSC or HSR may consider that the headaches could be work-related. It seems obvious that something has changed and is causing the headaches, because the frequency of headaches in the department is something new.

Research may assist in finding a reasonable explanation for this occurrence. The questions to be answered by research are:

- Are the headaches caused only by something in the workplace?

- What may be the cause?

To find answers to these questions, one begins a research plan.

The Research Plan

The goal of health and safety research is to attempt to determine the cause of a health concern so that action may be recommended to control or eliminate the problem. Being properly prepared is essential since the credibility of a research project depends on the thoroughness of the research team. Research plans are guidelines that enable the researcher to stay on track. The research plan involves several steps.

Defining the Objective
The first step in a research plan is to determine its objective, and the questions that should be answered within that objective. In our example, the objective is to find out why the workers are getting headaches and if the cause is workplace-related.

Stating the Hypothesis
Before starting the research, one may have a theory as to why a health and safety concern exists. This theory is sometimes called a hypothesis. A hypothesis is an educated guess and its correctness must be tested by research to determine its accuracy and validity. A hypothesis is not just a wild guess; it must have some reasonable basis in theory.

Before research begins, any hypothesis should be clearly stated.

Headaches are caused by toxic substances and are therefore work-related.

Listing Information Needs
The hypothesis creates research questions. In our example, if the hypothesis is that the headaches may be caused by exposure to toxic substances, then researchers will attempt to find out the following:

- To what substance or agent are employees exposed?

- What are the properties of this substance or agent?

- Are they known to cause headaches?

- What exposure levels of the substance or agent are known to cause headaches?

- What are actual workplace exposure levels to that substance and are they high enough to create a potential hazard?

- What are the possible solutions if a problem is determined to exist?

Although information needs may change as the research unfolds, it is worth making the initial list of questions as complete as possible.

Planning Information Collection

Because occupational health and safety information comes from many sources, it is important to plan how it will be gathered and from where. A detailed list of potential sources can be used later to assign work to research team members. Certain kinds of information, including the results of monitoring or sampling, may require special planning.

Report Outline

Although a report will not be written until the research is complete, it is useful to prepare a preliminary report outline during the planning phase. This outline will point to information that should be collected during the other phases of the project and will help to focus the work. The research report outline might contain the following sections:

Introduction: A statement of the health and safety concern and the hypotheses considered;

Research Methods: An explanation of how information was collected and analyzed, and the sources of that information;

Findings: A review of the relevant facts;

Conclusions: A statement of the apparent cause of the health and safety concern based on the facts and the data gathered, and how that may be affecting the employees;

Recommendations: Specific proposals for eliminating or controlling the health and safety concern.

Research Schedule

If more than one person is involved in the research project, a schedule is needed to coordinate their activities. As well as deadlines for the completion of each project phase, the schedule should include time for review meetings, production (typing, photocopying), and keeping the committee informed.

Once the research plan is written and agreed upon, the actual research — tracking down the needed information — can begin. The information may be found both inside and outside the workplace as follows:

Workplace Information
The workplace will be the source of all primary information.

Inspections, Concerns, Suggestions, and JHSC Meetings
First-hand observation of the workplace is an important source of information. The reports of inspections carried out by JHSC members, or by the employer, may help in identifying a specific health and safety concern. Concerns raised or suggestions made to the JHSC by workers or supervisors as well as reports of the JHSC meeting are other good sources. In smaller workplace the health and safety representative may be alone in this endeavour.

Employer Disclosure
The *OHSA* requires employers to provide health and safety information to the JHSC and HSR. This information may include:

- identification of hazardous materials present in the workplace;

- health and safety practices or standards used in other workplaces;

- monitoring results;

- first aid treatment statistics;

- assessments conducted by the employer under the designated substance regulations;

- safety data sheets; and

- general medical information about health effects in the workplace.

Some information about hazardous chemicals or health effects may be confidential. Examples are trade secrets that the employer wishes to keep competitors from learning and the results of medical examinations.

Workplace Safety and Insurance Board
The Board is required by law to provide an annual summary of incidents or lost time upon request, both for a specific workplace and an entire industrial sector.

The WSIB provides and online data service where interested parties can find and compare health and safety statistics for businesses across the province. This is in keeping with Ontario's Open Data Directive. Go to safetycheck.onlineservices.wsib.on.ca.

Anyone can search the health and safety record of an Ontario workplace, discover the types and number of injuries and compare those statistics to other businesses.

External Information
External information ranges from scientific studies of health hazards in various workplaces to general health and safety research papers from outside experts. Examples of various sources of information include:

Canadian Centre for Occupational Health and Safety (CCOHS)
The CCOHS is a federal crown corporation made up of labour, management and government members. It keeps legal, scientific, medical and statistical health and safety data on file. CCOHS can also access material from both the National Institute for Occupational Safety and Health in the United States and the International Labour Organization in Geneva, Switzerland, through its computer database.

University Resource Centres
As part of their post-graduate programs in occupational health and safety, some Ontario universities offer advice and information through special resource centres. Centre staff will also perform workplace testing for a small fee.

Industry Associations
The employer may belong to an industry or sector association. The association may have up-to-date information about potential hazards or adverse health effects that are specific to the kinds of workplaces found in that sector.

Unions or Labour Organizations
As well as collecting general research and other health and safety literature, some unions also have health and safety specialists on staff. Central labour bodies can provide contacts who may have data on a particular hazard.

Health and Safety Associations (HSAs)
These health and safety training bodies deliver education and training to various employment sectors in Ontario. Most of them are associated with specific sectors, such as industrial, forestry, construction and health care. They are likely to be good sources of information about the particular sector they serve.

Workers Health and Safety Centre (WHSC)
The WHSC delivers health and safety training to workers in general. The Centre maintains regional offices across Ontario that provide health and safety information.

Occupational Health Clinics for Ontario Workers (OHCOW)

These clinics, staffed by occupational health physicians, nurses and hygienists, maintain extensive libraries on occupational health subjects.

Community Health Clinics

Some clinics are available to conduct health tests on groups of workers. Government funding may be available to support specific projects.

Private Consultants

Consultants provide a range of health and safety services. This can include safety, industrial hygiene, and training. Along with their services, most consultants come with a wealth of experience and information. Most will speak to you initially, at no cost, to assist you in formalizing plans for your workplace.

Government

The Ontario Ministry of Labour, Training and Skills Development has extensive reference libraries. There are also several government publications relating to the *OHSA* and its regulations. Since health and safety provisions are set out in the *OHSA* and regulations, it can be a good starting point for identifying a problem. Information about the Ontario Gazette, the Revised Statutes of Ontario, the Revised Regulations of Ontario and Office Consolidations of the *OHSA* is given in Chapter 3.

Libraries

Since the information available in libraries depends on their size, university or college libraries are usually best for research purposes. However, even the smallest local libraries may be able to acquire specialized material such as reference books, periodicals or studies, if they are requested.

Computer Database Services

Computer databases are usually found at the library or at certain other institutions. The service saves time and energy by "searching" for all the available information on a given subject at once, rather than looking up each book or periodical individually. In addition to title and publication information, the database may also include a short outline of a document's contents or even the full text. Charges for this service are based on how long the search takes. The Canadian Centre for Occupational Health and Safety is a good example of where this type of service may be found.

Organizing Material

As the collection of health and safety information grows, a good filing system can save time when members try to find specific data or contact names for a new information. A good filing system will identify the collected material and where this information can be found in the books, periodicals or reports themselves. Inhouse experts may have up-to-date electronic files or articles and information which are workplace specific.

In research, it is not the amount of information that counts, but rather its quality and how well it relates to the health and safety concern at hand. Evaluating and analyzing that information are the last two stages in preparing for the main events: drawing conclusions and making recommendations.

Evaluation

It is important to know how to judge the quality of information before using it to test hypotheses. Internal information is easier to evaluate because it is generated within the workplace, sometimes specifically for the research project itself. Because outside information is prepared by outsiders to meet different objectives, it may not always be appropriate and should be carefully checked for relevance and bias.

Relevance

If the information doesn't deal directly with the issue being researched, then conclusions are difficult to draw. It must at least share a common element with the issue.

Bias

Researchers must watch for bias on the part of a report's author, since this may reduce its worth. Asking a series of questions is the best way to determine whether or not there is potential bias. A positive answer to any of the following questions is not necessarily an indication of bias but merely warns the researcher to be cautious.

- Who funded the research and why?

- Does the author work for the firm whose product is discussed in the report?

- Has the study been reviewed and accepted by other authorities in the field?

- Is the study full of inconsistent facts or erroneous comparisons?

- Does the study give notice of its limitations by warning that some of its conclusions may not be applicable to certain industries?

- Does the study avoid relevant issues or attempt to mislead the reader?

Report Quality

The best gauge of a report's quality is accurate up-to-date information:

- Date: Usually, recent studies are more useful than old ones, although this is not always the case.

- Size of Sample: The broader the sample studied, the better, as there is less chance for random events to bias the results.

- Effectiveness of Control: As an example, to accurately measure the potential effects of exposure to a toxic substance in a group of workers, they should be compared with a group of unexposed workers. Both groups must be isolated from other substances known to cause similar effects to the one being studied.

- Duration of Exposure: If the research study deals with a substance whose harmful effects take years to develop, then the study itself must cover a long enough period to observe that development.

- Consistency: If more than one study exists on the subject, ideally the results will be consistent. If not, the reader should check the research methods for an explanation.

A person doing research may not be able to determine from a report the various items in the above checklist. The researcher must then weigh the merits of the report against other criteria.

Analysis

During the analysis stage, all material must be considered, whether supportive or not. The related material from each source document should be tested against the hypotheses. If any data is dismissed because of bias, technical fault or lack of relevance, this should be stated with reasons given in the report or the new research itself may appear biased.

Sometimes data must be combined in a more compact form before conclusions can be drawn from it. This may require statistical analysis of the data, such as calculating averages of data gathered from a workplace monitoring system. Statistical analysis can be complicated and if no one on the research team is fully qualified in this concept, it would be advisable to seek assistance.

Conclusions

When all the information has been gathered, read, evaluated, and analyzed, the researchers can begin testing each of their original hypotheses in order to draw conclusions. For example, in the example cited earlier, to agree with the hypothesis that headaches are caused by toxic substances and are therefore work-related, researchers must be able to answer yes to the following questions on the basis of the facts:

- Are workers exposed to a substance known to cause headaches after exposure to certain levels?

- Are the levels in the workplace high enough to cause those symptoms?

How researchers arrive at that "yes" answer also depends partly on other factors.

The Concept of Proof and the Balance of Probabilities

Whether or not there is conclusive proof regarding any issue, a hypothesis should always be tested to determine whether or not anything was found to disprove the hypothesis. The balance between evidence that tends to prove or disprove the hypothesis must be weighed and the side that is more compelling should be accepted. Both kinds of evidence must be given equal consideration. A particular hypothesis can only be accepted as long as it is consistent with a good proportion of the evidence and not actually contradicted by the rest.

In a health and safety situation, this balance of probabilities is likely to be enough. The person who claims that a specific substance may cause a particular health effect, for example, must provide evidence sufficient and conclusive enough to make the case.

There is no question that research is a painstaking and deliberate process, but the more systematically the project is developed, the more confidence the researchers can have in their final results.

Recommendations

All the work done so far culminates in recommendations that relate to the health and safety concern. Recommendations must be specific and practical. They should outline proposed methods of controlling the health and safety concern in the short term and potentially eliminating or reducing it in the long term. If the research project cannot arrive at a conclusion, the recommendation might be to conduct further research studies or suggest that the employer carry out a full-scale assessment.

Writing the Research Report
The final report is a detailed record of the entire research process. By taking the reader through the project step by step, the report adds to the strength of the final conclusions and recommendations. Clarity and good organization are crucial. The report outline prepared at the beginning of the project is especially helpful now.

The report must be clearly written, without jargon, so that people unfamiliar with a particular workplace can still understand it. This means the report should:

- Address the subject directly;
- Present technical information in plain language;
- Support all findings and conclusions with good factual information; and
- List supporting documents so that sources can be checked.

Report writing is further described in Chapter 22, "Communication Skills".

Review

This chapter explains the basic principles of research, and provides a step-by-step guide to conducting a research project.

Research is the systematic gathering and evaluation of information. That information may be required when the JHSC or HSR believes that a health and safety concern in the workplace should
be investigated. Research may help to determine the possible causes of the concern and may recommend effective ways of controlling or eliminating it.

The process begins with the creation of a research plan. This plan serves as a guideline for the entire project, broken down into:

- Defining the objective;
- Stating the hypothesis;
- Listing information needs;
- Planning information collection;
- Detailing a report outline; and
- Documenting a research schedule.

Sources of information include inspection or assessment reports, employer information and other information gathered in the workplace. Other sources are more varied, including universities, computer databases, unions, trade or employer associations, health and safety delivery organizations, libraries and other resource centers.

After information has been gathered, it must be evaluated and analyzed. Data generated from within the workplace is usually considered reliable. Outside information must be carefully assessed because it was prepared by others for different objectives. Researchers should check for relevance, bias, and technical accuracy in the information before using it to reach conclusions.

Evaluating and analyzing materials as to the quality and relevance of the information is more important than the quantity of the material. Related material from various source documents can be combined to test hypotheses.

The two final stages of any research project are conclusions and recommendations. Conclusions are reached when original hypotheses are tested against the facts collected, and either accepted or rejected. This is done under two basic research principles, the concept of proof and the balance of probabilities.

Practical and specific recommendations are made on the basis of the conclusions drawn. If the committee has not been able to reach definitive conclusions, it may recommend further research and investigation.

The final report is a detailed record of the whole project. Clarity and good organization are crucial. When putting the report together, the writer should remember to consider the readers, avoid jargon, address the subject directly, and present technical information in plain language. All findings must be supported by relevant facts with a list of supporting material.

Chapter 21
Health and Safety Statistics

- Types of Statistics

- Statistical Presentation

- Sources of Health and Safety Statistics

- Using Health and Safety Statistics

- Review

Health and Safety Statistics

Joint health and safety committee members and health and safety representatives need information to identify a health or safety hazard, assess the severity and frequency of its effects, determine its cause, and find ways of controlling and evaluating the hazard controls. Information comes in all shapes and sizes — articles, books, scientific studies and reports — and it often consists of numbers. Researchers compare numbers in order to show facts and draw conclusions. The numbers might show, for example, that lost-time compensation claims for musculoskeletal injuries increased over the past year from the level of the year before. When researchers compare numbers, or use comparisons prepared by others, they are dealing with statistics.

Statistics can paint a quick, simple picture of a health and safety hazard in a particular workplace or industry, or across the province. They are often used to present research material, because they express facts or measurements in a short, precise way.

Statistics can be used to examine everything from processes and materials to work stations and occupations for causes of injuries or illness. They can measure the effectiveness of an existing workplace health and safety program and help in the design of a new one. They can often help make a persuasive case for a committee recommendation.

Many groups with a stake in health and safety share statistics. Industry, labour, and other groups who seek improvements in regulations use statistics to support their positions. Employers, JHSCs, and HSRs use statistics to evaluate the effectiveness of health and safety programs.

Types of Statistics

The effects of workplace hazards are often described in statistical terms. There are several kinds of health and safety statistics.

The raw materials of statistics are total numbers, or counts. Counts kept regularly by the WSIB include the following:

Days Lost (Lost-time)
Days lost is the number of full calendar days a person is off work due to temporary disability, not counting the day the injury happened or the day the person returned to work. Days lost include all the days in between, including weekends and holidays. They also include any other full days off due to the original injury once the employee has returned to work.

Disabling Injury

Disabling injury means any work injury, including a fatality, that prevents a person from coming to work or doing their job effectively on any day after the injury.

Occupational Illness

Occupational illness in compensation statistics is specifically defined by the statistical classification standard, but in broad terms can be defined as a sickness caused by factors in the work environment or by activities performed on the job.

Work Injury

A work injury describes any injury, disease, or illness incurred in connection with the job. It is called a lost-time injury if it keeps an employee off work for more than the day the injury occurred.

Health Care (No Lost-time)

The term "health care" is used to identify injury claims for "health care only" where the injury or illness is not severe enough to warrant more than one day (day of injury) off work but where treatment by a doctor, chiropractor, registered nurse (extended class), or dentist is paid for through the compensation system. This can also be called a 'no lost-time' claim.

First Aid Case

A first aid case is an injury that can be treated on the job without any days lost. It should be noted that the definitions outlined above have been defined by and are interpreted in light of compensation policy. In other contexts, or applications these same terms may have different meanings or interpretations and therefore produce very different numerical results.

Rates

Raw numbers become more meaningful and useful when they are turned into rates.

For example, the number of lost-time injuries in a particular year or period of years could be compared for different occupations, departments, or industrial sectors. This could show which one is having the best or worst experience. The result might be a decision to study the worst to learn what is going wrong or perhaps to study the best to find out what they are doing right.

Rates usually consist of the number of events averaged over both the number of people involved and the length of time during which the events occurred. Sometimes the number of people involved and the length of time involved are combined into one unit. Examples of rates include the number of fatalities per 1,000 workers per year or the number of injuries per 100 person years. Percentages are also rates. *Percent* is the Latin phrase for "in every hundred". A 10 percent lost-time rate, for example, could mean that 10 person-days out of every 100 person-days of work are eaten up by lost-time injuries or illnesses. Five kinds of rates are commonly used in health and safety statistics.

Frequency Rates

Frequency rates describe how often an illness or injury happens over time. Injuries that keep an employee off work for one or two days count the same as permanently disabling injuries. Frequency rate measurements are normally applied to lost-time injuries, medical aid cases, first aid cases, or combinations of all three. They are useful as a rough measure of health and safety performance, but don't provide much detail.

Severity Rates

Severity rates provide a better picture of the seriousness or extent of an injury or illness. They do so by calculating the number of days lost per total person-hours worked, rather than just the total number of injuries or illnesses. For example, one workplace might have a lower frequency of injuries than another, but because more working days were lost as a result, the injuries were more severe.

Fatality Rates

Fatality rates measure the number of fatalities for a given number of workers at risk from a given hazard, for example, fatalities per 100 or per 1000 workers. While frequency and severity rates may be applied to individual workplaces or employers, fatality rates are normally calculated for entire sectors, such as mining, construction, or manufacturing.

Incidence Rates

Incidence rates describe, in the form of a percentage, how many workers out of every 100 suffer an injury or contract an illness. They can be applied to a particular workplace or an entire sector. Incidence is measured against the number of persons exposed, whereas frequency and severity rates are based on total working time.

Epidemiological Rates

Epidemiology is the study of the causes, occurrence, and control of disease. Epidemiological studies aim to discover why a disease is concentrated in a certain part of a population. An epidemiological rate or ratio is one that compares illness or death from a certain cause among a particular group of people with the numbers that would normally be expected. There are many kinds of epidemiological studies. The science of epidemiology deals with deaths and illnesses that have already happened. It is nevertheless useful in the long run because it can lead to further investigation. It may also help to bring about preventive measures, both in individual workplaces and in laws and regulations.

How statistical data is arranged or presented depends on which facts are to be emphasized. There are two distinct forms of presentation: numerical and graphic. In addition, such details as the size of headings, small print explanations, definitions and labels on columns can influence the meaning of statistics.

Numerical Presentation
Numerical presentation consists of numbers – raw numbers, percentages, averages or ratios – stated in the body of a report or recommendation or included in a separate table.

Percentages
For efficiency, percentages are often used instead of actual numbers. Percentages make it possible to compare things of different sizes on the same basis. For example, 20 lost-time injuries per year in workplace A with 1,000 workers may be considered unacceptably high by the employer and the joint health and safety committee or health and safety representative. Two per year is a much smaller number, but if it occurs in workplace B with 10 workers, it is actually much worse. The annual lost-time injury rate in workplace A is 2 percent, while the rate in B is 20 percent. Caution is needed in dealing with percentages, as with all statistics. Because data is so easy to manipulate, percentages mean nothing unless related back to original data.

Things can be even more confusing when several different sets of statistics are used.

Example: Out of every 100 injuries in a workplace, 20 percent are related to Operation X. Fifty percent of Operation X's injuries happen on a Wednesday.

The key here is that the 50 percent doesn't apply to the original total, but only to Operation X. Twenty of every 100 injuries occur in Operation X. Ten of those 20 occur on a Wednesday. Percentages of percentages can be confusing. The researcher or presenter of the research should take adequate precautions to avoid these problems.

Averages
Averages provide a common standard by adding the quantities in a series of elements, and then dividing the total by the number of elements.

Example: If the incidence of lost-time illness in 10 workplaces adds up to 30 per month, then the average incidence for each of them is 30 divided by 10, or an average of 3 lost-time illnesses per workplace per month.

Averages can be either useful or misleading, depending on how big the numbers are, and depending on the variation between the numbers. As a rule of thumb, the more data points there are, the more valid the average.

Ratios

A ratio is another kind of numerical statistic. Ratios are usually used to express relative proportions. For example, the difference between two plants, given 50 percent foot injuries in Plant C and 10 percent foot injuries in plant D, may also be expressed as a 5:1 ratio, or five times the proportion of foot injuries observed in plant C relative to plant D. Ratios are often more dramatic and a bit easier to understand. They are more likely to be used when the incidence rate is high.

Tables

Tables are the simplest numerical presentation because they often use actual counts of injuries or illnesses. The counts are then arranged in columns with explanatory headings. Tables can also be used to present averages, ratios, or percentages in addition to, or instead of, raw numbers.

Table		Year aLLOWeD					
		2018		2019		2020	
	Diseases	98	30%	87	28%	77	29%
	Immediate deaths	141	42%	128	42%	119	44%
	Not immediate deaths	21	6%	31	10%	28	10%
	100% pensions	72	22%	61	20%	45	17%
	Total	332	100%	307	100%	269	100%

Graphic Presentation

Graphic presentations are those that present statistics in the form of a picture or image. Line graphs, bar charts and pie charts are familiar examples. The aim is to appeal to the reader's visual faculties. Graphs make it easier for the reader to visualize the relative sizes of the numbers presented.

Line Graphs

Line graphs show trends, or compare several trends, over a given period of time. In a line graph, the horizontal movement of the line often represents time in months or years, while vertical movement of the line represents increases or decreases in the number of incidents. For example, a line graph might be used to illustrate a declining or rising trend in the incidence of medical aid cases over a 10-year period.

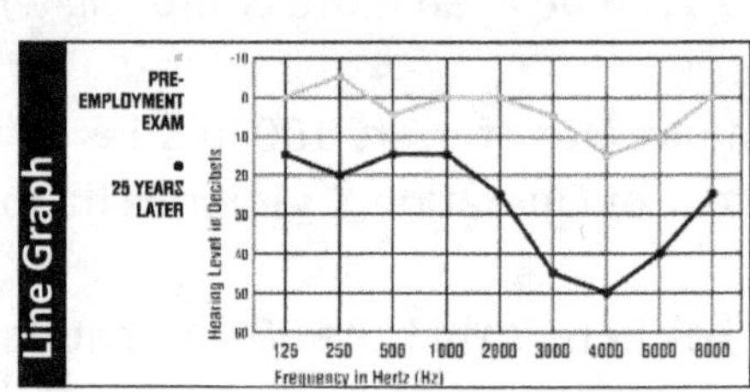

Pie Charts

Pie charts are round, like a pie. Different-sized slices of the pie can be used to show the divisions within a given category of information. An example might be a pie chart representing the hazards that caused lost-time injuries and illness. The whole pie represents 100 percent of the lost-time injuries. Different-sized slices might illustrate the comparisons among falls, strains, burns, illnesses of the lungs, and illnesses of the digestive tract.

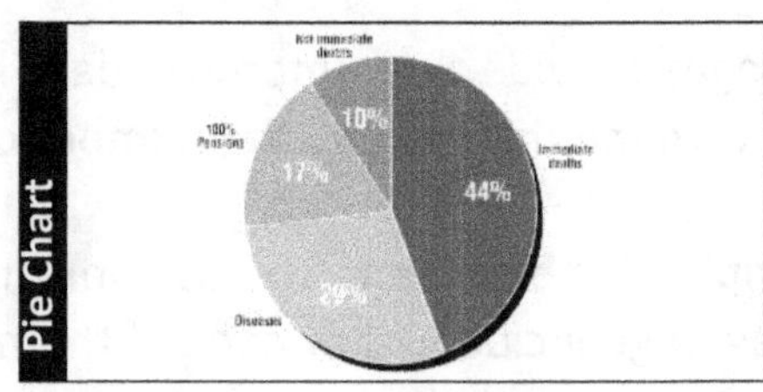

Bar Charts

The bar chart is another simple and practical way to
compare different statistics. Different numbers are
represented by bars of differing lengths.

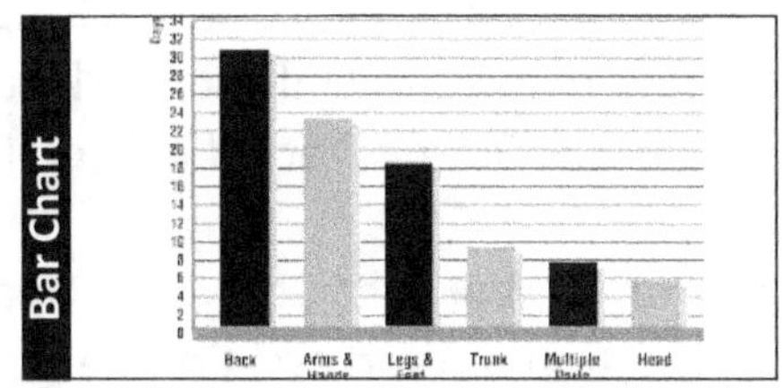

Histograms

A histogram is a kind of bar chart. The histogram is
used to show a range of numerical values – years,
ages, temperature, income brackets, and so on. For
example, a histogram might be used to illustrate the
varying number of years of experience among a group
of workers.

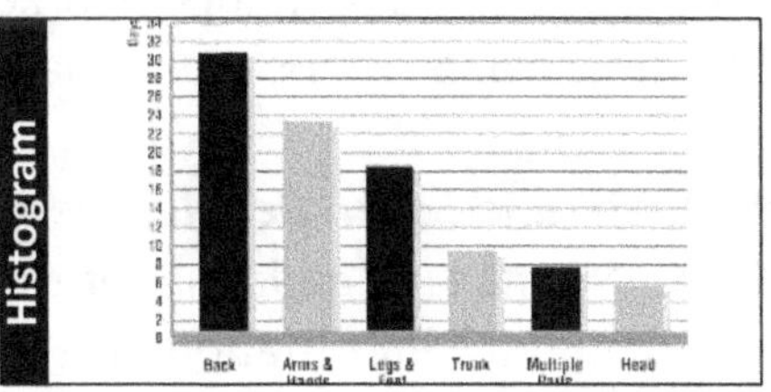

Combinations

Some studies and reports use combinations of statistical presentation methods. Most
presentation methods allow the user of statistics to explain a great deal in a small amount of
space.

Sources of Health and Safety Statistics

Statistics can be collected as part of either primary or secondary research. Primary statistics are
found in the workplace itself. They may be gathered by the JHSC, HSR, or the employer from
injury or illness reports, first aid and hygiene monitoring reports, inspection reports, and from
compensation claims and first aid treatment records. Secondary statistics come from a variety
of external sources.

Statistics can be obtained from the sources reviewed in Chapter 20 which deals with research.
The types of statistics available from some of those sources are described here.

WSIB (www.wsib.on.ca)

Workplace Safety and Insurance Board (WSIB) data are both primary and secondary,
depending on whether it refers to a specific workplace, an industry sector, or the province as a
whole. The information can be requested from the Board's Freedom of Information Office.

WSIB statistical information comes in several forms, including:

- annual summaries of workplace incidents and fatalities, lost work days, first aid cases,
  occupational injuries, and incidence of occupational illness;

- the annual report of the board reviews injury and illness trends across the province for
  the preceding year; and

- An online data service which is updated each July, that allows open access to health and safety records of Ontario workplaces. Interested parties can compare statistic between business. Go to safety check. onlineservices.wsib.on.ca.

Association of Workers' Compensation Boards of Canada
The Association of Workers' Compensation Boards of Canada collect work-related statistics for approximately 84% of Canadian workers. The national statistics include work-related fatalities and lost-time claims for occupational injuries and illnesses.

Employment and Social Development Canada
The Government of Canada, under the auspices of Employment and Social Development Canada, maintains information on employment standards, health and safety, workers compensation, and particularly labour as it pertains to federal employees. A federal government employee is covered both in Canada and abroad for workplace injuries, occupational illness, and fatalities.

Ontario Ministry of Labour, Training and Skills Development
The mandate of the Ministry of Labour, Training and Skills Development is to prevent workplace injuries and illnesses, promote and enforce employment standards, settle workplace disputes, and support apprenticeships, skilled trades, industry training and employment services in Ontario. Workplace health and safety is one part of their mandate

As well as providing general injury and illness statistics, the Ontario Ministry of Labour, Training and Skills Development provides data on work refusals, inspections, and rehabilitation. It lists Ministry of Labour, Training and Skills Development compliance initiatives each quarter (such as checking musculoskeletal injuries in workplaces) and court bulletins resulting from Ministry of Labour, Training and Skills Development charges laid and convictions rendered.

National Institute of Occupational Safety and Health
The National Institute of Occupational Safety and Health (NIOSH) is a useful source of information on workplace safety and health topics, including chemicals. It is affiliated with the Centre for Disease Control and Prevention.

International Labour Organization
With its motto "advancing social justice, promoting decent work" the International Labour Organization (ILO) is a tripartite United Nations agency with government, employer, and worker representatives pursuing social and scientific issues in the world of work. The ILO tracks and produces international statistics for its 187-member states and is a world authority on labour and work issues.

World Health Organization
WHO is the directing and coordinating health authority within the United Nations System. It is an international public health organization, and a source of information on health-related topics.

Like any other research information, statistics must be carefully evaluated before they are used to draw conclusions. Statistics are, after all, only as good as the information they describe, and they are only useful if they are properly applied. Because primary statistics are generated in the workplace, their reliability is easier to check. The same is not true for secondary statistics. The user of secondary statistics must be sure of their source and their relevance to the issue.

Source and Purpose

All occupational health and safety statistics originate in the workplace in some way, but different organizations compile them for different reasons. As a result, methods and definitions may vary, and data become more and more refined. To really understand a set of secondary statistics, it is useful to discover who prepared them, why, and for whom.

Research Methods

How statistical information is collected affects its validity. As a rule, direct observation and measurement is considered more reliable than studying a sample using a questionnaire. If the questionnaire method was used, the sample itself should be checked both for size and relevance. The use of substitute information, for example, payroll data versus actual hours worked, can also affect the outcome of statistics.

Technical accuracy is another element to check. If statistics are comparing injury frequency in several different workplaces, both the definition of injury and the means of determining hours of exposure must be consistent. Without a common base, the whole comparison becomes invalid.

What gets left out of statistics is just as important as what stays in. When measuring fatalities, for instance, it's crucial to know whether the total includes all compensable occupational deaths including heart attacks and motor vehicle crashes, or just those resulting from on-the-job incidents. This becomes even more important when statistics from different sources are being compared.

Limitations of Statistics

As convenient as they are, statistics aren't foolproof and shouldn't be overrated. With so much other data available, there would be no reason to delay making recommendations for change – and thereby exposing workers to continued risk – just because statistics don't exist to support those recommendations.

Statistics should never be used independently of the full data they represent. Nor do they apply to every situation.

Even if statistics are accurate and complete, they can still distract researchers from the real problem to be solved. It is important to look at what the numbers are saying, rather than constantly refining the numbers themselves. At the end of the day, the goal is to correct the problem – not simply to measure it.

Statistics are a compact, convenient form of presenting research information. JHSCs, HSRs and employers can use them to help assess the workplace for causes of injuries or illness, to measure the effectiveness of workplace health and safety programs, to raise awareness of health and safety in the workplace, and to support conclusions and recommendations. Statistics are also used by many other groups, from governments enacting health and safety laws to employers and unions lobbying for improvements to those laws.

Statistics measure workplace injuries or illness in several ways. Frequency rates describe how often an illness or injury happens over time; severity rates calculate the number of days lost due to injury over the same period. Both usually apply to individual workplaces. Fatality rates measure the number of deaths among a given number of workers in entire industry sectors. Incidence rates are a percentage of how many workers out of 100 suffer an injury or contract an illness. Epidemiology measures the incidence of an illness in specific parts of the general population.

Statistical data can be presented in either numerical or graphic form. Numerical statistics include percentages, averages, ratios, and tables. Graphic forms – line charts, pie charts, bar charts, and histograms – show trends and divisions and compare a variety of data. Alternately, they may show a sequence within a body of information.

Statistics can be calculated from events that occur within the workplace (primary data), or from external sources (secondary data). Primary data includes statistics from such sources as injury and illness reports, first aid and monitoring reports, and inspection reports.

A great deal of secondary data on workplace health and safety originates with the WSIB. The WSIB provides summaries of workplace incident data to individual workplaces, Statistics Canada, and Labour Canada. The summaries may cover one workplace, an industry sector, or the whole province.

Data on work refusals, inspections, and rehabilitation, as well as government papers on topical health and safety hazards, are available from the Ontario Ministry of Labour, Training and Skills Development For comparative purposes, statistics from the National Institute of Occupational Safety and Health or the International Labour Organization may also be useful.

Before using statistics to draw any conclusions, the researcher must discover who prepared them, for what purpose, and by what method. This checking will highlight any potential bias on the part of the author and will also establish the validity of the statistics. Statistical method, technical accuracy, content and coding are important factors in the reliability or usefulness of statistics.

Statistics have limitations. They are not necessarily any more effective than other kinds of information. They should never be used independently of the data they represent, and they do not apply to every situation. In fact, they can sometimes distract researchers from the real problem at hand. As a result, it is always important to understand what the numbers are saying.

Chapter 22
Communication Skills

- Modes of Communication

- Communication Techniques

- Training

- Evaluating Training Needs

- Evaluating Training Programs

- Review

Communication Skills

Two of the most important jobs for JHSCs and HSRs are setting out recommendations in written reports and consulting with the employer. This consultation many involve the evaluation or design of training programs dealing with hazardous materials and physical agents. Success in either job depends on a clear understanding of how communications work and what techniques and tools are available. At the same time, good communicators must avoid the barriers that can block a message.

The Communications Cycle

For communication to take place, there must be a sender, a message, a means of sending that message and a receiver. The sender creates and sends a message verbally, on paper, electronically, or through visual means. The receiver gets the message, interprets it, and acts upon it.

Most people aren't aware of this sequence as they're using it. If a message isn't properly received, knowing the separate steps enables the sender to backtrack and find out where the cycle broke down. In other words, the whole cycle must be completed for every successful communication.

Modes of Communication

Communications are flexible. Once the content of a message is set, there are four different ways of sending it. Deciding which technique to use is as much a part of effective communications as actually using it. The key is to choose the mode of communication that is most convenient and effective under a particular set of circumstances.

Oral Communications

Face-to-face, over the telephone, on radio or on television, the spoken word is one of the most versatile modes of communication. From conversations and meetings to training sessions, oral communications are ideal when a lot of information needs to be exchanged between the sender and the receiver. The whole cycle can be completed quickly, information is exchanged freely, and other tasks can be performed during the exchange.

Written Communications

Written communication can be a slower, more measured exchange of information. If a JHSC or HSR is recommending ways to correct a hazardous condition in the workplace, written communication is essential, because descriptions, diagrams and specifications are likely to be more precise.

Written communications also provide a permanent record of important information.

Computers provide for a faster means of exchanging written communications. Email has taken the place of letters and reaches the recipient in less time. Texting, which is less formal, may also be used. Both email and texting speed up the mode of written communication, provide a permanent record of communication, but because of its hurried fashion, could lead to misunderstandings.

Visual Communications

Visual communications such as charts, graphs, pictures, illustrations or videos, are usually an aid to effective communication, because they illustrate or show information instead of explaining it with words alone. Used together, written and visual communications can often promote better understanding on the part of the person receiving the message.

Body Language

Faces and bodies are indirect factors in communications, but they can directly affect the quality of the message. In any oral communication, body movements and gestures can support or contradict what is being said. Tone of voice and emphasis also add meaning. Since a high percentage of understanding comes from non-verbal clues, it is important to the sender to be sure that body language supports the message, and does not become a barrier.

Combinations

The most effective communications are those that use more than one mode, and therefore more than one human sense. Studies have shown that people retain only 20 percent of what they hear, and only 30 percent of what they read. When people both hear and read information, the total percentage of information retained rises to 50 percent. A good program, for instance, might start with a short oral introduction, illustrate the message with a video presentation, follow it with a discussion, and close with reference to a written text or manual.

Listening

A common error is to think of communications only in terms of sending written or verbal messages. The best communications are two-way. The ability to listen carefully with an open mind -- rather than just hearing -- is one of the most important communication skills.

Skills are needed to make the best use of each communications mode. Most communication skills are a combination of basic grammar and vocabulary.

Communications Techniques

Oral Communication

Members of the joint health and safety committee and health and safety representatives need effective oral communication techniques. A thorough knowledge of those techniques is also essential when it comes to evaluating workplace training programs.

Effective oral communication starts before a word has been spoken. Positive body language, good eye contact, and a warm tone of voice help ensure that the audience -- whether it is one person or a group -- never feels talked down to and stays interested.

Oral messages should be kept simple. Big, complex words can be confusing. Different cultural meanings of certain words should be checked to make sure no one is offended. Jargon should not be used unless the communicator is sure that the listener understands it.

Effective Listening

Good listening is not just an important communication skill. It is also one of the most difficult and the most neglected.

The first step in effective listening is to pay close attention to what the speaker is saying and to listen to the whole idea, not just the individual words. By keeping distractions to a minimum, the listener stays focused and lets the speaker know the message is of interest.

Listening is not passive. Active listeners make better communicators. At the end of the message they may ask open-ended questions to obtain more information and to keep the discussion focused. When the speaker has finished, the active listeners may repeat the message in their own words to show that it was correctly understood.

Good listening means keeping an open mind. Personal likes or dislikes of the sender or the subject of the message must be put aside. Listening to the whole message before making a judgment is essential.

Written Communication

To some people, the prospect of writing can be intimidating. Writing requires more specialized skills than speaking. However, good writing in a report on health and safety questions should not prove difficult. It must simply be clear, direct, and well organized. An understanding of the basic elements of writing -- words, sentences, paragraphs, and headings -- can help.

When writing, words should be chosen with care. They should be familiar, preferably short, gender-neutral if possible, and non-technical unless those who will read the report are familiar with the technical language or jargon. Often several words have a similar meaning; the writer should try to select the one that describes the thought most precisely.

Sentences should be kept short and each sentence should contain only one idea. Avoid excess words and phrases. For example, the word 'if' takes up a lot less room than the phrase 'in the event that'; yet their meanings are identical.

Paragraphs organize information into a logical order. Short paragraphs are best and should be limited to one topic or part of a topic. The first sentence of the paragraph should introduce the idea, and the remaining sentences provide detail.

Before starting to write, it is often useful to plan or outline. The outline divides the report into main sections with major headings. The outline keeps the report organized by dividing the material into sections.

Reports

A badly written report –- say an inspection report -– wastes the work of the committee member or health and safety representative. Information has been gathered, the physical inspection completed, and the results noted and analyzed. Conclusions have been drawn and recommendations carefully considered. A badly organized or poorly written report may turn an otherwise effective and thorough process into an unreadable and confusing puzzle. A carefully organized and well-written report presents that work and those recommendations in a persuasive and convincing way. It should state the gathered information precisely, noting the results of the inspection, and any conclusions and recommendations that have been considered.

In preparing a report, the writer should apply the writing techniques described here to the following five-part structure or outline.

Introduction and Purpose

This section introduces the report and generally explains what is contained in the report and its purpose.

Methods

The second section describes the methods used to gather the information or observations.

Findings

A review of the information gathered and observations made are contained in this section. For clarity, information may be divided into categories. An incident investigation report, for instance, might contain the following sub-sections:

- A brief description of incident;

- The names of persons interviewed or contacted; and

- The causes of incident.

Conclusions

This section contains a statement of the underlying cause of a given situation, in the opinion of the writer, based on the data which were gathered and analyzed. Each conclusion should be separately identified and explained. Where the report reflects the consensus of the JHSC, this should be indicated.

Recommendations

Recommendations flow from the conclusions. They are specific proposals for decisions or actions. They must be clearly stated.

Introduction, method, findings, conclusions, and recommendations make up the body of the report. The following two kinds of attachments may be useful as well.

Supporting Documentation

Other documents which provide information that has been considered in the report should be attached. This might include an official report from a recognized authority. The main conclusion drawn from this official report can be explained in the findings or conclusions with a note that a copy of the original is attached.

Bibliography

In some cases, the employer or other person receiving a report will want to check original sources that are described or referred to in the report. If copies of these sources are not attached to the report, a bibliography should be attached, to show the reader where this material can be obtained. Each reference should include title, author, publisher, and where the material can be found. An example is:

A Guide to the Occupational Health and Safety Act; Ontario Ministry of Labour, Training and Skills Development. Available from www.ontario.ca

Workplace Communication Tools

Workplace communications can be enhanced with a variety of practical tools.

Bulletin Boards

Bulletin boards are useful for communicating health and safety information because people are used to checking them. Bulletins should have a simple layout, a large headline, and a very brief message. Bulletin boards are not appropriate for communicating lengthy or detailed information.

Posters

Posters can also be used to quickly call attention to an issue. Larger than a bulletin, they use illustrations and slogans instead of text to get across simple ideas: for example, the importance of reading WHMIS labels.

Internet Sources

There has been a huge increase in the volume of reputable research information on the internet. If this information is quoted in a report, it is frequently cited following American Psychological Association writing guidelines (APA Publication Manual). See official information available at http://www.apastyle.org/

Newsletters

Newsletters provide a permanent record of information that can be read at leisure outside the workplace. Like any other formal publication, they need a name to establish continuity from one issue to the next. Newsletters can often be produced in the workplace.

Safety Talks

Safety talks can involve a small group of people from a specific part of the workplace. These personal presentations by JHSC members or HSRs encourage feedback that may in itself suggest topics for future talks.

Special Bulletins

Special bulletins, sometimes called flash reports, are designed to communicate urgent information when other channels are too slow. The design should be accordingly different so that flash reports are not ignored or lost amongst other information.

Barriers to Communication

Knowledge of effective communication techniques is only half the battle. JHSC members and HSRs may still come up against barriers that interfere with important messages. Training programs may also miss their target if barriers to communication are not removed. Recognizing the barriers is the first step in their removal.

In a multicultural province like Ontario, workers speak many languages. Many are fluent in English or French. Some speak other languages. Others may have differing levels of language skill in their own language. JHSC members and HSRs should find out what languages and levels of language skill exist in the workplace and adapt to them. If simplifying vocabulary isn't enough, it may be necessary to have written materials and instructions translated. Sometimes co-workers can do this, but sometimes outside help may be needed. The Ministry of Labour, Training and Skills Development has translated materials available in several languages.

Specialized terminology -— or jargon —- can be a foreign language itself. Using jargon with new workers is not only ineffective but potentially dangerous, especially if hazardous conditions are involved. Levels of understanding should be considered both in normal communications and training.

Personality conflicts are also harmful. It is always important to put personal differences aside when dealing with health and safety issues. A common solution is training. Training is knowledge, knowledge builds confidence, and confidence improves attitudes.

Body language usually enhances communication, but if gestures and expressions contradict the message being delivered, the receiver can become confused. Being aware of the power of body language enables communicators to tap this resource rather than letting it get in the way.

One of the most important applications of communication skills is in the design and evaluation of workplace training programs. Adult education is an integral part of building awareness of occupational health and safety. When developing training programs, it is important to remember how adults learn and to make the most of the many strengths they bring to the process. Successful adult learning depends on some basic principles.

- New concepts and information should relate back to the life and work experience of the adults involved, as far as possible.

- Facts and ideas must not be presented in a narrow or rigid framework.

- Good or bad past learning experiences affect how adults learn.

- The work and life experience of adults must be recognized and reinforced as an advantage in training.

- The motivation of adults, who are volunteer participants, should also be taken into account in the preparation and presentation of training.

How Adults Learn
The principles described in the previous section can be broken down into separate characteristics of adult learning. Those who evaluate training should be aware of them.

Adults learn best what is most relevant or most needed. New information and skills are accepted sooner if trainees can relate them immediately and directly to actual health and safety issues they deal with at work.

Participants have different approaches to learning and problem solving. Learning can be divided into four stages: feeling or experience; observation (as a result of experience); thought (developing new theories about that experience); and action (testing the theory in an everyday situation). Since some people learn more at one stage than another, the program should feature all four stages. The learning atmosphere is improved when a variety of techniques is used.

Adults learn more when they participate in the process. A one-sided lecture is less effective because the participants have no control over the learning process. Training should be interactive or two-way, based on cooperation and discussion between trainer and trainee.

Learning is the result of experience and practice. Skills that are practiced are retained sooner and for longer. Adults don't change behaviour patterns because they're told to. They accept something when they can see for themselves that it works. Training programs should include opportunities for participants to experiment with new facts and concepts.

Learning is an emotional and intellectual process. Adults don't learn unless they believe or feel that what is being presented is correct and relevant. Programs must be centered on the participants themselves rather than a specific task or piece of information. Adult motivation to learn is usually strong in this kind of environment.

Delivery Techniques

The following delivery techniques can be matched to stages in learning.

Stage	Techniques
Feeling	• Role plays • Field trips *(to other workplaces/site surveys)* • Feedback and discussion
Observing	• Learning journal *(participant's daily record of learning)* • Individual exercises/activity • Self-tests • Discussion groups
Thinking	• Lecture • Theory readings • Debate
Doing	• Case studies • Role plays (assuming a different role in a learning exercise) • Projects

Objectives are important. By setting goals, participants know where learning is headed. Frequent opportunities to check progress against those goals should be built into the program.

Adult Education Techniques

Experienced adult educators or trainers use a variety of techniques. Some of the more common techniques are described briefly here.

- **Brainstorming:** Ideas are shared, combined and fine-tuned by the entire group.

- **Lecturette:** A brief oral description of a topic by the instructor or facilitator before, after, or during other activities in the program.

- **Small Groups/Workshops/Buzz Groups:** Study, research, and analysis of a specific topic in groups of three to four people.

- **Role Playing:** A simulated real-life situation in which learners play roles and use a pre-set background and conditions to solve a problem.

- **Case Study:** The oral and written presentation of a real situation which is analyzed by a group of learners, who then make recommendations for solution by applying skills learned during earlier parts of the program.

- **Participative Lecture:** An oral presentation that includes questions and answers, reports, group work and quizzes.

- **Group Discussion:** A conversation among participants focused on a specific learning objective.

- **Debate:** A formal activity in which two teams of learners argue for and against a given proposition or idea.

Those who conduct adult learning are variously known as instructors or facilitators. The terms are used interchangeably here. Health and safety delivery agencies can supply more information. They may also offer training for instructors or facilitators.

Educational Tools

Educational tools are instruments that help participants to learn and retain information. Tools should never be used simply to replace interaction between instructor and participants or to fill in time. Their purpose is to enhance the learning experience and save time. Some of the most commonly used educational tools are described briefly here.

Printed materials range from participant and instructor manuals outlining the course content to reference materials and handouts. Handouts may include case studies, problems, and quizzes that provide background to group discussions or workshops.

Audio tools are usually recordings. In a health and safety context, they are most often used to study problems associated with noise. As a rule, they work better when they are combined with visual aids.

Flip charts, chalkboards, and whiteboards are traditional visual tools. All are useful for recording ideas during brainstorming sessions. They can also be used to draw flow charts or diagrams that illustrate an idea. Flip charts are most flexible, because they can be used as permanent records during the program. They can also be prepared in advance to provide a starting point for a group discussion.

Audio-visual (AV) aids that combine sight and sound have expanded tremendously. Whereas at one time, VHS videotapes were popular, CD/DVD formats are already outdated. With flash drives and WiFi availability, an individual with a laptop computer and projector, can go to the internet to show YouTube, podcasts, and online visuals for their health and safety programs. College and universities have a 'blackboard' where course can be delivered completely 'online.' There are also webinars where training from one central point is relayed to computers elsewhere to view live or in delayed time. This technology was critical during the COVID-19 pandemic in 2020.

The *OHSA* gives JHSCs and HSRs a role in training. Developing training programs depends on knowing what needs those programs must meet. There are a number of ways that these needs may be identified.

- An incident may reveal a lack of knowledge or understanding about a hazard.

- A health problem may be found to have a workplace cause.

- A work refusal is not properly handled.

- A worker feels ill-equipped for her or his new responsibilities.

- An amendment to the *OHSA* is passed, or new regulations are adopted.

To translate needs into effective training, several decisions are required. They include who may need to be trained and why, what must be learned, and how this goal can be achieved.

Who may need to be trained can be identified by analyzing incidents in the workplace, and through consultation with the people in the workplace. Absenteeism, injury, or compensation records may also provide an objective indicator of training needs.

A needs analysis may identify people who need different training than that of the general workforce. For example, those who dispose of hazardous wastes might require more specialized training than those who occasionally handle or use hazardous materials in their jobs.

Once an assessment of training needs has been completed, the next step is setting objectives for training. The objectives should state the desired results of the training and a blueprint of the information that should be included in the training. The training objectives should include the following elements:

- Program content;

- The purpose of the training and what may be required by the trainees during the process; a statement of what participants will be able to do by the end of the session; and

- The estimated time which may be required to achieve the training goal

Evaluating Training Programs

Since health and safety training needs can constantly change, the training program must be flexible. The ability of JHSC members and HSRs to evaluate the effectiveness of existing or new programs is important to the ongoing development of training programs.

Program Evaluation
Evaluating training means finding out if the goals of the program itself and of the participants were met. If not, why not; and what elements contributed to the success or failure of the program? This can be done by formal or informal evaluations both during and after the program.

In-Program
Observing participants' responses to the training material and analyzing their reaction during the program provides a good indication of the effectiveness of the training.

Surveys filled out by participants or informal interviews between trainer and participants, are also practical ways to evaluate training programs.

After-Program
Conducting follow-up surveys and observing how participants deal with real situations in the workplace after the training program are the most useful way to evaluate training programs. These techniques will provide an indication of the effectiveness of the training materials and methods used by the program. Was the training applied outside of the classroom?

Whatever methods are used to evaluate training programs, the results must always be fed back into the training design process to ensure that any needed improvements are implemented.

Review

Effective communication skills are important to the work of JHSC members and HSRs especially in the areas of report writing and assessing training effectiveness.

Communication is a means of sharing information. The communications cycle consists of a sender, a message, a way of sending that message, and a receiver. The cycle can be completed in either a formal or informal way.

There are three basic modes of communication. Oral communications allow for a quick, free exchange of information. Written communications are ideal when a precise, permanent record is needed. Visual communications can illustrate messages and enhance oral or written communication.

Sometimes, no one mode is appropriate, and combinations are used to get a message across. Effective listening is an essential communication skill.

Written communications should use simple words and short, clear sentences. Paragraphs should be used to organize thoughts, and outlines should be used to organize entire documents. These principles should be applied to report writing.

Various tools are available to enhance communication. These include bulletin boards, posters, newsletters, informal safety talks, and flash reports.

Communication barriers – from poor language skills, jargon and noise, to personality conflicts and confusing body language – can prevent messages from getting through. By recognizing potential barriers, JHSC members can work towards eliminating them.

To help develop training programs, the JHSC member and health and safety representative must first understand how adults learn and make the most of the strengths that adults bring to the learning process: past experience, motivation, ideas, and work and learning abilities.

The principles of adult education should be incorporated into the design of any program.

A program can be delivered by several educational techniques, including group discussions, workshops, role playing, case studies, and formal debates. A range of audio and visual aids tools are available to enhance each of these activities.

To assist in the development of effective training programs, there must be a clear idea of training needs. Those needs may be identified through simple observation of the workplace, safety audits, surveys, outside consultation, group discussions, and the study of professional literature or internal records.

Once needs have been identified, objectives can be established. The training outline should estimate the time which may be required to achieve each training goal. It should state the purpose of the training and what participants should be able to do by the end of the program. It should also describe the training content itself.

No matter how carefully training is designed, there may be room for improvement after evaluating its effectiveness.

To evaluate effectiveness, it must be determined whether the objectives of the program and its participants were met. This may be done through informal interviews or on-the-job analysis. Whatever methods are used, the results must be fed back into the training process to help ensure that it is serving the purpose for which it was established

Chapter 23
Occupational Health and Safety Management Systems

- Leading Versus Lagging Indicators

- Critical Elements of a Managed System

- Chief Prevention Officer's Role

- Ontario's Required OHSMS Elements

- Ontario's OHS Employer Recognition Program

- Review

Occupational Health and Safety Management Systems

Management systems have been around since the 1920s. An Occupational Safety and Health Management System (OHSMS) is defined in the *OHSA* as a "coordinated system of procedures, processes and other measures that is designed to be implemented by employers in order to promote continuous improvement in occupational health and safety". All management systems include a version of Plan, Do, Check, Act.

Many companies implement health and safety programs, but not systems.

An occupational health and safety program is a set of policies and procedures which meets minimum legal requirements. Training typically consists of certified member, violence and harassment, and WHMIS training. A program includes inspections done by the designated worker member of the joint health and safety committee or health and safety representative filed in a binder so that an inspector can see them when requested. A health and safety program is minimalist in its approach.

A system is much more. A system ensures regular review of policies and procedures and assigns responsibility to someone to ensure that updates are completed on a regular basis and communicated to those that need to know about the changes. A system tracks training and identifies who needs which training and when it expires. A system ensures follow up on workplace inspections and assigns responsibility with timelines. When a workplace has an OHSMS in place, there is a coordinated effort aimed at maintaining and improving occupational health and safety measures in the workplace.

Leading Versus Lagging Indicators

Lagging indicators focus on things that have already happened. One often says that lagging indicators are like "looking in the rearview mirror." Examples of lagging indicators in occupational health and safety include lost-time and no-lost time incidents, or the number of days without an injury. Those numbers may give us some indication of our safety systems, but not necessarily.

Consider the company that boasts 567 days with no lost-time injury. What does it tell us? It tells us that in 567 days, the WSIB has not recorded a lost-time injury for that workplace. Recall that in order for a lost-time injury to be counted, the worker has to miss the next regularly scheduled day of work, after the injury occurred. It does not account for a worker that lost a finger on Friday morning, got stitches in the emergency department and recovered enough over the weekend to participate in a modified workplan on Monday. The 567 days does not identify the worker who strained his or her back and was afraid to tell the supervisor because he or she didn't want to be the one to cancel the company bonus or jackets. Numbers can be deceiving, as can a focus on lagging indicators.

Leading indicators help us to look to the future. While there is no agreement in OHS circles about which leading indicators are the most helpful in workplaces, there is certainly agreement that changing our focus from lagging to leading indicators helps to move OHSMSs forward. Every workplace needs to set targets. The JSHC and HSR should be involved in this process.

Examples of measurable leading indicators include:

- the number of employees who are up-to-date on their mandatory training. The target is 100%.

- the number of new hires who receive OHS orientation before they start work. The target is 100%.

- the number of supervisors who receive due diligence and competent supervisor training as they transition into their new role. The target is 100%.

- the number of management/staff meetings that have health and safety as an agenda item. This is not legally required but workplaces which practice this begin to instill safety into their culture. The target is 100%.

- the number of JHSC/HSR workplace inspections completed in one year. The target is 12.

- the number of JHSC meetings in one year. This target is at least four but may be more in some workplaces where the JHSC meets more often.

- the number of workers who receive some type of safety training in one year. The target is 100%.

- the number of recommendations to which management responds within 21 days. The target is 100%.

- the number of action items from JHSC minutes, incident investigations, and recommendations completed within the designated timeframes. The target is 100%.

- the number of policies and procedures reviewed on a regular basis. Some may need to be reviewed yearly (Health and Safety Policy, Violence and Harassment Policy) while others may be on a three-year cycle. The target is 100%.

It is the role of the joint health and safety committee and health and safety representative to be involved in setting targets for occupational health and safety in the workplace. It is management's role to have enough resources in place to reach the targets. All targets are managed efficiently with the use of data management systems.

Occupational health and safety management systems are multi-faceted. They exceed minimum legislative requirements and contain many elements, including document control. Here are some very important parts of any OHSMS.

Senior Management Commitment

In order for a workplace to implement an Occupational Health and Safety Management System, there needs to be buy-in and commitment from the top. This means that the person who leads the organization and all senior managers must be invested in health and safety and show it through their actions. Some evidence of senior management commitment includes supporting the joint health and safety committee or health and safety representative at the workplace, responding to recommendations within the 21-day timeframe, and consulting with the JSHC/HSR on safety-related issues. The CEO needs to champion health and safety through actions like sending out regular safety messages or visiting workers in their work areas.

Risk Management

Every workplace needs to understand the occupational health and safety hazards associated with its workplace. For example, a construction project has many safety hazards such as heavy equipment, vehicles, machinery, and potential falls from heights. A healthcare facility faces biological hazards which are not found on a construction site. A mine is concerned with potential fires, flood, collapse, toxic atmospheres, and dust or gas explosions.

Once the hazards are identified, their risk is analyzed, and control measures put in place. An occupational health and safety system ensures that programs are in place to monitor the control measures.

Hazard Management Tools are discussed in more detail in Chapter 16.

Continual Improvement

Every occupational health and safety management system is a living system. It cannot stay stagnant. Legislative updates happen on a regular basis and need to be added into policies and procedures. Workers need to receive training on the updates. When an incident happens, lessons learned from the incident investigation may change protocols, policies, or forms. Risk assessments completed in an organization must be reviewed on a regular basis. At times, the job changes, no longer exists, or new technology allows the job to be done safer. These changes are reflected in a managed system.

Competence

Every job has competencies, including health and safety competencies. For example, a registered nurse must remain in good standing with the College of Nurses of Ontario in order to work as an RN. As well, depending on the setting, the RN may require extra training for donning and doffing personal protective equipment or safe driver training. In Ontario's underground mines, mandatory training programs exist, called Common Core.

Each workplace, and each position has a level of competency. An OHSMS ensures that each job category identifies the necessary credentials, type of experience, skills training, and occupational health and safety training required. The workplace training is completed within pre-determined time frames. Annual employee evaluations include a review of the identified competencies.

A review of the OHSMS compares the identified competencies to the completeness for all staff in the pre-determined time frames.

Communication

Communication is a critical part of the OHSMS. It starts with the policies and procedures. Where are they kept? Does everyone have access to them? Training is part of communication. This includes new hires and contractors. In a fully functioning OHSMS, the person in charge can easily access who receives communication, and how often. For example, did the three contractors and each of their employees coming on site, receive the safety induction? On which date, and from whom? All of this should be easily available. If a new worker shows up, it needs to be apparent that he or she also needs the safety induction prior to beginning work. The OHSMS tracks who and how many received safety messages or training throughout the year.

Employee Involvement

Responsibility for occupational health and safety belongs to more than the joint health and safety committee or health and safety representative. Senior management cannot implement a safety system on its own. If each employee has involvement with occupational health and safety on some level, there is more buy-in to the system. There needs to be meaning for each employee. A workplace can do this by involving workers in training decisions and programs, incident investigations, workplace inspections, wellness initiatives or home-based safety messaging. The goal is to have as many "fingers in the OHS pie" as possible.

Sections 7.6.1 to 7.6.5 of the *Occupational Health and Safety Act* explain how the Chief Prevention Officer (CPO) may establish standards and accredit an OHSMS in Ontario. The CPO may recognize an employer for certification of a recognized system based on established criteria. The CPO may also recognize employers and publish their names along with the accredited health and safety management system used by the employer.

Currently, the following systems are accredited by the CPO:

- ISO 45001:2018: Occupational health and safety management systems — Requirements with guidance for use

- CSA Z45001-19: Occupational health and safety management systems — Requirements with guidance for use

- BS OHSAS 18001: 2007: Occupational health and safety management system — Requirements

- COR™ (2020) updated standard available for implementation January 2020

An employer may have their own occupational health and safety management system accredited by the CPO. The employer-specific OHSMS must be evaluated by the Ministry of Labour, Training, and Skills Development. It will be compared to the CPO OHSMS Accreditation Standard.

What the Law Says

CPO's Role

- Establish standards which OHSMSs must meet in order to be accredited

- Accredit OHSMSs that meet the standards

- Revoke or amend an accreditation or recognition for a standard or employer

- Establish criteria for employer recognition

- Recognize employers who meet the CPO's criteria

- Publish names of accredited OHSMS and recognized employers

- Accredit an individual employer's OHSMSs

Any CPO-accredited OHSMS includes the broad categories of leadership, commitment and participation; planning and implementation; and evaluation.

Leadership and Commitment
Senior management is ultimately responsible for the success and implementation of the OHSMS. Management defines, assigns, and communicates roles and responsibilities for all workplace parties. The leaders review and evaluate the OHSMS regularly.

Worker Participation
Each workplace establishes, implements, monitors and maintains a process to ensure worker participation in the planning, implementation and evaluation of the occupational health and safety management system. This includes, but is not limited to hazard identification, risk assessments, controls, incident investigations, development and review of OHS policies, procedures, processes and objectives, and access to relevant reports. The joint health and safety committee, health and safety representative, and all workers have a role to play.

Communication
Communication includes internal parties and external stakeholders. The OHSMS has processes in place to report workplace incidents, and actual and potential hazards. The employer communicates information about the OHSMS and the implementation progress to all workplace parties and interested stakeholders.

OHS Policy
The scope of the OHS policy matches the complexity of the workplace. It takes into account the size, nature and needs of the organization, and is reflective of the operations and/or activities of the organization. The policy, which is approved by senior management, focuses on prevention of injury and occupational illness and compliance with applicable OHS legislation. The policy supports continual improvement of the company's OHSMS and OHS performance.

Identification of Hazards, Risk Assessment and Determination of Controls
The workplace establishes, implements and maintains a hazard identification and risk assessment process to recognize hazards and manage risks for each of its routine and non-routine operations and/or activities. The hazard assessments are completed by a competent person. The control measures utilize the hierarchy of controls; elimination, substitution, engineering, administrative, and personal protective equipment. This process is documented, shared with affected parties, and continually improved.

Preventative and Protective Control Measures
Based on the process above, the workplace establishes, implements, monitors and maintains control measures to manage risks. Control measures aim to eliminate the risk or reduce the risk to as low as reasonably achievable (ALARA). Control measures are communicated to the affected parties.

Legal and Other Requirements
The workplace follows and applies all legal requirements for the establishment, implementation and maintenance of the OHSMS. At regular documented intervals, the workplace reviews and evaluates compliance, any changes to legislation, and updates the OHSMS as necessary.

OHS Objectives
The workplace sets OHSMS targets. They must be simple, measurable, achievable, realistic, and timely (SMART). Previous targets are reviewed, and new ones set, with attention to time frames and responsibility for achieving them.

Competency and Training
Any worker, including contractors, performing a task must be competent to do so. The workplace completes a training needs assessment for each position and training is provided by a competent person. Records of training are kept.

Emergency Prevention, Preparedness and Response
The employer establishes, implements, monitors, and maintains emergency procedures. This includes identifying and trying to prevent potential emergency situations, establishing written emergency response plans, preventing or minimizing injury or occupational illness for the identified emergency situations, and testing identified emergency situations. Emergency plans are updated regularly and communicated to internal and external stakeholders.

Documentation
The employer establishes, implements, monitors, and maintains a procedure for the control of documents and retention of records. This includes the scope of the OHSMS, the OHS Policy, objectives and leading and lagging performance measures, as well as documents and records required by the organization.

Control of Documents
Documents contain information related to the OHSMS. They are approved prior to issue, have titles, dates, a reference number, and version control. All documents are legible, and easy to identify.

Control of Records
Records are documents which show the results achieved or provide evidence of activities performed. The employer maintains records to demonstrate conformity to the requirements of its OHSMS. There is a process to identify, store, protect, retrieve, retain and dispose of records. The employer considers privacy and confidentiality in record control.

Management of Change

There is a process to manage changes to work processes, control measures, procedures, equipment, organizational structure, staffing, products, workplace parties, physical locations or services, or when new products, processes or services are introduced. Changes also occur in legislation and OHS knowledge and technology. The workplace ensures hazard identification, risk assessment, and determination of controls is completed according to established workplace processes. All changes are communicated to the affected workplace parties.

Procurement

The employer establishes, implements, monitors and maintains a procedure to evaluate and manage the procurement of products, supplies, equipment, materials and other goods and services. The process follows the workplace's established protocols of hazard identification, risk assessment, control, and evaluation of controls. The procurement process is monitored.

Management of Contractors

The employer establishes, implements, and maintains criteria to monitor and evaluate contractors on OHS performance during all phases of the work cycle. This includes the identification of hazards and control of risks, and the competency and ability of the contractor to control the risks.

Performance Measuring and Monitoring

The employer regularly measures and monitors the OHSMS performance. This includes qualitative and quantitative measurement of leading and lagging indicators, the extent to which the organization's OHS policy and objectives are being met, conformance to the OHSMS, monitoring the effectiveness of the control measures, and the extent to which legal and other requirements are fulfilled. The results are recorded and communicated with workplace parties and interested stakeholders.

Incident Investigation and Analysis

Investigations are conducted in a timely manner, and by a competent person, including subject matter experts when warranted. The employer has processes in place to report, investigate, analyze, document and maintain records for incidents. The process includes roles and responsibilities of the workplace parties including the JHSC and HSR, which incidents are investigated, a focus on contributing factors, and opportunities for corrective action and continual improvement.

Non-Conformity, Preventative and Corrective Action

A nonconformity is when there is evidence that a process has not been performed as it was required in the employer's OHSMS and according to the overall OHS standard being used. The employer has processes in place which deal with non-conformities, risk controls, corrective actions, and preventative actions.

Internal Audit

Internal audits are conducted regularly and are based on OHSMS requirements as well as results of previous audits. The audit program is in accordance with ISO 19011 – Guidelines for managing auditing systems. The audit program includes responsibilities for the audit team, the audit scope, frequency of audits, audit planning, how to document and report on audit findings, addressing non-conformities, continual improvement, JHSC/HSR involvement, and communication with relevant stakeholders.

Management Review

Senior management regularly reviews the OHSMS, focuses on opportunities for improvement, and looks for OHS trends within the organization. The review includes results from the annual audit, compliance evaluations, JHSC/HSR recommendations, incident investigations, and other communication received from interested stakeholders. Furthermore, senior management also reviews the extent to which their annual OHSMS targets have been met, the effectiveness of their hazard assessment and control program, incident investigation trends and preventative actions, follow-up actions from previous management reviews, legislative changes that affect the OHSMS, and recommendations for improvement. The review is recorded and communicated to the JSHC/HSR in the workplace.

Ontario's OHS Employer Recognition Program

The Chief Prevention Officer of Ontario has the authority to recognize employers who use a CPO-accredited OHSMS in their workplace. There is an application process and the employer must meet all applicable criteria established by the CPO.

Employers who apply for CPO recognition must successfully meet the objectives for third-party audits, the *OHSA*, and worker participation and commitment to the IRS. The MLTSD has ongoing reporting and quality assurance processes to ensure the employer is maintaining and continuously improving their CPO-accredited OHSMS. This is verified by internal and third-party audits and CPO-recognition criteria. The CPO has the authority to revoke an employer's recognition.

Third-Party Audits

The employer must first complete an internal audit of its OHSMS. In order to receive CPO recognition, the employer provides proof of a completed third-party audit. There are stringent rules for the lead auditor and certification bodies.

The *Occupational Health and Safety Act*
Employers must show compliance with the *OHSA*. This includes having a worker and management certified member for the JHSC, and a health and safety representative, where required. The MLTSD ensures that there are no ongoing prosecutions or past (within the last three years) convictions under the *Provincial Offences Act*.

Worker Participation and Employer Commitment to the Internal Responsibility System
Employers wishing to pursue a CPO designation must demonstrate worker participation and commitment to the IRS. The employer must be free of reprisal convictions, based on an Ontario Labour Relations Board (OLRB) decision, against a worker for the previous three years. Further, an employer cannot have a conviction in the three years prior to applying for CPO designation, for failing to establish a JHSC or HSR, if applicable, in the workplace. There can be no ongoing prosecution for failing to establish a JHSC or HSR. The employer must provide proof of training of the chosen health and safety representative, if required, in the workplace.

Review

Occupational Health and Safety Management Systems are complex and coordinated systems of processes and procedures aimed at managing occupational health and safety in workplace. These systems focus on leading indicators as senior leaders set targets for their organizations.

Some important, aspects of an OHSMS include, but are not limited to, senior management commitment, risk management, continual improvement, competence, communication, and employee involvement.

In Ontario in late 2019, the Chief Prevention Officer established an occupational health and safety management system accreditation standard. The CPO can publicly recognize employers who meet certain criteria. Employers who believe they have an OHSMS that meets the CPO's accreditation standard can apply to the MLTSD to have their system accredited.

The Chief Prevention Officer's accredited occupational health and safety management system includes 21 elements. They are:
- Leadership and Commitment
- Worker Participation
- Communication
- OHS Policy
- Identification of Hazards, Risk Assessment and Determination of Controls
- Preventative and Protective Control Measures
- Legal and Other Requirements
- OHS Objectives
- Competency and Training
- Emergency Prevention, Preparedness and Response

- Documentation
- Control of Documents
- Control of Records
- Management of Change
- Procurement
- Management of Contractors
- Performance Measuring and Monitoring
- Incident Investigation and Analysis
- Non-Conformity, Preventative and Corrective Action
- Internal Audit
- Management Review

Employers who apply for CPO recognition must successfully meet the objectives for third-party audits, the *OHSA*, and worker participation and commitment to the IRS.

Glossary

Absorption Passage through the skin.

Accuracy (in monitoring) How close the measurement comes to true value.

Acoustic trauma Loss of hearing caused by a rupture of the eardrum.

Acute exposure A short contact with a hazard, for example, chemical, noise

Additive (health effects) The health effects of a mixture which are equal to the sum of the effects of the components of the mixture. This is the case when two or more hazardous substances act upon the same organ system.

Adrenalin A hormone secreted by the adrenal glands affecting circulation and muscular action and causing excitement and stimulation. It is called into play in the stress response.

Aerosol A suspension of fine solid or liquid particles (dust, fume, mist, smoke) in a gas (air). The particle size ranges from .001 micron to 100 micron.

Airborne Carried by or through the air.

ALARA: As Low As Reasonably Achievable. Where it is assumed that there is a risk of health effects associated with doses below the recommended limits, these doses should be minimized. The doses should be kept as low as reasonably achievable, economic and social factors being taken into account.

Allergen A substance which reacts with the body's immune system to produce a type of irritation known as an allergic reaction.

Alveoli The tiny air sacs of the lungs which allow for rapid gaseous exchange (e.g., oxygen, carbon dioxide).

Anthropometry The study and measure of the physical dimensions (size) of the human body.

Antibody A protein substance developed in response to and counteracting antigens such as bacteria, toxins and foreign blood cells.

Anvil (incus) One of the three small bones of the ear.

Asphyxiant Any agent or substance that interferes with the supply of oxygen to the blood.

Audit A systematic, independent and documented process for obtaining audit evidence and evaluating it objectively to determine the extent to which audit criteria are fulfilled

Backdrafting When the air pressure inside a ventilated area is less than the pressure outside that area, contaminants may be drawn back into the area through the ventilation system.

Biological hazard Biological substance that poses a threat to the health of living organisms, primarily humans. They include bacteria, viruses, fungi as well as larger organisms such as parasites and plants.

Biomechanics The study of the forces required to manually lift, lower, push, pull or carry objects or people, and the effects of these forces on the body.

Boiling point The temperature at which a liquid changes to a vapour. The boiling point varies with pressure and the nature of the liquid.

Bronchi The large air tubes leading into the lungs from the trachea.

Bursa A very thin, fluid-filled sac that helps reduce friction where tendons rub against bones, ligaments and other tendons, or where bones come close to the surface of the skin.

Bursitis An inflammation of a bursa.

Cancer A group of diseases characterized by malignant, uncontrolled growth of cells of body tissue.

Capillaries The smallest blood vessels of the body.

Carcinogen A substance that causes cancer.

Carcinoma Cancer of lining tissues such as tissue that makes up the skin or lines the intestine, kidneys, mouth, uterus, lungs, and other organs.

Cardiovascular System The system of the body that includes the heart and blood vessels (veins and arteries).

Carpal Tunnel A tunnel, formed by the carpal bones of the hand and a tough fibrous band, through which nerves, tendons, and blood vessels run to and from the hand.

Cartilage A smooth, gristle-like connective tissue that surrounds joint surfaces.

CAS Number The unique identification number assigned to specific chemicals by the Chemical abstract Services Division of the American Chemical Society.

Cell The basic building block of all life. each cell is specialized to perform a particular function.

C or Ceiling Limit The maximum airborne concentration of a biological or chemical agent beyond which a worker should not be exposed at any time.

Chemical families Compounds sharing similarities of chemical structure.

Chemical hazard Any substance that can cause harm to people. Chemical hazards take the form of solids, liquids, vapours, gases, dusts, fumes, or mists.

Cilia Hair-like projections of the cells of the large airways that trap dust and bacteria and move them toward the mouth.

Circadian rhythm The rhythms of our physiological system that function in a pattern approximating a 24- hour period.

Cochlea A small snail-shaped organ containing the hearing mechanism, located in the inner ear.

Contaminant A chemical that does not have a purpose in a compound or mixture.

Continual improvement A recurring process of enhancing any system in order to achieve improvements in overall performance consistent with the organization's goals and objecectives

Contractor Person or organization providing services to another organization in accordance with agreed-upon specification, terms and conditions

Controlled products Hazardous materials covered by the Controlled Products Regulation under the federal *Hazardous Products Act*. The classes of controlled products are compressed gases, flammable and combustible materials, oxidizing materials, poisonous and infectious materials, and dangerously reactive materials.

Cortisone A hormone secreted by the adrenal glands that, when converted to cortisol, helps to mobilize body fuels. It is called into play in the stress response.

Cumulative trauma disorder
Musculoskeletal disorder:

Cumulative Increasing in amount by one addition after another;

Trauma Bodily injury from mechanical stress;

Disorder Physical ailment or abnormal

Decibel A unit for measuring sound intensity or loud ness.

Decomposition products Material produced by the chemical or physical degradation of a parent material.

Density Ratio of weight (mass) of volume of a material, usually in grams per cubic centimetre.

Dermatitis Inflammation of the skin, characterized by reddened, cracked and blistered skin.

Directors of a Corporation A body of elected or appointed members who jointly oversee the activities of a company

Disabling injury An injury that disables a worker from doing his or her usual work.

Disc (vertebral) The structure that separates each pair of vertebrae, gives the spine flexibility, and absorbs shock; made up of a tough, elastic-like outer shell and a jelly-like centre.

DNA Short for deoxyribonucleic acid. It is a complex chemical blueprint for growth and development.

Document Medium containing information

Duct velocity Air speed through a ventilation duct.

Dust Solid particles suspended in air produced by agitation, crushing, grinding, abrading, or blasting. Ranges in size from 0.1 to 50 micron and larger.

Effects

    Acute Occurring immediately or very soon after exposure.

    Chronic Occurring long after exposure.

Employer Means a person who employs one or more workers or contracts for the services of one or more workers and includes a contractor or subcontractor who performs work or supplies services and a contractor or subcontractor who undertakes with an owner, constructor, contractor or subcontractor to perform work or supply services

Epicondylitis Inflammation of the area around the elbow joint.

Ergonomics The study of human characteristics for the appropriate design of living and work environments.

Exposures

    Acute Brief, intense or short-term exposure, sometimes referring to brief exposure of high intensity.

    Chronic Prolonged or long-term exposure, often with specific reference to low-intensity.

Exposure Monitoring Evaluation of employee exposure to hazardous substances (chemicals, noise, radiation) by taking quantitative measurements and interpreting those measurements using experience, legislative standards, and professional judgement.

Flashpoint The lowest temperature at which a flammable material gives off sufficient vapour to form an ignitable mixture with air near its surface or in a vessel.

Freezing point The temperature at which a material changes from a liquid to a solid at normal atmospheric pressure.

Frequency (or pitch) The number of sound vibrations which occur each second.

Fume An airborne dispersion consisting of minute solid particles arising from the heating of a solid (such as molten metal).

Ganglion cyst a disorder of the tendon sheath or joint capsule, which causes a nodule filled with fluid or semi-solid material to develop.

Gas A formless substance that expands to occupy the space of its container.

Gastric acid Hydrochloric acid secreted by cells in the stomach.

Grab samples Samples of air removed for analysis (in a lab or on the spot).

Guard Any device, barrier, or equipment used to protect workers from contact with the moving parts of a machine

Hammer (malleus) One of the three small bones of the ear.

Hazard Potential source of harm to a worker.

Hazardous material In a broad sense, any substance or mixture of substances having properties capable of producing adverse effects on the health or safety of a human.

Health Care (in terms of WSIB Form 7) Services provided at hospitals and health facilities, and services that can only be provided by one of the following health care professionals: chiropractor, physician, physiotherapist, registered nurse (extended class), or dentist.

Hemoglobin A protein found in red blood cells which is specialized to transport oxygen.

Herniated disc A back injury in which some of the jelly-like centre of the vertebral disc protrudes through small tears in the tough outer shell of the disc.

Hierarchy of controls A principle used to describe the order in which controls should be implemented. It takes into consideration the effectiveness of controls, within the hierarchy: elimination (including substitution); engineering; administrative; and personal protective equipment.

Housekeeping A control "along the path" including proper cleaning, disposal of wastes, the clean-up of spills, and maintaining clear aisles and passageways.

Hypothesis A statement of belief which guides research.

Incident An occurrence, condition, or situation arising in the course of work that resulted in, or could have resulted, in injuries, illnesses, damage to health or fatalities.

Independent (health effects) When two or more substances act on different organs of the body, the health effects are considered independently of one another.

Industrial hygiene See Occupational hygiene.

Infectious agent An organism that is capable of producing infection or infectious disease.

Ingestion A route of entry. The taking in of a substance through the mouth and its passage through the digestive tract.
Inhalation A route of entry. The breathing in of a substance in the form of a gas, vapour, fume, mist, smoke, or dust.

Injection A subsurface placement of a liquid or waste.

Integrated sampling method A class of sampling methods that involves the collection of a sample in a collection medium that must be analyzed in a lab.

Irritant A substance that causes pain and reddening of the exposed areas, most often the eyes, skin, and respiratory tract.

Labour Relations Officer The occupational health and safety adjudicator appointed under subsection 20(1) of the *OHSA*.

Latency period The time period between exposure to a substance and the appearance of disease.

LC50 of ingredient Lethal Concentration. The concentration in air of a material that causes the death of 50 percent of a group of test animals when inhaled over a set period of time, usually one to four hours.

LD50 of ingredient Lethal Dose. The dose of a substance that causes the death of 50 percent of an animal population from exposure to the substance by any route other than inhalation when given all in one dose.

Leukemia Cancer of blood-forming tissue in the bone marrow and lymph nodes.

Ligaments A short band of tough, flexible fibrous connective tissue linking bones together.

Liquid A formless fluid that takes the shape of its container, but does not necessarily fill it.

Local effects Effects at the site of direct contact of a harmful agent with the body.

Lockout A specific set of procedures to secure against the start-up or movement of parts of circuits, systems or equipment that are temporarily out of service.

Lost-time injury A work-related injury/disease which results in being off past the day of the incident, loss of wages/earning, or a permanent disability/impairment.

Lower explosive limit (LEL) The lowest concentration, expressed as a percent volume/volume ratio, of a vapour or gas in air that can burn or explode if ignited.

Lymphoma Cancer of lymphatic tissue.

Median nerve A motor and sensory nerve that passes through the carpel tunnel.

Micron A unit of length equal to one--millionth of a meter.

Mist An airborne cloud of tiny liquid droplets.

MLTSD Ministry of Labour, Training and Skills Development

Monitoring strategy A plan of action for measuring the level of hazardous agents in the workplace.

Musculoskeletal disorder (MSD) Disorders of the system of muscles, tendons, ligaments, joints, bones, and related structures of the human body.

Musculoskeletal hazard A hazard which poses a risk to the musculoskeletal system, and may lead to a musculoskeletal disorder.

Mutagen An agent causing genes in an organism to mutate or change.

Nervous system The nervous system is divided into two divisions, the central nervous system, which includes the brain and spinal cord, and the peripheral nervous system, which includes all the other neural elements.

No lost-time injury A work-related injury where no time is lost from work other than on the day of the incident, but where health care is required. The health care costs resulting from the injury are paid by the WSIB.

Occupational illness A condition that results from exposure in a workplace to a physical, chemical, or biological agent to the extent that the normal physiological mechanisms are affected and the health of the worker is impaired.

Occupational injury Any injury that leads to bodily harm, that was incurred by an employee in the performance of, or in connection with his or her work.

Occupational hygiene Sometimes called industrial hygiene. The science devoted to the anticipation, recognition, evaluation, and control of health hazards in the workplace.

Odour threshold The lowest concentration of a materials vapour (or a gas) in air that can be detected by odour.

OHSA Occupational Health and Safety Act

Organs Structures in the body that perform particular functions, e.g., stomach, tongue, bladder.

Ovary The female organ that produces ova or eggs.

Owner includes a trustee, receiver, mortgagee in possession, tenant, lessee, or occupier of any lands or premises used or to be used as a workplace, and a person who acts for or on behalf of an owner as an agent or delegate

pH value The value that represents the acidity or alkalinity of an aqueous solution.

Physical hazard A type of occupational hazard that involves environmental hazards that can cause harm with or without contact. Physical hazards include electricity, noise hazards, vibration hazards, heat and cold stress, and radiation.

Pituitary gland A gland that secretes a number of hormones that regulate many bodily processes including growth, reproduction, and various metabolic activities. It is often referred to as the master gland of the body.

Precision A method is said to be precise when the values obtained can be consistently reproduced or repeated.

Prescribed As set out in the regulations under any Act.

Principles of control Control measures discussed on the basis of where the control is applied:

> at the source (of the hazard);
> along the path (between the hazard and the worker;
> at the worker.

Product information (WHMIS) Identifies the product, the supplier/manufacturer, and the use(s) of the product.

Psychosocial hazard Any hazard that affects the mental well-being or mental health of a worker.

Quorum The minimum number of officers and members of a constituted body necessary for the valid transaction of business.

Radiation Energy that is emitted, transmitted, or absorbed in wave or energetic-particle form.

Reagent A substance used in a chemical reaction to detect, measure, or yield other substances.

Record Document stating results achieved or providing evidence of activities performed

Routes of entry See inhalation, absorption, ingestion, injection.

Safety hazard Hazard associated with equipment, contact between the body and an outside agent. It can range in severity from a minor scratch or burn to the loss of a limb or even death. They include but are not limited to machine hazards, confined space hazards, hand tool hazards, and ladder hazards.

Sampling The use of monitoring equipment to take samples of substances and agents in the workplace.

Sarcoma Cancer of bone, connective tissues, and muscles.

Schedule 1 employer Employers for whom the WSIB pays benefit compensation for workers' claims. Schedule 1 employers are required by legislation to pay premiums to the Board and are protected by a system of collective liability. Since the Board pays benefits to injured workers out of money pooled in the insurance fund, Schedule 1 employers are relieved of individual responsibility for actual incident costs.

Schedule 2 employer Employers that self-insure the provision of benefits under the *WSIA*. Schedule 2 employers pay all benefit compensation and administration costs for their workers' claims. The WSIB administers the payment of the benefits for workers of Schedule 2 employers and recovers the cost of these benefits plus administration fees from the employers.

Sensitivity The ability of an analytic procedure to measure small amounts of the contaminant in the sample.

Sensitization The development, over time, of an allergic reaction to a chemical. The chemical may cause a mild response initially, but as the allergy develops the response becomes worse with subsequent exposures. Ultimately, even brief exposures to low concentrations can cause a very severe reaction.

Smoke Airborne particles that are the result of the incomplete combustion of materials consisting of or containing carbon.

Solubility The capacity of a material to dissolve in water or another liquid.

Specific gravity The ratio of the density of a material to the density of water. Materials that are lighter than water (specific gravity less than 1.0) will float. Materials that are heavier than water (specific gravity greater than 1.0) will sink.

Specificity The ability of an analytical method to measure accurately one contaminant in a sample without interference from any other contaminants in the same sample.

STEL or Short-Term Exposure Limit means the maximum airborne concentration of a biological or chemical agent to which a worker is exposed in any 15-minute period, no more than four times during an eight-hour workshift, and with at least an hour between exposures.

Stirrup (stapes) One of the three small bones of the ear.

Stressor A cause of stress.

Supervisor Means a person who has charge of a workplace or authority over a worker

Supplier A person or entity that is the source for goods or services

Syndrome A group of signs or symptoms that collectively characterize or indicate a particular disease or abnormal condition.

Synergy An interaction of materials to give an effect greater than the sum of their separate effects.

Synovial fluid A fluid that supplies nutrients to, and lubricates the cartilage inside joints.

Systemic effects Effects on the organs or systems of the body as the result of a harmful substance entering the bloodstream.

Tarsal tunnel A tunnel formed by the tarsal bones of the ankle and a tough fibrous band, through which nerves, tendons and blood vessels run to and from the foot.

Tendinitis Inflammation of the tendons.

Tendons Bands of fibrous connective tissue that attach muscles to bones.

Tenosynovitis Inflammation of the tendon and its sheath.

Teratogen A substance that produces abnormalities in the embryo or fetus by changing the balance of the environment in the womb or by directly affecting the embryo or fetus.

Terms of reference A written statement of the functions and operating procedures of a committee.

Testis The gland in men that produces sperm.

Threshold shift

Temporary Temporary loss of hearing.

Permanent Permanent loss of hearing.

Toxic substances Substances able to cause harmful health effects.

TWA or Time-Weighted Average Limit means the time weighted average airborne concentration of a biological or chemical agent to which a worker is exposed in a work day or a work week. (Normally an 8-hour work day).

Upper explosive limit The highest concentration, expressed as a volume/volume ratio, of a vapour or gas in air that will burn or explode if ignited.

Vapour The gaseous state of a material suspended in air that would normally be a liquid or solid at room temperature and normal atmospheric pressure.

Vapour density The weight of a vapour or gas com- pared to the weight of an equal volume of air. Light gases (density less than 1.0) rise in air. Heavy gases (density greater than 1.0) can accumulate in low-lying areas.

Vapour pressure A measure of the tendency of a material to form a vapour. The higher the vapour pressure, the higher the potential vapour concentration.

Vector-borne The transmission of infectious agents by insects.

Vehicle-borne The transmission of infectious agents through contact with contaminated materials or objects.

Ventilation

Local The removal of contaminated air directly at its source.

General Also known as dilution ventilation (along the path), it is the removal of contaminated air from the general area and the bringing in of clean air.

Vertebrae The 33 bones that make up the spine.

Volatility The measure of a material's tendency to vapourize or evaporate at room temperature and normal atmospheric conditions.

Wind chill index Indication of coldness arrived at by a combination of wind speed and temperature factors.

Workers' Compensation A system of insurance funded by employers and administered by the government to pay for the medical treatment and lost wages of employees who are injured or made ill from work exposures/incidents.

Worst-case strategy (monitoring) Monitoring those at the highest risks of exposure to determine whether their exposure is below the level considered safe. This helps to determine whether further monitoring is required.

WSIB Workplace Safety and Insurance Board

Worker Means any of the following, but does not include an inmate of a correctional institution or like institution or facility who participates inside the institution or facility in a work project or rehabilitation program:
- A person who performs work or supplies services for monetary compensation.
- A secondary school student who performs work or supplies services for no monetary compensation under a work experience program authorized by the school board that operates the school in which the student is enrolled.
- A person who performs work or supplies services for no monetary compensation under a program approved by a college of applied arts and technology, university, private career college or other post-secondary institution.
- Such other persons as may be prescribed who perform work or supply services to an employer for no monetary compensation.

Workplace Any land, premises, location or thing at, upon, in or near which a worker works

Workplace harassment Engaging in a course of vexatious comment or conduct against a worker in a workplace that is known or ought reasonably to be known to be unwelcome, or workplace sexual harassment.

Workplace sexual harassment Engaging in a course of vexatious comment or conduct against a worker in a workplace because of sex, sexual orientation, gender identity or gender expression, where the course of comment or conduct is known or ought reasonably to be known to be unwelcome, or making a sexual solicitation or advance where the person making the solicitation or advance is in a position to confer, grant or deny a benefit or advancement to the worker and the person knows or ought reasonably to know that the solicitation or advance is unwelcome.

Workplace violence The exercise of physical force by a person against a worker, in a workplace, that causes or could cause physical injury to the worker; an attempt to exercise physical force against a worker, in a workplace, that could cause physical injury to the worker; or a statement or behavior that it is reasonable for a worker to interpret as a threat to exercise physical force against the worker, in a workplace, that could cause physical injury to the worker.

Index

of noise, 138
of non-ionizing
   radiation, 148
of psychosocial hazard,
209
on reproductive system,
158
of vibration, 143

Health Hazards, 10

**Health Protection and
   Promotion Act**, 34

Hearing Loss, 139

Heart, 99

Heat Stress
assessing exposure, 144
controlling exposure,
145
exposure to, 144
health effects of, 144

Herniated Disc, 192

Hierarchy of Controls, 121

Highway Traffic Act, 35

Histograms, 293

Hoods, 168

Housekeeping, 125, 171

Human Body, 99, 196

I

Identification
hazard, 160

Infectious Agents
direct transmission of,
178
diseases caused by, 179
indirect transmission of,
179

Incident
defined, 252
follow-up, 257
interview witnesses, 255
investigate causes, 254
investigation
procedures, 253
reporting, 254, 257
secure and manage
   scene, 253
survey the scene, 254

Incident Investigations,
analyzing facts, 256
organize facts, 255
physical, 255
prepare report, 255
procedures, 253
right of JHSC to
investigate, 253
secure and manage
   scene, 253
taking part in, 85
techniques, 255-257
using photographs and
   drawings, 256

**Incidents and
   Occupational Illnesses**,
6

Indirect-Reading Method,
268

Industry Associations, 279

Information
disposal, 162
ecological, 162
gathering, 278-280
other, 162
regulatory, 162
required for sampling,
264
toxicological, 161
transport, 162

Injury
disabling, 289
lost-time, 288
no lost-time, 289
work, 289

Inspections, 59, 239-249,
278
conducting, 243
follow-up, 247
four stages, 239, 248-
249
pre-inspection, 239
review and reporting,
244-246
tools, 240
writing report, 245

Inspectors, 89-90
dealing with, 74
legal enforcement of
   orders, 90
orders, 89

Instrument Displays,
198

Interaction of Factors,
195

ACGIH American Conference of Governmental Industrial Hygienists

ALARA As Low As Reasonably Achievable

C Ceiling Limit

CCOHS Canadian Centre for Occupational Health and Safety

GHS Globally Harmonized System of Classification and Labelling of Chemicals

COVID-19 Coronavirus Disease 2019

Gy Gray (SI Unit of radiation)

HSA Health and Safety Association

HSPI Health & Safety Professionals Inc.

HSR Health and Safety Representatives

IHSA Infrastructure Health and Safety Association

JHSC - Joint Health and Safety Committee

MLTSD Ministry of Labour, Training and Skills Development

NIHL Noise-Induced Hearing Loss

OELs Occupational Exposure Limits

OHSA Occupational Health and Safety Act

PEMEP People, Equipment, Materials, Environment, Process

PPE Personal Protective Equipment

PSHSA Public Services Health & Safety Association

SI International System of Units

STEL Short-Term Exposure Limit

Sv Sievert (SI Unit of radiation)

TLV Threshold Limit Value

TWA Time Weighted Average

WBGT Wet-Bulb Globe Temperature

WHMIS Workplace Hazardous Materials Information

WSIA Workplace Safety and Insurance Act

WSIB Workplace Safety and Insurance Board

WSN Workplace Safety North

WSPS Workplace Safety & Prevention Services

About the Author

Louise Caicco Tett is passionate about occupational health and safety (OHS). She began her career as a registered nurse in the intensive care unit (ICU) and saw first-hand the devastating effects of preventable injuries, both at home and at work. When she left the ICU, Louise worked as a Public Health Nurse and gravitated towards injury prevention and workplace health. It was great planning and some good luck that allowed Louise and her family to relocate to Sault Ste. Marie where she opened her Occupational Health and Safety (OHS) training and consulting business in 1998. As the company grew, so did Louise's thirst for knowledge; first an OHS certificate, then her Canadian Registered Safety Professional designation, and finally her Master's in Public Health, with a specialty in OHS Management.

Louise has taught Basic Certification since 1999 and believes that knowledge is power. Those workplaces that educate more people have stronger occupational health and safety systems in place because employees and managers speak the same safety language and have the same goals.

This book had its start in the 1990s with the Workplace Health and Safety Agency, and later the Workplace Safety and Insurance Board. It would have been but a distant memory, if Louise hadn't brushed it off, revised, reorganized, and added new material. *It's such a great reference. It would have been a shame to lose all of that information.* Louise is committed to reviewing this reference guide, and bringing updates to members of Joint Health and Safety Committees, Health and Safety Representatives, safety and human resources professionals, students, and supervisors/managers across Ontario.